SAMUEL TAYLOR COLERIDGE

SAMUEL TAYLOR COLERIDGE *a selective bibliography of criticism, 1935-1977*

WITHDRAWN

Compiled by
Jefferson D.Caskey and
Melinda M. Stapper

GREENWOOD PRESS
WESTPORT, CONNECTICUT • LONDON, ENGLAND

Library of Congress Cataloging in Publication Data

Caskey, Jefferson D
    Samuel Taylor Coleridge : a selective bibliography of
criticism, 1935-1977.

    Includes index.
    1. Coleridge, Samuel Taylor, 1772-1834—Bibliography.
I. Stapper, Melinda M., joint author.
Z8182.C37   [PR4483]   016.821'7   78-57765
ISBN 0-313-20564-7

Library of Congress Catalog Card Number: 78-57765
ISBN: 0-313-20564-7

First published in 1978

Greenwood Press, Inc.
51 Riverside Avenue, Westport, Connecticut 06880

Printed in the United States of America

10 9 8 7 6 5 4 3 2 1

Contents

Preface

Samuel Taylor Coleridge: A Selective Bibliography of Criticism, 1935-1977, had its beginning in the summer of 1966 when I had the privilege of taking a course in the English Romantic Movement under the late Dr. James V. Baker, Professor of English, at the University of Houston. It was the inspired teaching of this scholar that made me realize for the first time that Samuel Taylor Coleridge was not just another poet to be passed over quickly but a profound thinker who was far ahead of his time.

As a librarian and professor of library science I came to realize, even from a cursory investigation, that Coleridge was receiving attention: from students who were writing dissertations and theses about him and his works; from scholars who were writing books and articles about him; from psychiatrists, psychologists, and theologians who were interested in what he wrote about dreams, guilt, and the subconscious mind long before Sigmund Freud did his research; and from undergraduates who were discovering that he had something to say to them in the twentieth century.

It was this brief investigation and interest that brought to my attention that the only extant bibliography available to aid in the study of Coleridge at any level was the work compiled in 1935 by Virginia Wadlow Kennedy with the assistance of Mary Neill Barton: *Samuel Taylor Coleridge: A Selected Bibliography of the Best Available Editions of His Writings, of Biographies and Criticisms of Him, and of References Showing His Relations with Contemporaries for Students and Teachers* (Baltimore: The Enoch Pratt Free Library).

With the assistance of Mrs. Melinda Stapper, an instructor of high school English and one of my students in library science, plans were formulated to prepare and make available a bibliography of the criticism that has been published on Coleridge and his writings since 1935, the publication date of Kennedy's work, continuing through 1977.

The bibliography is selective. We have limited our entries to criticism. Coleridge's writings are cited only when critical material was found in their prefaces or introductions or when they furnished biographical information. With few exceptions, the material listed in this bibliography was located and examined with the intention of including sources that are readily available in American university and college libraries. The major exception to this is the listing of abstracts of dissertations taken almost exclusively from *Dissertation Abstracts International*.

This bibliography includes chapters on criticism of individual works, general criticism found in books and in periodicals, biography, and abstracts of dissertations. Annotations have been kept brief, and when titles seemed to make them unnecessary, they were omitted. Citations to reviews of books have been included.

Many individuals at Western Kentucky University have helped to make this bibliography possible, and we acknowledge them with deep gratitude: Dr. James L. Davis, Vice-President for Academic Affairs; Dr. William R. Hourigan, Dean of the College of Applied Arts and Health; Dr. Vera Grinstead Guthrie, Head of the Department of Library Science and Instructional Media, and Dr. Robert C. Smith, Assistant Professor of Library Science and Instructional Media, for their support and encouragement. Appreciation also goes to the Faculty Research Committee—Dr. Bruce Goodrow, Dr. William Lane, Dr. Gene Harryman, Dr. John Wassom, Mr. Curtis Logsdon, Dr. Jack Thacker, and Mrs. Eunice Wells—for making a grant available to complete this project.

We are also grateful to the many librarians who assisted us in their libraries at the University of Houston, Rice University, the University of Texas at Austin, Texas A & I University at Kingsville, Del Mar College at Corpus Christi, George Storch Memorial Library of Trinity University in San Antonio, Southwest Texas State University at San Marcos, and Western Kentucky University.

We are especially grateful to the two faithful typists for their endurance and unselfish devotion to the task of preparing the manuscript: Miss Jo Lynn Hickman of Taft, Texas, who typed the first draft of the work; and Mrs. Earlene Cantrell, who prepared the final copy and assisted faithfully and well.

JEFFERSON D. CASKEY
Bowling Green, Kentucky

List of Serials and Abbreviations

ABC	American Book Collector
AFF	Anali Filoskog Fakulteta
AI	American Imago
AL	American Literature
ALJ	Australian Library Journal
AN&Q	American Notes & Queries
AP	Aryan Path
AQ	Arizona Quarterly
AS	American Speech
A Sch	American Scholar
ATR	Anglican Theological Review
Adam	Adam: International Review
Agenda	
Alphabet	
ANGL	Anglia
ARIEL	A Review of International English Literature
Arion	Arion (University of Texas)
Art I	Art International
Athen	The Athenaeum

BB	Bulletin of Bibliography
BC	The Book Collector
BFA	Bulletin of the Faculty of Arts
BJA	British Journal of Aesthetics
BJRL	Bulletin of the John Rylands Library
BLR	Bodleian Library Record
BMQ	British Museum Quarterly
B Mag	Blackwood's Magazine
BNYPL	Bulletin of the New York Public Library
BS	Bibliotheca Sacra
BSUF	Ball State University Forum
BUSE	Boston University Studies in English
Barat R	Barat Review
BuR	Bucknell Review
CCTE	Conference of College Teachers of English of Texas
CE	College English
CEA	CEA Critic
CJ	Classical Journal
CL	Comparative Literature
CLAJ	College Language Association Journal (Morgan State College, Baltimore)
CLC	Columbia Library Columns
CLJ	Cornell Library Journal
CLS	Comparative Literature Studies
CM	Carleton Miscellany
CP	Concerning Poetry (West Washington State College)
CS	Critical Survey
CamJ	Cambridge Journal
CamR	Cambridge Review
Carrell	
CentR	The Centennial Review (Michigan State University)

ChLB	Charles Lamb Bulletin
Com	Commonweal
Conrad	Conradiana: A Journal of Joseph Conrad
CONT	Continuum
Coronet	
Costerus	
CRIT	Criticism (Wayne State University)
Crit Q	Critical Quarterly
DA	Dissertation Abstracts
DESB	Delta Epsilon Sigma Bulletin (Alton, Ill.)
DIAC	Diacritics
DR	Dalhousie Review
DUJ	Durham University Journal
DilR	Diliman Review
DuR	Dublin Review
Daedalus	
EA	Etudes Anglaises
EAOB	English Association of Ohio Bulletin
E&S	Essays and Studies by Members of the English Association
ECS	Eighteenth-Century Studies (University of California)
EDH	Essays by Divers Hands
EIE	English Institute Essays
EIC	Essays in Criticism (Oxford)
EJ	English Journal
ELH	Journal of English Literary History
ELN	English Language Notes (University of Colorado)
EM	English Miscellany
ES	English Studies
ESC	Eighteenth Century Studies
ESELL	Essays and Studies in English Language and Literature (Sendai, Japan)
ESQ	Emerson Society Quarterly

ESA	English Studies in Africa
EStudien	Englissche Studien
EUQ	Emory University Quarterly
EIGO S	Eigo Seinen—(The Rising Generation, Tokyo)
EngR	English Record
English	
EXPL	Explicator
Forum	
GR	The Georgia Review
HAB	Humanities Association Bulletin (Canada)
HLB	Harvard Library Bulletin
HLQ	Huntington Library Quarterly
HTR	Harvard Theological Review
IJES	Indian Journal of English Studies (Calcutta)
IJP	International Journal of Psycho-Analysis
IL	Indian Literature
Invitation to Learning	
Isis	
JA	Jahrbuch fur Amerikastudien
JAAC	Journal of Aesthetics and Art Criticism
JAS	Journal of American Studies
JEGP	Journal of English and Germanic Philology
JHI	Journal of the History of Ideas
JJQ	James Joyce Quarterly
JP	Journal of Philosophy
JR	Journal of Religion
JWIC	Journal of the Warburg and Courauld Institutes
KM	Kansas Magazine
KR	Kenyon Review
KSJ	Keats-Shelley Journal
KSMB	Keats-Shelley Memorial Bulletin (Rome)
L&P	Literature and Psychology
LC	Library Chronicle (University of Pennsylvania)

LCUT	Library Chronicle of the University of Texas
LCrit	Literary Criterion (University of Mysore, India)
LHR	Lock Haven Review (Lock Haven State College, Pa.)
LL	Life and Letters
LM	London Magazine
LT	London Times
Listen	Listener (British Broadcasting Corporation)
MB	More Books—Bulletin of the Boston Public Library
MCR	Melbourne Critical Revue
MFS	Modern Fiction Studies
MLJ	Modern Language Journal
MLN	Modern Language Notes
MLQ	Modern Language Quarterly
MLR	Modern Language Review
MP	Modern Philology
MQ	Midwest Quarterly (Pittsburg, Kans.)
MR	Massachusetts Review
MS	Medieval Studies (Toronto)
MSCS	Mankoto State College Studies
MSE	Massachusetts Studies in English
Meanjin	Meanjin Quarterly (University of Melbourne)
Merc	London Mercury
Mill N	Mill Newsletter
Mon/HES	Monograph Series-Harvard English Studies
Mon/TUMS	English Monograph Series (University of Tulsa)
NALF	Negro American Literature Forum
N&Q	Notes and Queries
NB	New Blackfriars
NCS	Nineteenth Century Studies
NDEJ	Notre Dame English Journal
NDQ	North Dakota Quarterly
NEQ	New England Quarterly

NLWJ	National Library of Wales Journal
NM	National Review
NRRSL	Notes and Records of the Royal Society of London
NS	Die Nueren Sprachen
NSN	New Stateman and Nation
NSta	New Statesman
NYPLB	New York Public Library Bulletin
NYT	The New York Times
NEOPHIL	Neophilolgus (Groningen)
OL	Orbis Litterarum
Orcrist	
PAPS	Proceedings of the American Philosophical Society
PBA	Proceedings of the British Academy
PBSA	Papers of the Bibliographical Society of America
PCP	Pacific Coast Philology
PHR	Philosophical Review
PLL	Papers on Language and Literature
PMASAL	Papers of the Michigan Academy of Science, Arts, and Letters
PMLA	Publication of the Modern Language Association of America
PQ	Philogical Quarterly
PS	Prairie Schooner
PTRSC	Proceedings and Transactions, Royal Society of Canada
PULC	Princeton University Library Chronicle
Person	The Personalist
PoeN	Poe Newsletter
PetR	Poetry Review
Poetry	
PsyR	Psychoanalytic Review
QJCA	Quarterly Journal of Current Acquisitions

QJS	Quarterly Journal of Speech
QQ	Queen's Quarterly
QR	Quarterly Review
R&E	Review and Expositor
RBPH	Revue Belge de Philologie et d'Histoire
RdE	Rivista di Estetica (University di Padova)
REL	Review of English Literature
RES	Review of English Studies
RLC	Revue de Litterature Comparee
RLV	Revue Des Langues Vivantes (Bruxelles)
RMS	Renaissance & Modern Studies (University of Nottingham)
RORD	Research Opportunities in Renaissance Drama
RS	Research Studies—State College of Washington
REN	Renascence
SAQ	South Atlantic Quarterly
SB	Studies in Bibliography
SCB	South Central Bulletin Studies
SE	Studies in English (University of Texas)
SEL	Studies in English Literature
SEL-Japan	Studies in English Literature (Japan)
SGG	Studia Germania Gandensia
SH	Scripta Hierosolymitana
SHR	Southern Humanities Review
SIR	Studies in Romanticism (Boston University)
SLJ	Southern Library Journal
SLL	Studies in Literature and Language—University of Texas
SM	Smallwood's Magazine
SP	Studies in Philology
SQ	Shakespeare Quarterly
SR	Sewanee Review
SRL	Saturday Review of Literature

SS	Science and Society
SSF	Studies in Short Fiction (Newberry College, S.C.)
SSL	Studies in Scottish Literature
ST	Sky and Telescope
STC	Studies in the Twentieth Century
SatR	Saturday Review of Literature
Scrut	Scrutiny
Serif	Serif (Kent, Ohio)
ShN	Shakespeare Newsletter
ShQ	Shakespeare Quarterly
ShS	Shakespeare Survey
SoR	Southern Review (University of Adelaide)
Stand	Standpunte
StwenC	Studies in the Twentieth Century
Style	Style (University of Arkansas)
TDR	Tulane Drama Review (Now, The Drama Review)
TLS	Times Literary Supplement (London)
TQ	Texas Quarterly (University of Texas)
TSE	Tulane Studies in English
TSL	Tennessee Studies in English
TSLL	Texas Studies in Literature and Language
TRI-Q	Tri-Quarterly
TxSE	Texas Studies in English
THOTH	Thoth (Dept. of English, Syracuse University)
UCPE	University of California Publications in English
UDR	University of Denver Quarterly
UTQ	University of Toronto Quarterly
UWR	University of Windsor Review (Windsor, Ontario)
VH	Vermont History
VP	Victorian Poetry (West Virginia University)
VPN	Victorian Periodicals Newsletter
VQR	Virginia Quarterly Review
VS	Victorian Studies (Indiana University)

Ven	Venture: Magazine of the Yale Graduate School
WAL	Western American Literature
WASAL	Wisconsin Academy of Science, Arts, and Letters
WC	The Wordsworth Circle
WCS	Wordsworth Centenary Studies
WHR	Western Humanities Review
WL	Women & Literature
WisSL	Wisconsin Studies in Literature
YFS	Yale French Studies
YR	Yale Review
YULG	Yale University Library Gazette
ZAA	Zeitschrift fur Anglistuk and Americanistik (East Berlin)

SAMUEL TAYLOR COLERIDGE

Criticism of Individual Works

BIOGRAPHIA LITERARIA

1   Adams, Robert M. "Poetry in the Novel; or, Faulkner Esemplastic."
VQR, 29 (Summer, 1953), 419-34.

2   Barcus, James E. "The Homogeneity of Structure and Idea in
Coleridge's Biographia Literaria, Philosophical Lectures, and Aids
to Reflection." University of Pennsylvania, DA, 29 (January, 1969),
2205A-06A.

3   Brooks, Jerome. "Coleridge's Biographia Literaria." EXPL,
1 (December, 1942), Item 21.

4   Cairns, Huntington. "Coleridge: Biographia Literaria." (In
Cairns, Huntington and others. Invitation to Learning. New York:
Random House, 1941), 241-55.

5   Christensen, Jerome C. "Coleridge's Marginal Method in the
Biographia Literaria." PMLA, 92 (October, 1977), 928-40.

6   Cooke, M. G. "Quisque Sui Faber: Coleridge in the Biographia
Literaria." PQ, 50 (April, 1971), 208-29.

7   D'Avanzo, Mario L. "Yeats' 'Long-Legged Fly'." EXPL, 34
(November, 1975), Item 23.

8   Eliot, Thomas Stearns. "Wordsworth and Coleridge." (In Eliot,
T. S. The Use of Poetry and the Use of Criticism: Studies in the
Relation of Criticism to Poetry in England. London: Faber and Faber,
1948), 67-85.

9   Fogel, Daniel Mark. "A Compositional History of the Biographia
Literaria." (In Virginia. University. Bibliographical Society.
Studies in Bibliography. Edited by Fredson Bowers, v. 30. Published
for the Bibliographical Society of the University of Virginia by
University Press of Virginia, 1977), 219-34.

10   Hall, Roland. "Words from Coleridge's Biographia Literaria."
N&Q, 17 (May, 1970), 171-74.

11   Hayden, John O. "Coleridge, the Reviewers, and Wordsworth."
SP, 68 (January, 1971), 105-19.

12   Hocks, Richard Allen. "'Novelty' in Polarity to 'the Most
Admitted Truths': Tradition and the Individual Talent in S. T.
Coleridge and T. S. Eliot. (In Evolution of Consciousness: Studies
in Polarity. Edited by Shirley Sugerman. Middletown, CT: Wesleyan
University Press, 1976), 83-97.

13   Howells, Coral Ann. "Biographia Literaria and Nightmare Abbey."
N&Q, 16 (February, 1969), 50-51.

14   Hume, Robert D. "Coleridge's Retention of Primary Imagination."
N&Q, 16 (February, 1969), 55-56.

15   Knoepflamacher, Ulrich Camillus. "A Nineteenth-Century Touch-
stone: Chapter XV of Biographia Literaria." (In Nineteenth-Century
Literary Perspectives: Essays in Honor of Lional Stevenson. Edited
by Clyde de L. Ryals with the assistance of John Clubbe and Benjamin
Franklin Fisher IV. Durham, N.C.: Duke University Press, 1974), 3-16.

16   Leavis, F. R. "Coleridge in Criticism." Scrut., 9 (June,
1940), 57-69.

17   Little, Geoffrey. "A Note on Wordsworth and Blair." N&Q,
7 (July, 1960), 254-55.

18   McFarland, Thomas Alfred. "The Origin and Significance of
Coleridge's Theory of Secondary Imagination." (In Hartman, G. H.,
ed. New Perspectives on Coleridge and Wordsworth: Selected Papers
From the English Institute. Edited with a foreword. New York:
Columbia University Press, 1972), 195-246.

19   Mallette, Richard. "Narrative Technique and Structure in the
Biographia Literaria." MLR, 70 (January, 1975), 32-40.

20   Montgomery, Marion. "Around the Prickly Pear." (In Montgomery,
Marion. The Reflective Journey Toward Order: Essays on Dante,
Wordsworth, Eliot, and others. Athens: University of Georgia Press,
1973), 179-97.

21   Orsinski, Sister Mary Lucilla, O. S. F. "A Study of the
Structure of Coordination in a Representative Sample of the Biographia
Literaria. The Catholic University of America, DA, 24 (March 19),
3731-32.

22   Parrish, Stephen Maxfield. "The Wordsworth-Coleridge
Controversy." PMLA, 73 (September, 1958), 367-74.

      Extends from the collaboration on Lyrical Ballads (1797) to
      Biographia Literaria (1817).

23   Pollin, Burton R. and Redmond Burke. "John Thelwall's
Marginalia in a Copy of Coleridge's Biographia Literaria." BNYPL,
74 (February, 1970), 73-94.

24   Pradhan, S. V. "Coleridge's 'Philocrisy' and His Theory of
Fancy and Secondary Imagination." SIR, 13 (Summer, 1974), 235-54.

      Revision of a paper presented at the annual meeting of the
      Pacific Division of the American Society for Aesthetics at
      Squaw Valley, California, April 20, 1973.

25   Rauber, D. F. "The Fragment as Romantic Form." MLQ, 30
(June, 1969), 212-21.

26   Raysor, Thomas M. "Coleridge's Criticism of Wordsworth."
PMLA, 54 (June, 1939), 496-510.

27   Richards, Ivor Armstrong. "Literature for the Unlettered."
(In Uses of Literature. Edited by Monroe Engel. Cambridge, Mass.:
Harvard University Press, 1973. Harvard English Studies, 4),
207-24.

28   Rogers, William E. "Yeats 'Long-Legged Fly' and Coleridge's
Biographia Literaria." CP, 8 (1975), 11-21.

29   Shaffer, Elinor S. "The 'Postulates in Philosophy' in
Biographia Literaria." CLS, 7 (September, 1970), 297-313.

30   Teich, Nathaniel. "Coleridge's Biographia and the Contemporary
Controversy about Style." WC, 3 (Spring, 1972), 61-70.

31   Watson, George. "The Text of the Biographia Literaria." N&Q,
199 (June, 1954), 262-63.

32   Whalley, George. "The Integrity of Biographia Literaria."
E&S, 6 (1953), 87-101.

33   Wright, G. W. "Coleridge and Dr. Hartley." N&Q, 177
(September 2, 1939), 179.

CHRISTABEL

34   Adams, Maurianne S. "Coleridge and the Victorians: Studies
in the Interpretation of Poetry, Scripture, and Myth." Indiana
University, DA, 28 (Mar. 1968), 3662A-63A.

35   Adlard, John. "The Quantock Christabel." PQ, 50 (April, 1971), 230-38.

36   Alley, Alvin D. "Coleridge and Existentialism." SHR, 2 (Fall, 1968), 451-61.

37   Angus, Douglas. "The Theme of Love and Guilt in Coleridge's Three Major Poems." JEGP, 59 (October, 1960), 655-68.

38   Basler, Roy P. "Christabel: A Study of Its Sexual Theme." SR, 51 (January-March, 1943), 73-95.

39   _____. "Coleridge's Christabel." (In Basler, Roy P. Sex, Symbolism, and Psychology in Literature. New Brunswick: Rutgers University Press, 1948), 25-72.

40   Berkoben, Lawrence D. "Christabel: A Variety of Evil Experience." MLQ, 25 (December, 1964), 400-11.

41   _____. "Varieties of Evil Experience, II: Christabel." (In Berkoben, Lawrence D. Coleridge's Decline as a Poet. The Hague: Mouton, 1975), 93-107.

42   Bostetter, Edward E. "Christabel: The Vision of Fear." PQ, 36 (April, 1957), 183-94.

43   Brooks, E. L. "Coleridge's Second Packet for Blackwood's Magazine." PQ, 30 (October, 1951), 426-30.

      Concerning articles on witchcraft that may be by Coleridge; if authentic, they pertain, for example, to Christabel.

44   Chayes, Irene H. "Coleridge, Metempsychosis, and Almost All the Followers of Fenelon." ELH, 25 (December, 1958), 290-315.

45   Coburn, Kathleen. "Who Killed Christabel?" TLS (May 20, 1965), 397.

46   Dowden, Wilfred S. "Thomas Moore and the Review of Christabel." MP, 60 (August, 1962), 47-50.

47   Dramin, Edward I. "'Amid the Jagged Shadows': Parody Moral Realism, and Metaphysical Statements in Coleridge's Christabel." Columbia University DAI, 34 (July, 1973), 310A.

48   Edwards, Paul, and MacDonald, Emslie. "'Thoughts So All Unlike Each Other': The Paradoxical in Christabel." ES, 52 (June, 1971), 236-46.

49   Emslie, MacDonald, and Paul Edwards. "The Limitations of Langdale: A Reading of Christabel." EIC, 20 (January, 1970), 57-70.

50   Enscoe, Gerald E. "Eros and the Romantics: Sexual Love As a Theme in Coleridge, Shelley, and Keats." University of Washington, DA, 24 (July, 1963), 296-97.

51   Erdman, David V. ed. "A New Discovery: The First Review of
Christabel." TxSE, 27 (1958), 53-60.

52   Everett, Edwin M. "Lord Byron's Lakist Interlude." SP, 55
(January, 1958), 62-75.

53   Farrison, W. Edward. "Coleridge's Christabel: The Conclusion
of Part II." CLAJ, 5 (December, 1961), 83-94.

54   Fields, Beverly Franke. "Reality's Dark Dream: A Study of
Dejection in Coleridge." Northwestern University, DA, 26 (December,
1965), 3333-34.

55   Flory, Wendy Stallard. "Fathers and Daughters: Coleridge and
'Christabel'." Women & Literature, 3 (Spring, 1975), 5-15.

56   Fogle, Richard Harter. "Christabel." (In R. H. Fogle. The
Idea of Coleridge's Criticism. Berkeley: University of California
Press, 1962), 130-59.

57   French, Richard. "Sir Walter Scott and His Literary Contemporaries." CLAJ, 11 (March, 1968), 248-54.

58   French, Warren G. "Coleridge's Christabel." EXPL, 13 (June,
1955), Item 48.

      Suggests that the oak tree in Stanza 4 has druidical associations.

59   Garvin, Katherine. "Snakes in the Grass with Particular
Attention to Satan, Lamia, Christabel." REL, 2 (April, 1961), 11-27.

60   Green, Andrew J. "Essays in Miniature: The Resistless Eye."
CE, 3 (May, 1942), 722-3.

      Coleridge's obsession with the mesmeric eye in Christabel,
      Rime of the Ancient Mariner, and Kubla Khan.

61   Griggs, Earl L. "An Early Defense of Christabel." (In Wordsworth
and Coleridge: Studies in Honor of George McLean Harper. ed. by Earl
L. Griggs, New York: Russell and Russell, 1962), 173-91.

      An unpublished review preserved in the handwriting of John J.
      Morgan, and apparently written by Morgan with Coleridge's help.

62   Griggs, Earl L. "The Willing Suspension of Disbelief."
(In Elizabethan Studies and Other Essays in Honor of George F.
Reynolds. University of Colorado Studies. Series B. Studies in
the Humanities, v. 2, no. 4), 272-85.

63   Haven, Richard. "Anna Vardill Niven's 'Christobell': An
Addendum." WC, 7 (Spring, 1975), 117-18.

64   Holstein, Michael E. "Coleridge's 'Christabel' as Psychodrama:
Five Perspectives on the Intruder." WC, 7 (Spring, 1976), 119-28.

65   Horrell, Joseph. "The Demonic Finale of Christabel." MLR,
37 (July, 1942), 363-64.

66   Hunting, Constance. "Another Look at 'The Conclusion to
Part II' of Christabel." ELN, 12 (March, 1975), 171-76.

67   Johnson, Mary Lynn. "Gillman's Discovery of the 'Lost'
Times Review of Christabel." WC, 6 (Winter, 1975), 55-58.

68   Jones, Edgar. "A New Reading of Christabel." CamJ, (November,
1951), 97-112.

69   Jordan, Hoover H. "Thomas Moore and the Review of Christabel."
MP, 54 (November, 1956), 95-105.

      (Also in Evidence for Authorship, ed. by David V. Erdman and
      Ephim G. Fogel, New York: Cornell University Press, 1966, 355-69.)

70   Katsurada, Rikichi. "Appreciation of Christabel." ESELL,
45-46 (December, 1964), 127-45.

71   Kitzhaber, Annabel W. "David Hartley in Christabel." RS,
9 (December, 1964), 213-22.

      Traces Hartley's optimism and determinism in the poem and
      suggests that Coleridge's failure to finish it may have been
      due in part to his abandonment of Hartley's philosophy.

72   Knight, G. Wilson. "Coleridge's Divine Comedy." (In M. H.
Abrams, ed. English Romantic Poets: Modern Essays in Criticism.
London, New York: Oxford University Press, 1960), 158-69.

73   _____. The Starlit Dome: Studies in the Poetry of Vision.
London, New York: Oxford University Press, 1941, 83-84 et passim.

74   Kroeber, K. "The Poetic Tale." (In K. Kroeber. Romantic
Narrative Art. Madison: University of Wisconsin Press, 1960), 64-77.

75   Kuic, Ranka. "Three Levels of Reality in Coleridge's Christabel
and an Anatomy of Christabel's Psyche." Zbornik radova. Odsek za
anglistidu. Beograd, 145-96.

76   Little, G. L. "Christabess: by S. T. Colebritchie, Esq."
MLR, 56 (April, 1961), 215-20.

      Discusses an anonymous parody of Coleridge.

77   _____. "An Important Unpublished Wordsworth Letter:
December 28, 1800." N&Q, 6 (September, 1959), 313-16.

78   McElderry, B. R., Jr. "Christabel, Coleridge, and the
Commentators." RS, 9 (September, 1941), 206-12.

      Discusses the sources of the poem and restates his opinion
      that Gillman's report of Coleridge's plan is authentic.

79 _____. "Coleridge's Plan for Completing Christabel."
SP, 33 (July, 1936), 437-55.

80 _____. "Coleridge's 'Preface' to Christabel." (In Wordsworth
and Coleridge: Studies in Honor of George McLean Harper. ed. by
Earl L. Griggs. New York: Russell and Russell, 1962), 166-72.

An examination of two letters of Coleridge which constitute
virtually a first draft of the Preface.

81 Maier, Rosemarie. "The Bitch and the Bloodhound: Generic
Similarity in Christabel and The Eve of St. Agnes." JEGP, 70
(January, 1971), 62-75.

82 Marsh, Florence G. "Christabel and Coleridge's 'Recipe' for
Romance Poems." N&Q, 5 (November, 1958), 475-76.

Miss Marsh now identified by N&Q as the author.

83 Nethercot, Arthur H. "Christabel's Wild Flower Wine." MLQ,
1 (December, 1940), 499-501.

84 _____. "Coleridge's Christabel and LeFanu's Carmilla."
MP, 47 (August, 1949), 32-38.

LeFanu's story lends some support to the theory that Coleridge's
Geraldine was conceived...as a vampire.

85 _____. The Road to Tryermaine: A Study of the History,
Background, and Purposes of Coleridge's Christabel. Chicago:
The University of Chicago Press, 1939.

Reviews: H. E. Arntston in LQ, 10 (1940), 451; G. M. Harper in
SRL (June 15, 1940), 18-19; R. W. King in RES, 16 (July, 1940),
350-53; Rene Wellek in MP, 38 (November, 1940), 218-21; Richard
F. Jones in JEGP, 40 (1941), 154-55; Arno Esch in Ang. Bbl. 52
(1941), 121-24; E. C. Batho in MLR, 36 (1941), 127-29; E. L.
Griggs in SR, 49 (April-June, 1941), 385-88; Mario Praz in MLN,
56 (May, 1941), 381-84; H. W. Hausermann in ES, 24 (1942), 95-96.

86 Nethercot, Arthur H. & Charles I. Patterson, Jr. "On Coleridge's
'Kubla Khan' and 'Christabel'." PMLA, 90 (1975), 927-29.

87 O'Hear, Michael F. "The Constant Dream: Coleridge's Vision of
Woman and Love." University of Maryland, DAI, 37(February, 1971),
4174A-75A.

88 Otten, Terry. "Christabel, Beatrice, and the Encounter with
Evil." BuR, 17 (May, 1969), 19-31.

89 Ousby, Heather Dubrow. "Coleridge's 'The Ballad of the Dark
Ladie'." EXPL, 35 (Fall 1976), 21-22.

90   Patrick, Michael D. "Christabel: A Brief Critical History
and Reconsideration." (In Hoggs, James, ed. Romantic Reassessment XI.
Inst. Fur Englische Sprache und Literature, University Salzbur, 1972),
A-5020.

   Review: Anya Taylor in WC, 5 (Summer, 1974), 191-94.

91   Patterson, Charles I. "An Unidentified Criticism by Colerdige
Related to Christabel." PMLA, 67 (December, 1952), 973-88.

   Coleridge's review of Horsley's book on classical prosody
   (Critical Review, 19, 1797) throws light on the preface to
   Christabel.

92   Peckham, Morse. "Poet and Critic (or the Damage Coleridge
Has Done)." STC, 6 (Fall 1970), 1-11.

93   Pollin, B. R. "Poe's Use of the Name 'Ermengarde' in Eleonora."
N&Q, 19 (September, 1970), 332-33.

94   Preston, Thomas R. "Christabel and the Mystical Traditions."
ESELL, 5 (1964), 138-57.

95   Radley, Virginia L. "Christabel: Directions Old and New."
SEL, 4 (Autumn, 1974), 531-41.

96   Reiman, Donald H. "Christabel; or, The Case of the Sequel
Preemptive." WC, 6 (Autumn, 1975), 283-89.

97   Richards, I. A. "Coleridge: The Vulnerable Poet." YR, 48
(June, 1959), 491-504.

98   Rickey, Mary Ellen. "Christabel and Murder in the Cathedral."
N&Q, 10 (April, 1973), 151.

99   Schneider, Elisabeth. "Notes on Christabel." PQ, 32 (April,
1953), 197-206.

100   _____. "Tom Moore and Edinburgh Review of Christabel."
PMLA, 77 (March, 1962), 71-76.

101   _____. "The Unknown Reviewer of Christabel: Jeffrey
Hazlitt, Tom Moore." PMLA, 70 (June, 1955), 417-32.

102   Schulz, Max F. "Coleridge, Wordsworth, and the 1800 Preface
to Lyrical Ballads." SEL, 5 (Autumn, 1965), 619-39.

103   Schwartz, Lewis M. "A New Review of Coleridge's Christabel."
SIR, 9 (Spring, 1970), 114-24.

   Review attributed to Lamb.

104   Siegel, Robert H. "The Serpent and the Dove: Christabel and
the Problem of Evil." (In Huttar, Charles A. ed. Imagination and
the Spirit: Essays in Literature and the Christian Faith Presented
to Clyde S. Kilby. Grand Rapids, Michigan: Eerdmans, 1971), 159-86.

105   Smith, J. Percy. "Criticism and Christabel." UTQ, 21
(October, 1951), 14-26.

106   Smith, Raymond. "Christabel and Geraldine: The Marriage of
Life and Death." BuR, 13 (March, 1954), 63-71.

107   Smith, Raymond D., Jr. "The Imagery for Christabel." McNeese
Review, 14 (1973), 32-44.

108   Spatz, Jona. "The Mystery of Eros: Sexual Initiation in
Coleridge's Christabel." PMLA, 90 (January, 1975), 107-16.

      A psychological study.

109   Starr, Nathan C. "Coleridge's 'Sir Leoline'." PMLA, 61
(March, 1946), 157-62.

      Suggests that Coleridge may have found the name of Christabel's
      father in a story told by Camden and Burton of Leolin Prince
      of Wales and King Edward the Elder meeting at Aust Cliff in
      Gloucestershire, a place associated with Coleridge's quarrel
      with Southey.

110   Stebelman, Scott David. "The Theme of Betrayal in Coleridge's
Poetry." University of Wisconsin, DA, 134 (July, 1974), 418A.

111   Stevenson, W. "Christabel: A Re-Interpretation." Alphabet,
4 (June, 1962), 18-35.

112   Sullivan, Ruth E. "Some Variations on the Oedipal Theme in
Three Pieces of Fiction: A Rose for Emily, Three Hours After Marriage,
and Christabel." Tufts University DAI, 33 (February, 1973), 436A.

113   Taylor, Anya. "A Review: Christabel, A Brief Critical History
and Reconsideration by Michael D. Taylor in Vol. 2 (Salzburg, 1973),
1-35." WC, 5 (Summer 1974), 191-94.

114   Thumboo, Edwin. "Christabel: Poem of Fragment." LCrit, 2
(Winter, 1973), 13-19.

115   Tomlinson, Charles. "S. T. Coleridge: Christabel." (In
Interpretations: Essays on Twelve English Poems. ed. by John Wain,
London: Routledge and K. Paul, 1955), 86-112.

116   Tuttle, Donald R. "Christabel Sources in Percy's Reliques and
the Gothic Romances." PMLA, 53 (June, 1938), 445-74.

      Sources and parallels in three ballads in Percy's Reliques
      and in Mrs. Radcliffe and others of the School of Terror.

117 Twitchell, James B. "Coleridge's Christabel." EXPL, 35 (Winter, 1976), 28-29.

118 _____. "Desire with Loathing Strangely Mixed: The Dream Work of Christabel." PsyR, 61 (Spring, 1974), 33-34.

119 Ware, J. Garth. "Coleridge's Great Poems Reflecting the Mother Image." AI, 18 (Winter, 1961), 331-52.

120 Willis, Richard. "Another Source of Christabel?" N&Q, 194 (March 19, 1949), 126.

    Joseph Warton's Ode to Solitude, 1746.

121 Woodring, Carl. "Christabel of Cumberland." REL, 7 (January, 1966), 43-52.

122 Wormhoudt, Arthur. "Christabel." The Demon Lover: A Psychoanalytic Approach to Literature. New York: Exposition Press, (1949), 17-29, 42-47.

DEJECTION: AN ODE

123 Bewley, Eugene M. "The Poetry of Coleridge." Scrut., 8 (March, 1940), 406-20.

124 Bhattacharya, Biswanath. "Mismanaged Sensibility." LCrit, 9 (Winter, 1970), 81-83.

125 Bloom, Harold. "Samuel Taylor Coleridge." (In Bloom, Harold. The Visionary Company. New York: Doubleday, 1961), 216-23.

126 Bostetter, Edward E. The Romantic Ventriloquists: Wordsworth, Coleridge, Keats, Shelley, Byron. Seattle: University of Washington Press, 1963. 132-33.

127 Boulger, James D. "Imagination and Speculation in Coleridge's Conversation Poems." JEGP, 64 (October, 1965), 691-711.

128 Bouslog, Charles S. "Structure and Theme in Coleridge's Dejection: An Ode." MLQ, 24 (March, 1973), 42-52.

129 Bowra, C. M. The Romantic Imagination. New York: Oxford University Press, 1961, 85-91 et passim.

130 Broughton, Panthea R. "The Modifying Metaphor in Dejection: An Ode." WC, 4 (Autumn, 1973), 241-49.

131 Burke, Charles B. "Coleridge and Milton." N&Q, 176 (January 21, 1939), 42.

    Notes a parallel in Samson Agonistes and Dejection: An Ode.

132 Chayes, Irene H. "Rhetoric as Drama: An Approach to the Romantic Ode." PMLA, 79 (March, 1964), 67-79.

133 Daniel, Robert. "Ode to a Dejection." KR, 15 (Winter, 1953), 129-40.

Studies particularly Coleridge's Dejection: An Ode and Keats' Ode To A Nightingale with some reference to other poems in the same tradition.

134 D'Avanzo, Mario L. "Wordsworth's and Coleridge's 'Genial Spirits'." WC, 2 (Winter, 1971), 17-20.

An explanation of the two poets' use of the term "my genial spirits."

135 De Selincourt, Ernest. "Coleridge's Dejection: An Ode." E&S, 22 (1936), 7-25.

Reviewed by Raymond D. Havens in MLN, 53 (May, 1938), 395-96.

136 Dickstein, Morris. "Coleridge, Wordsworth and the Conversation Poems." CentR, 16 (Fall, 1972), 367-83.

137 Dunlap, Rhodes. "Verses by Coleridge." PQ, 42 (April, 1963), 282-84.

Six unpublished lines in ms. in University of Iowa Library reflecting the central theme in Dejection...: "Sing and rejoice."

138 Elledge, W. Paul. "Fountains Within: Motivation in Coleridge's Dejection: An Ode." PLL, 7 (Summer, 1971), 304-8.

139 Evans, B. Ifor. "Coleorton Manuscripts of Resolution and Independence and Ode To Dejection." MLR, 46 (July-October, 1951), 355-60.

140 Fairbanks, A. Harris. "The Form of Coleridge's Dejection Ode." PMLA, 90, (October, 1975), 874-84.

141 Fogle, Richard H. "The Dejection of Coleridge's Ode." ELH, 17 (March, 1950), 71-77.

An analysis of Dejection: An Ode indicates that the poem is less gloomy than has usually been thought.

Reprinted in Fogle, R. H. The Permanent Pleasure: Essays on Classics of Romanticism. Athens: University of Georgia Press, 1974, 53-9.

142 Fogle, Stephen F. "The Design of Coleridge's Dejection." SP, 48 (January, 1951), 49-55.

The differences between the original and the revised version of the poem are all fully justified on aesthetic as well as on those of caution.

14 SAMUEL TAYLOR COLERIDGE

143   Frese, John J.   "Four Voices: Studies in Consciousness and the Romantic Ode." University of Iowa, DAI, 33 (October, 1972), 1681A.

144   Galinsky, Hans. "Echowirkungen von Coleridge's Kubla Khan and Dejection: An Ode in Longfellow's ersten Heine-Essay. (1842)." JA, 3 (1958), 112-35.

145   Gay, R. M. "Coleridge's Dejection: An Ode." EXPL, 2 (November, 1943), Item 14.

146   Hardy, Barbara. "Keats, Coleridge and Negative Capability." N&Q, 197 (July 2, 1952), 299-301.

147   Harper, George M. "Coleridge's Conversation Poems." (In Abrams, M. H. English Romantic Poets. New York: Oxford University Press, 1960), 144-57.

148   Hayden, John O. "Coleridge's Dejection: An Ode." ES, 52 (April, 1971), 132-6.

149   Kelly, Michael J. "Coleridge's 'Picture; or, The Lover's Resolution': Its Relationship to 'Dejection' and Its Sources in the Notebooks." Costerus, 5 (1972), 75-96.

150   Knight, G. Wilson. The Starlit Dome: Studies in the Poetry of Vision. London: Oxford University Press, 1941; New York: Barnes & Noble, 1960, passim.

151   Lefcowitz, Barbara F. "Omnipotence of Thought and the Poetic Imagination: Blake, Coleridge, and Rilke." PsyR, 59 (1972), 417-32.

152   Little, Geoffrey. "'Lines Written at Shurton Bars': Coleridge's First Conversation Poem?" SoR, 2 (1966), 137-49.

153   Lovejoy, Arthur O. "Coleridge and Kant's Two Worlds." ELH, 7 (December, 1940), 341-62.

      Influence of Kant upon Dejection: An Ode.

154   Lupton, Mary J. "The Dark Dream of Dejection." L&P, 18 (1968), 39-47.

155   _____. "A Psychoanalytic Study of the Poetry of Samuel Taylor Coleridge." Temple University, DAI, 30 (October, 1969), 1531A-32A.

156   Magnuson, Paul A. "The Problems of Personal Identity and Guilt in Coleridge's Poetry." University of Minnesota, DAI, 30 (February, 1970), 3466A-67A.

157   Marsh, Florence G. "Coleridge: 'A Mountain-birth'." N&Q, 2 (June, 1955), 261-62.

158   Matthews, Jerry B. "Coleridge's Principle of the Reconciliation of Opposition as Manifested in His Poetry." University of Texas at Austin, DAI, 35 (February, 1975), 5354A.

159   Mays, Morley J. "Coleridge's Dejection: An Ode." EXPL, 2 (February, 1944), Item 27.

160   Meyer, George Wilbur. "Resolution and Independence: Wordsworth's Answer to Coleridge's Dejection: An Ode." TSE, 2 (1950), 49-74.

161   Mounts, Charles E. "Coleridge's Self-Identification with Spenserian Characters." SP, 47 (June, 1950), 522-33.

162   Pafford, Ward. "Samuel Taylor Coleridge." EUQ, 21 (Spring, 1965), 3-14.

163   Purves, Alan C. "The Verse Technique of Samuel Taylor Coleridge." Columbia University, DA, 21 (July, 1960), 190-1.

164   Rapin, René. "Coleridge's Dejection: An Ode." ES, 45 (1964), 76-94.

165   Read, Herbert. "Two Kinds of Poetry." Agenda, 7 (Spring, 1969), 34-40.

166   Rhodes, Jack L. "A Study in the Vocabulary of English Romanticism: Joy in the Poetry of Blake, Wordsworth, Coleridge, Shelley, Keats, and Byron." The University of Texas at Austin, DA, 27 (April, 1967), 3434A.

167   Ridénour, George M. "Source and Allusion in Some Poems of Coleridge." SP, 60 (January, 1963), 73-95.

      An examination of Coleridge's poems including "An Ode."
      Comments on Coleridge's use of borrowed material.

168   Scarfe, Francis. "Coleridge's Nightscapes." EA, 18 (January - March, 1965), 27-43.

169   Seturaman, V. S. "Coleridge's Dejection: An Ode: A Reconsideration." (In Seturaman, V. S. ed. Critical Essays in English Literature...Bombay: Orient Longmans, 1965), 32-39.

170   Simmons, J. L. "Coleridge's Dejection: An Ode: A Poet's Regeneration." UK, 33 (Spring, 1967), 212-18.

171   Smith, Fred M. "The Relation of Coleridge's Ode On Dejection to Wordsworth's Ode on Intimations of Immortality." PMLA, 50 (March, 1935), 224-34.

172   Starzyk, Lawrence J. "Emily Brontë: Poetry in a Mingled Tone." CRIT, 14 (Spring, 1972), 119-36.

173   Suther, Marshall. "'Dejection.'" (In Suther, Marshall.
The Dark Night of Samuel Taylor Coleridge. New York: Columbia
University Press, 1960), 119-151.

174   Swanson, Donald R. "The Growth of a Poem: Coleridge's Dejection."
BSUF, 12 (Autumn, 1971), 53-57.

175   Teichman, Milton. "Wordsworth's Two Replies to Coleridge's
Dejection: An Ode." PMLA, 86 (October, 1971), 982-89.

176   Thompson, William I. "Collapsed Universe and Structured Poem:
An Essay in Whiteheadian Criticism." CE, 28 (October, 1966), 25-39.

177   Wendling, Ronald C. "Dramatic Reconciliation in Coleridge's
Conversation Poems." PLL, 9 (Spring, 1973), 145-60.

178   Whalley, George. "'Late Autumn's Amaranth': Coleridge's Late
Poems." PTRSC, 2, 4th Series (June, 1964), 159-79.

179   Woodring, Carl R. "Coleridge and Mary Hutchinson." N&Q, 4
(May, 1957), 213-14.

180   Yamanouchi Hisaaki. "The Implications of Dejection: An Ode."
English Criticism in Japan. Compiled by Carl Miner, Tokyo: University
of Tokyo Press, 1972, 199-232.

THE EOLIAN HARP

181   Abrams, M. H. "Structure and Style in the Greater Romantic
Lyric." Essays Presented to Frederick A. Pottle. ed. by Frederick
W. Hilles and Harold Bloom, New York: Oxford University Press, 1965,
527-60.

      "Coleridge's 'A Light in Sound': Science, Metascience, and
      Poetic Imagination." PAPS, 116 (1972), 458-76.

182   Beer, J. B. "Coleridge and Boehme's Aurora." N&Q, 10
(May, 1963), 183-87.

183   Boulger, James D. "Imagination and Speculation in Coleridge's
Conversation Poems." JEGP, 64 (October, 1965), 691-711.

184   Burke, Kenneth. "The Eolian Harp." (In Burke, Kenneth.
The Philosophy of Literary Form. Baton Rouge: Louisiana State
University Press, 1941.) 93-98

185   Dickstein, Morris. "Coleridge, Wordsworth, and the Conversation
Poems." CentR., 16 (Fall, 1972), 367-83.

186   Fairbanks, A. Harris. "The Form of Coleridge's Dejection Ode."
PMLA, 90 (October, 1975), 874-84.

187   Fogle, Richard H. "Coleridge's Conversation Poems." TSE, 5
(1955), 108-09.

188 Frese, John J. "Four Voices: Studies in Consciousness and the Romantic Ode." University of Iowa, DAI, 33 (October, 1972), 1681A.

189 Gaskins, Avery F. "Coleridge: Nature, the Conversation Poems, and the Structure of Meditation." NEOPHIL, 59 (1975), 629-35.

190 Gerard, Albert. "Counterfeiting Infinity. The Eolian Harp and the Growth of Coleridge's Mind." JEGP, 60 (July, 1961), 411-22.

191 _____. "The Systolic Rhythm: The Structure of Coleridge's Conversation Poems." EIC, 10 (July, 1960), 307-19.

   The structures of The Eolian Harp, Frost at Midnight, Fears in Solitude, and Reflections on Having Left a Place of Retirement.

192 Harper, George McLean. "Coleridge's Conversation Poems." (In English Romantic Poets. ed. by M. H. Abrams, New York: Oxford University Press, 1960), 144-57.

193 Henry, William Harley. "Coleridge's Meditative Poems and Early Religious Thought: The Theology of The Eolian Harp, This Lime-Tree Bower My Prison, and Frost at Midnight. The John Hopkins University, DAI31 (November, 1970), 2345A.

194 Hoyle, James F. "The Coleridgean Landscape: An Essay in Historical Criticism of His Poetry." Princeton University, DA, 22 (December, 1961), 1999.

195 Magnuson, Paul A. "The Dead Calm in the Conversation Poems." WC, 3 (Spring, 1972), 53-60.

196 Marshall, William H. "The Structure of Coleridge's The Eolian Harp." MLN, 76 (March, 1961), 229-32.

197 Martin, C. G. "Coleridge and Cudworth: A Source for The Eolian Harp." N&Q, 13 (May, 1966), 173-6.

198 Milley, Henry J. W. "Some Notes on Coleridge's Eolian Harp." MP, 36 (May, 1939), 359-75.

   Attributes the change in Coleridge's poetry not to the influence of Wordsworth, but to his own newly awakened appreciation of nature; shows that the poem is a fusion of two pieces written on different occasions; notes its influence on Wordsworth's Tintern Abbey; finds traces of it in flux of ideas, images, words, etc., that found expression Kubla Khan.

199 Pachori, Satya S. "The Transcendentalism of Samuel Taylor Coleridge." University of Missouri (Columbia), DAI, 30 (April, 1970), 4421A-22A.

200   Paris, Bernard J. "Coleridge's The Eolian Harp." PMASAL,
51 (1965), 571-82.

201   Piper, H. W. "The Eolian Harp Again." N&Q, 15 (January, 1968),
23-25.

202   Rubenstein, Jill. "Sound and Silence in Coleridge's Conversation
Poems." English, 21 (Summer, 1972), 54-60.

203   San Juan, E., Jr. "Coleridge's The Eolian Harp as Lyric
Paradigm." Person, 48 (January, 1967), 77-88.

204   Scarfe, Francis. "Coleridge's Nightscapes." EA, 18 (January –
March, 1965), 27-43.

205   Scheuerle, William H. "A Reexamination of Coleridge's The
Eolian Harp." SEL, 25 (Autumn, 1975), 591-99.

206   Schnier, Jacques. "Free Association and Ego Function in
Creativity: A Study of Content and Form in Art." AI, 17 (Spring,
1960), 61-74.

207   Schulz, Max F. "The Wry Vision of Coleridge's Love Poetry."
Person, 45 (Spring, 1964), 214-26.

208   Ward, Patricia. "Coleridge's Critical Theory of the Symbol."
TSLL, 8 (Spring, 1966), 15-32.

209   Wendling, Ronald C. "Coleridge and the Consistency of The
Eolian Harp." SIR, 8 (Autumn, 1968), 26-42.

210   Wilkinson, Loren E. "Meaning, Man, and Earth: A Romantic
Dilemma in Contemporary Art." Syracuse University, DAI, 34 (April,
1974), 6609A.

211   Wilson, Douglas B. "Two Modes of Apprehending Nature: A
Gloss on the Coleridgean Symbol." PMLA, 87 (January, 1972), 42-52.

212   Woodring, Carl. "A Coleridge Miscellany." CLC, 24 (May,
1975), 26-32.

FROST AT MIDNIGHT

213   Fogle, Richard H. "Coleridge's Conversation Poems." TSE,
5 (1955), 110.

214   Hanson, Lawrence. "Frost at Midnight." (In Hanson, Lawrence.
The Life of S.T. Coleridge: The Early Years. New York: Russell,
Russell, 1962), 247-49.

215   Kaplan, F. "Coleridge's Aesthetic Ministry." (In Kaplan,
Fred. Miracles of Rare Device: The Poet's Sense of Self in Nineteenth Century Poetry. Detroit: Wayne State University, 1972),
44-61.

216   Landbaurn, Robert. "Frost at Midnight." (In Landbaurn, Robert.
The Poetry Experience: The Dramatic Monologue in Modern Literary
Experience. New York: Random House, 1957), 45-46.

THE FRIEND

217   Bailey, Dudley. "Coleridge's Revision of The Friend." MP,
59 (November, 1961), 89-99.

218   Bailey, June D. "Coleridge's Revisions of The Friend: A
Study of His Thought and Methods." University of Illinois, DA, 15
(January, 1955), 120-21.

219   Coburn, Kathleen. "Francis Bacon." N&Q, 2 (June, 1955), 273.

220   "Coleridge and the Background to The Friend." TLS, (January 8,
1970), 21-22.

221   Courthope, W. J. "Anti-Jacobinism in English Poetry." A
History of English Poetry, Vol. 6, New York: Russell, 1962, 124-40.

222   Di Pasquale, Pasquale, Jr. "Coleridge's Framework of Objectivity
and Eliot's Objective Correlative." JAAC, 26 (Summer, 1968), 489-500.

223   Good, James Milton. "The Coleridge-Figure in Wordsworth's
Prelude." Columbia University, DAI, 33 (July, 1972), 273A.

224   Griggs, Earl Leslie. "The Friend: 1809 and 1818 Editions."
MP, 35 (May, 1938), 369-73.

225   Heinemann, F. H. "Unknown Coleridge Marginalia." N&Q,
178 (June 29, 1940), 455-56.

226   Hunter, Parks C., Jr. "Coleridge's The Friend As the Probable
Source of the Wordsworth Quotation in the Preface to Shelley's
Alastor." N&Q, 5 (November, 1958), 474.

227   Landess, Thomas H. "The Politics of Samuel Taylor Coleridge."
SR, 81 (Autumn, 1973), 847-59.

228   Larkin, John E., Jr. "The Theory and Methods of Criticism in
Coleridge and Carlyle." Duke University, DAI, 34 (August, 1973),
729A-30A.

229   Lattin, Vernon E. "Samuel Taylor Coleridge's The Friend: A
Study in Argument and Methods of Expression." University of
Colorado, DAI, 31 (March, 1971), 4777A.

230   Mann, Peter. "Annotations by Coleridge in a Copy of The
Friend (1818)." SB, 26 (1973), 243-54.

231   Martin, C. G. "Sara Coleridge: (An Unpublished Letter)."
N&Q, 14 (February, 1967), 51-52.

232   Masterman, Neville. "Coleridge's Friend." TLS, (June 21,
1957), 381.

233   Mounts, Charles E. "Coleridge's Self-identification with
Spenserian Characters." SP, 47 (June, 1950), 522-33.

234   Nichelson, Floyd Patrick. "A Romantic Motif in Theological
Ethics: An Expository Study of the Doctrines of God and Original
Sin in Samuel Taylor Coleridge's Friend of 1818." University of
Southern California, DAI35 (December, 1974), 3872A-73A.

235   Robinson, Charles E. "The Shelley Circle and Coleridge's
The Friend." ELN, 8 (June, 1971), 269-74.

236   Rooke, Barbara E. "The Friend." TLS, (January 24, 1948), 51.

237   Ross, James. "The Friend." TLS, (February 7, 1948), 79.

238   Sanderson, David R. "Coleridge's Political Sermons: Discursive
Language and the Voice of God." MP, 70 (May, 1973), 319-30.

239   Seronsy, Cecil C. "Marginalia by Coleridge in Three Copies
of His Published Works." SP, 51 (July, 1954), 470-81.

240   Warner, Oliver. Coleridge's 'Naval Poetry' and Southey's
'Life of Nelson'." N&Q, 17 (May, 1970), 169-70.

241   Wells, John E. "Printer's Bills for Coleridge's Friend and
Wordsworth's Cintra." SP, 36 (July, 1939), 521-23.

242   Werkmeister, Lucyle. "Coleridge and Godwin on the Communication
of Truth." MP, 55 (February, 1958), 170-77.

243   _____. "The First Two Editions of Coleridge's Friend,
Edited by Lucyle Werkmeister." University of Nebraska, DA, 17 (July,
1957), 1560.

244   Wordsworth, Johnathan. "Some Unpublished Coleridge Marginalia."
TLS, (June 14, 1957), 369.

245   Wynn, Lawrence. "The Reputation of Samuel Taylor Coleridge
Among His Contemporaries in England." Princeton University, DA, 15
(May, 1955), 834-35.

KUBLA KHAN

246   Allen, N. B. "A Note on Coleridge's Kubla Khan." MLN,
57 (February, 1942), 108-13.

        Lines 1-30 are what Coleridge had written down before he
        was interrupted; lines 31-36 represent his effort to contiue
        the vision; and the lines 37-54 are his comment on the loss
        of the vision.

247   Anderson, Erland G. "Harmonious Madness: A Study of Musical
Metaphors in the Poetry of Coleridge, Shelley, and Keats." University
of Washington, DAI, 34 (January, 1974), 4185A.

248   Angus, Douglas. "The Theme of Love and Guilt in Coleridge's
Three Major Poems." JEGP, 59 (October, 1960), 655-68.

249   Archer, Jerome W. "Kubla Khan: Queen Mab, II, 4-79; VIII,
70-109, and Alastor, 81-94; 163-172." SP, 41 (October, 1960),
576-81.

250   Ashe, Dora J. "Byron's Alleged Part in the Production of
Coleridge's Remorse." N&Q, 198 (January, 1953), 33-36.

251   Baskett, Sam S. "A Damsel with a Dulcimer: An Interpretation
of Poe's Eleonara." MLN, 73 (May, 1958), 332-38.

252   Benoit, R. "The Tao of 'Kubla Khan'." (In Benoit, R. Single
Nature's Double Name. The Hague: Mouton, 1973), 29-40.

253   Beres, David. "A Dream, a Vision and a Poem." IJP, 32
(1951), 97-116.

254   Bewley, Eugen M. "The Poetry of Coleridge." Scrut, 8
(March, 1940), 406-20.

255   Beyer, Werner W. The Enchanted Forest. Oxford: Blackwell;
New York: Barnes and Noble, 1963.

        Wieland's Oberon and Coleridge.
        Reviewed in TLS (December 5, 1963), 1014.

256   Bishop, Marchard. "The Farm House of Kubla Khan." TLS (May
10, 1957), 293.

257   Bliss, H. S. and D. T. Bliss. "Coleridge's Kubla Khan." AI,
6 (1949), 261-73.

258   Bodkin, Maud. "Kubla Khan." (In Bodkin, Maud. Archetypal
Patterns in Poetry. London: Oxford University Press, 1934), 90-116.

259   Bogholm, N. "Uber die Genesis des Kubla Khan." EStudien,
73 (May, 1939), 220-26.

260   Borges, J. L. "The Dream of Coleridge." (In Borges, J. L.
Other Inquisitions, 1937-1952. Translated by Ruth L. C. Simms. Introduction by James E. Irby. Austin: University of Texas Press, 1964), 14-17.

261   Brammell, James. "Kubla Khan - Coleridge's Fall?" NM, 53
(December, 1952), 449-66.

262   Breyer, Bernard R. "Towards an Interpretation of Kubla Khan."
(In English Studies in Honor of James Southal Wilson. Edited by
Fredson Bowers. University of Virginia Studies, 4, 1951), 227-90.

263   Brooks, Cleanth, Jr., Purser, John Thibault, and Warren, Robert
Penn. Kubla Khan. (In Brooks, Cleanth, Jr., and Others. An
Approach to Literature. Rev. ed. New York: F. S. Crofts & Co., 1942),
376-378.

       Also in third edition, 1952.

264   Brown, Harry M. "Archetypal Patterns in Kubla Khan." CCTE,
33 (September, 1968), 13-17.

265   Burke, Kenneth. "Kubla Khan: Proto-Surrealist Poem." (In
Burke, K. Language as Symbolic Action. Berkeley: University of
California Press, 1966), 201-22.

266   _____. "On Musicality in Verse, As Illustrated by Some
Lines of Coleridge." Poetry, 57 (October, 1940), 31-40.

267   Cameron, Kenneth Neil. "Rasselas and Alastor: A Study in
Transmutation." SP, 40 (January, 1943), 58-78.

       Indebtedness to Kubla Khan.

268   Cannon, Garland. "A New, Probable Source for Kubla Khan."
CE, 17 (December, 1955), 136-42.

       Points out similarities between Coleridge's poem and Sir
       William Jones' A Hymn to Ganga.

269   Carswell, John. "Kubla Khan." TLS, (March 16, 1962), 185.

270   Cawly, A. C. "Love's Fool Paradise." MQ, 23 (June, 1964),
179-85.

       Kubla Khan's "pleasure dome."

271   Chambers, E. K. "The Date of Coleridge's Kubla Khan." RES,
11 (January, 1935), 78-80.

272   Chayes, Irene H. "Coleridge, Metempsychosis, and 'Almost All
the Flowers of Fenelon'." ELH, 25 (December, 1958), 290-315.

273   _____. "Kubla Khan and the Creative Process." SIR, 6
(Autumn, 1966), 1-21.

274   Coats, R. H. "Kubla Khan." TLS (December 18, 1937), 964.

Resembles Wordsworth's Solitary Reaper.

275   Copeland, Thomas. "A Woman Wailing for Her Demon Lover."
RES, 17 (January, 1941), 87-90.

Finds the suggestion for lines near the beginning of Kubla
Khan in the Book to Tobit and a passage in Paradise Lost.

276   Davis, Bertram R. "A Manuscript of Kubla Khan." TSL,
(January 26, 1951), 53.

277   Emerson, Francis Willard. "Joseph Sterling's Cambuscan in
Coleridge's Kubla Khan." N&Q, 7 (March, 1960), 102-03.

278   England, A. B. "Kubla Khan Again: The Oceans, the Caverns,
and the Ancestral Voices." ARIEL, 4 (October, 1973), 63-72.

279   Enscoe, Gerald E. "Ambivalence in Kubla Khan: The Cavern
and the Dome." BuR, 12 (March, 1964), 29-36.

280   _____. "Eros and the Romantics: Sexual Love as a Theme
in Coleridge, Shelley, and Keats." University of Washington,
DA, 24 (July, 1963), 296-97.

281   Fields, Beverly Frankel. "Reality's Dark Dream: A Study of
Dejection in Coleridge." Northwestern University, DA, 26 (December,
1965), 3333-34.

282   Fleissner, Robert F. "Examining Xanadu: Kubla Khan Revisited."
(In Chakrabarti, Dipendu, ed. Essays Presented to Prof. Amalendu
Bose. Bull. of the Department of English, 8 (1972-73). Calcutta:
Calcutta University Press, 1972), 38-43.

283   _____. "Hwaet! Wē Gardēnia: Kubla Khan and Those Anglo-
Saxon Words." WC, 5 (Winter, 1974), 50-54.

284   _____. "Kubla Khan and Tom Jones: An Unnoticed Parallel."
N&Q, 7 (March, 1960), 103-05.

285   _____. "Kubla Khan As an Integrationist Poem." NALF, 8
(1974), 254-56.

Suggests Coleridge's knowledge of Leo Africanus' History and
Description of Africa.

286   _____. "The Mystical Meaning of Five: A Notelet on Kubla
Khan." ES, 47 (February, 1965), 45.

287   _____. "Passage from Kubla Khan to Forster's India." ILU,
14 (September, 1971), 79-84.

288 _____. "Shakespeare in Xanadu." Shakespeare Studies
(University of Tokyo), 6 (1967-68), 94-102.

289 Fogle, Richard Harter. "The Romantic Unity of Kubla Khan."
CE, 13 (October, 1951), 13-18.

290 _____. "1951: The Romantic Unity of Kubla Khan." CE 22
(November, 1960), 112-16.

291 _____. "The Romantic Unity of Kubla Khan." (In Fogle,
Richard Harter. The Permanent Pleasure: Essays on Classics of
Romanticism. Athens: University of Georgia Press, 1974), 43-52.

292 Frankenbert, Lloyd. Invitation to Poetry. New York: Doubleday,
(1956), 45-48.

293 Galinsky, Hans. "Echowirkungen von Coleridge's Kubla Khan und
Dejection: An Ode in Longfellow's Ersten Heine-Essay, 1842." JA,
3 (1958), 112-35.

294 Gerber, Richard. "Cybele, Kubla Khan, and Keats." ES, 46
(October, 1965), 269-89.

295 _____. "Keys to Kubla Khan." ES, 44 (October, 1963),
321-41.

296 Gersch, Gabriel. "Palaces of Pleasure." Com, 63 (October
14, 1955), 33-5.

297 Gibson, Walker. "Coleridge: An Explanation by Literary Origins."
(In Gibson, Walker. Poems in the Making. Boston: Houghton Mifflin,
1963), 93-151.

298 Goldstein, Neal L. "Coleridge's Kubla Khan: Mythic Unity and
an Analogue in Folklore and Legend." QQ, 75 (Winter 1968), 642-50.

299 Graves, Robert. "The Integrity of the Poet." Listen,
(March 31, 1955), 579-80.

300 Green, Andrew J. "Essays in Miniature: The Resistless Eye."
CE, 3 (May, 1942), 722-23.

301 Greer, Michael. "Coleridge and Dante: Kinship in Xanadu." UDR,
10 (Summer, 1974), 65-74.

        Extensive echoes of Dante in Kubla Khan.

302 Hardy, Barbara. "Another Road to Xanadu." EIC, 6 (January,
1956), 87-94.

303 Harrex, S. C. "Coleridge's Pleasure Dome in Kubla Khan."
N&Q, 13 (May, 1966), 172-3.

304   Hassler, Donald M. "Coleridge, Darwin, and the Dome." Serif,
4 (September, 1967), 28-31.

305   Hayter, Alethea. "Xanadu at Lyme Regis." ARIEL, 1 (January,
1970), 61-64.

       Influence of Kubla Khan on Persuasion.

306   Heninger, S. K., Jr. "A Jungian Reading of Kubla Khan."
JAAC, 18 (March, 1960), 358-67.

307   Hennecke, Hans. (tr.) "Kubla Khan oder ein Traumgesicht.
Ein Bruchstuck von S. T. Coleridge." Die Neue Rundschau, 49 (1938),
338-41.

       A rhymed, metrical translation with brief critical comment
       by the translator.

308   Hoffpauir, Richard. "Kubla Khan and the Critics: Romantic
Madness as Poetic Theme and Critical Response." ESC, 2 (1976),
402-22.

309   House, H. "'Kubla Khan', 'Christabel', and 'Dejection'." (In
Kumar, S. K. ed. British Romantic Poets), 119-41.

310   Hoyle, James F. "Kubla Khan as an Elated Experience." L&P,
16 (Winter, 1966), 27-39.

       Followed by "comment" by Mrs. Mabel Worthington, 40-42.

311   Hussain, Imdad. "Orientalism and Coleridge." Ven, 1 (December,
1960), 336-46.

312   _____. "Orientalism and Coleridge." Ven, 2 (March,
1961), 44-55.

313   John, Brian. "Tennyson's Recollection of the Arabian Nights
and the Individuation Process." VP, 4 (Autumn, 1966), 275-79.

314   Karrfalt, David H. "Another Note on Kubla Khan and Coleridge's
Retirement to Ash Farm." N&Q, 13 (May, 1966), 171-72.

315   Kelly, Michael J. "Kubla Khan and Cowper's Task: Speculation
Amidst Echoes." BNYPL, 78 (1975), 482-89.

316   Kendle, Burton S. "Trillings 'Of This Time, Of That Place'."
EXPL, 22 (April, 1964), Item 61.

       Many references to The Ancient Mariner and Kubla Khan.

317   Knight, G. Wilson. "Coleridge's Divine Comedy." (In M.H.
Abrams, ed. English Romantic Poets: Modern Essays in Criticism.
London, New York: Oxford University Press, 1960), 158-69.

318   Knight, G. Wilson. "Coleridge's Divine Comedy." (In M. H.
Abrams, ed. English Romantic Poets: Modern Essays in Criticism.
London, New York: Oxford University Press, 1960), 158-69.

319 _____. "Coleridge's Divine Comdey." The Starlit Dome:
Studies in the Poetry of Vision. New York: Barnes & Noble, 1941,
83-178.

320 _____. "The School of Knight." EIC, 4 (October, 1954),
430-31.

321   Landow, George P. "Mount Abora." N&Q, 20 (August, 1973),
386-89.

322   Lefebure, Molly. "Kubla Khan." (In Lefebure, M. Samuel
Taylor Coleridge: A Bondage of Opium. New York: Stein and Day, 1974),
254-63, 481-85.

323   Lerner, Lawrence. "Roads to Xanadu and Back." EIC, 20
(January, 1970), 89-98.

324   MacKenzie, Norma. "Kubla Khan: A Poem of Creative Agony and
Loss." EM, 20 (1969), 229-40.

325   Marcovitz, Eli. "Bemoaning the Lost Dream: Coleridge's Kubla
Khan and Addiction." IJP, 45 (1964), 411-25.

326   Maxwell, J. C. "Kubla Khan." TLS (March 23, 1962), 201.

327   Meier, Hans Heinrich. "Ancient Lights on Kubla's Lines."
ES, 46 (February, 1965), 15-29.

328 _____. "Xanaduvian Residues." ES, 48 (April, 1967), 145-55.

329   Mercer, Dorothy F. "The Symbolism of 'Kubla Khan'." JAAC,
12 (September, 1953), 44-65.

330   Meyerstein, E. H. W. "Chatterton, Coleridge, and Bristol: The
Sacred River." TLS (August 21, 1937), 606.

331 _____. "The Completeness of Kubla Khan." TLS (October 30,
1937), 803.

332 _____. "Kubla Khan." TLS (December 4, 1937), 928.

333 _____. "A Manuscript of Kubla Khan." TLS (January 12, 1951),
21.

334 _____. "A Manuscript of Kubla Khan." TLS (February 9,
1951), 85.

335   Michaels, Judith Rowe. "The Bounds of the Self: Coleridge's
Philosophy of Love and Its Effect on His Poetic Vision." Bryn
Mawr College, DAI, 35 (April, 1975), 6674A.

336   Milner, R. H. "Coleridge's 'Sacred River'." TLS (May 18, 1951), 309.

337   Moorman, Charles. "The Imagery of Kubla Khan." N&Q, 6 (September, 1959), 321-24.

338   "MS of Kubla Khan." TLS (February 16, 1962), 112.

339   Mulvey, Thomas Vincent. "The Fractured Dome: A Study of the Unity of Coleridge's Kubla Khan." Fordham University, DAI, 35 (November, 1974), 3000A-01A.

340   Nelson, Carl. "The Ironic Allusive Texture of Lord Jim: Coleridge, Crane, Milton, and Melville." Conrad, 4 (1972), 47-59.

341   Ober, Warren U. "Southey, Coleridge, and Kubla Khan." JEGP, 58 (July, 1959), 414-22.

342   Oppel, Hurst. "Coleridge's Kubla Khan - zur Interpretation Remantischer Dichtung." NS (1952), 101.

343   Ower, John. "Another Analogue of Coleridge's Kubla Khan." N&Q, 14 (August, 1967), 295.

344   Pafford, Ward. "Samuel Taylor Coleridge." EUQ, 21 (Spring, 1965), 3-14.

345   Parsons, Howard. "A New Interpretation of Coleridge's Kubla Khan." PoetR, 34 (1943).

346   _____. "The Sources of Coleridge's Kubla Khan." N&Q, 196 (May 26, 1951), 233-35.

347   Passler, Susan Miller. "Coleridge, Fielding, and Arthur Murphy." WC, 5 (Winter, 1974), 55-58.

348   Patrick, John M. "Ammianus and Alpheus: The Sacred River." MLN, 72 (May, 1957), 334-37.

349   Patterson, Charles I., Jr. "The Daemonic in Kubla Khan: Toward Interpretation." PMLA, 89 (October, 1974), 1033-42.

350   Peckman, Morse. "Poet and Critic (or the Damage Coleridge Has Done.)" STC, 6 (Fall, 1970), 1-11.

351   Pettit, Henry. "Coleridge's Mount Abora." MLN, 54 (May, 1941), 376.

      Notes the mention of "Abur, a mountain in Arabia: in Clement Crutwell's New Universal Gazeteer-1798.

352   Piper, H. W. "Mount Abora." N&Q, 20 (August, 1973), 286-89.

353   _____. "The Two Paradises in Kubla Khan." RES, 27 (May, 1976), 148-58.

354   Purves, Alan C. "Formal Structure in Kubla Khan." SIR, 1 (Spring,1962), 187–91.

355   Raben, Joseph. "Coleridge As the Prototype of the Poet in Shelley's Alastor." RES, 17 (August, 1966), 278–92.

     Comment by Timothy Webb on this article: "Coleridge and Shelley's Alastor: A Reply." RES (November, 1967), 402–11.

356   Raine, Kathleen. "Traditional Symbolism in Kubla Khan." SR, 72 (Autumn,1964), 626–42.

357   Rauber, D. F. "The Fragment as Romantic Form." MLQ, 30 (June, 1969), 212–21.

358   Read, Herbert. "Two Kinds of Poetry." Agenda, 7 (Spring, 1969), 34–40.

359   Rhys, Keidrych. "Coleridge in Wales." TLS (August 16, 1947) 415.

360   Ridenour, George M. "Source and Allusion in Some Poems of Coleridge." SP, 60 (January, 1963), 73–95.

361   Robertson, Jean. "The Date of Coleridge's Kubla Khan." RES, 18 (November, 1967), 438–9.

362   Rodway, A. E.; Salgado, G.; Knight, G. Wilson; and Bateson, F. W. "The School of Knight." EIC, 4 (April, 1954), 212–24.

363   Ross, Donald, Jr. "The Prelude, VIII." AN&Q, 5 (June, 1967), 147–8.

364   Rothman, Richard M. "A Re-examination of Kubla Khan." EJ, 55 (February, 1966), 169–71.

365   Schneider, Duane B. "The Structure of Kubla Khan." AN&Q, 1 (January, 1963), 68–70.

366   Schneider, Elisabeth. Coleridge, Opium, and Kubla Khan. Chicago: University of Chicago Press, 1953; London: Cambridge University Press, 1954; New York: Octagon Books, 1966.

     Reviews: NSN, 47 (May, 29), 1954; Hugh Kenner in Poetry, 84 (1954), 179–84; Thomas M. Raysor in JEGP, 53 (July, 1954), 484–5; Thomas M. Raysor in TLS (July 16, 1954), 455; Henry Tyler in TLS (July 30, 1954), 485; Henry Tyler in Listen, 52 (September 9, 1954), 409; M. H. Abrams in MLN, 70 (January, 1955), 216–9; Erwin Wolff in Angla, 73 (1955), 245–6; Erwin Wolff in Person, 36 (1955), 82–3; B. Hardy in EIC, 6 (January, 1956), 87–94; J. P. Mann in RES, 7 (April, 1956), 207–9.

367 _____. "The 'Dream' of Kubla Khan. PMLA, 60 (September, 1945), 784-801.

Rejects, chiefly by appeal to medical testimony, the view that Kubla Khan is the product of a dream under the influence of opium, and discerns a meaning in the poem.

368   Schwegel, Douglas M. "Joyce's Ulysses, Calypso Episode." EXPL, 27 (March, 1969), Item 49.

369   Seronsy, Cecil C. "Poe and Kubla Khan." N&Q, 4 (May, 1957), 219-20.

370   Sgammato, Joseph. "A Note on Coleridge's 'Symphony and Song'." WC, 6 (Autumn, 1975), 303-06.

371   Shaffer, E. S. "Holderlin's 'Patmos' Ode and 'Kubla Khan': Mythological Doubling." (In Shaffer, E. S. 'Kubla Khan' and The Fall of Jerusalem: The Mythological School in Biblical Criticism and Secular Literature, 1770-1880. Cambridge: Cambridge University Press, 1975), 96-144.

372 _____. "The Oriental Idyll." (In Shaffer, E. S. 'Kubla Khan' and The Fall of Jerusalem: The Mythological School in Biblical Criticism and Secular Literature, 1770-1880. Cambridge: Cambridge University Press, 1975), 96-144.

373   Sharma, R. C. "Kubla Khan: An Interpretation." IJES, 7 (1966) 32-42.

374   Shelton, John. "The Autograph Manuscript of Kubla Khan and an Interpretation." REL, 7 (January, 1966), 32-42.

375   Sitwell, Osbert. "The Sole Arabian Tree." TLS (April 26, 1941), 199.

376   Sloane, Eugene H. "Coleridge's Kubla Khan: The Living Catacombs of the Mind." AI, 29 (Summer, 1972), 97-122.

377   Skeat, T. C. "Kubla Khan." BMQ, 26 (Spring, 1963), 77-83.

378   Smith, James. "The Poetry of Coleridge." Scrutiny, VIII. (March, 1940), 411-414.

379   Smith, Michael Harold. "The Measureless Caverns: Coleridge's Kubla Khan and the Critics." Pennsylvania State University. DAI, 36 (October, 1975), 2225A-26A.

380   Southam, Brian. "Letter to Editor." ARIEL, 3 (July, 1972), 79.

381   Starr, Nathan C. "Coleridge's Sacred River." PLL, 11 (Spring, 1966), 117-25.

382   Steiner, George. "On Reading Kenneth Burke." CamR, 89A (November 4, 1967), 69-70.

383   Stelzig, Eugene L. "The Landscape of Kubla Khan and the
Valley of the Rocks." WC,6 (Autumn, 1975), 316-18.

384   Stevenson, Warren. "Kubla Khan as Symbol." TSLL, 14
(Winter, 1973), 605-30.

385   Stoll, Elmer Edgar. "Symbolism in Coleridge." PMLA, 63
(March, 1948), 214-33.

386   Stovall, Floyd. "Poe's Debt to Coleridge." Studies in
English - University of Texas, 10 (July 8, 1930), 70-127.

387   Suther, Marshall. "On the Interpretation of Kubla Khan."
BuR, 7 (May, 1957), 1-19.

388   _____. Visions of Xanadu. New York, London: Columbia
University Press, 1975.

        Reviews: Robert F. Fleissner in Thought, 40 (1965), 601-3;
        Robert F. Fleissner in Choice, 2 (November, 1965), 584;
        James Benizger in CRIT, 8 (Summer 1966), 289-93; Richard
        Gerber in ANGL 84 (1966), 479-80; John Colmer in AUMLA, 26
        (1966), 321-2; Richard Martin in WHR, 20 (Summer 1966),
        255-6; James Hoyle in L&P, 16 (1966), 48-50; James Hoyle in
        TLS (February 3, 1966), 89; John Colmer in MLR, 62 (July,
        1967), 514-5; J. B. Beer in RES, 18 (February, 1967), 87-90;
        James R. Bennett in ES, 52 (February, 1971), 80-2.

389   Sypher, Wylie. "Coleridge's Somerset: A Byway to Xanadu."
PQ, 18 (October, 1939), 353-66.

        Possible presence of a bit of local scenery and legend in
        Kubla Khan.

390   Taylor, M. A. "Kubla Khan: The Well Ordered Fragment."
CEA Critic, 37 (March, 1975), 8-9.

391   Templeman, William D. "A Note on the Dulcimer." TLS
(April 2, 1931), 271.

392   Todd, Ruthven. "Coleridge and Paracelsus; Honeydew and LSD."
LM, 6 (March, 1967), 52-62.

393   Tyler, Henry. "Kubla Khan." TLS (July 30, 1954), 487.

394   Van Haitsma, Glen. "Notes Toward a Definition of a Romantic
Cosmology." WisSL, 3 (1966), 74-89.

395   Walsh, Dorothy. "Literature and Categories." JP, 55 (September
25, 1958), 846-55.

396   Ware, J. Garth. "Coleridge's Great Poems Reflecting the
Mother Image." AI, 18 (Winter, 1962), 331-52.

397   Warne, F. J. "Prester John in Coleridge's Kubla Khan,
MLR, 30 (January, 1935), 55-8.

398   Watson, George. "The Meaning of Kubla Khan." REL, 2
(January, 1961), 21-9.

399   Webb, Timothy. "Coleridge and Shelley's Alastor: A Reply."
RES, 18 (November, 1967), 402-11.

400   Wendling, Ronald C. "Dramatic Reconciliation in Coleridge's
Conversation Poems." PLL, 9 (Spring, 1973), 145-60.

401   Whalley, George. "Romantic Chasms." TLS (June 21, 1947), 309.

Calls attention to the possible connection between Kubla Khan
and the Gothic Garden at Crookham.

402   Woodring, Carl. "Coleridge and the Khan." EIC, 9 (October,
1959), 361-8.

403   Worthington, Mabel. "Comment on Kubla Khan As an Elated
Experience." L&P, 16 (Winter, 1966), 40-2.

404   Wright, John K. "From Kubla Khan to Florida." AQ, 8 (Spring,
1956), 76-80.

Indebtedness to Bartram.

LEWTI

405   Joughin, G. L. "Coleridge's Lewti: The Biography of a Poem."
TxSE (1943), 66-93.

THE RIME OF THE ANCIENT MARINER

406   Abel, Darrel. "Coleridge's 'Life-in-Death' and Poe's 'Death-
in-Life'." N&Q, 2 (May, 1955), 218-20.

407   Abrew, Kamal De. "Coleridge's Ancient Mariner--Rime or Ballad?"
University of Ceylon Rev., 17 (July-October, 1959), 90-98.

408   Adams, Maurianne S. "Coleridge and the Victorians: Studies
in the Interpretation of Poetry, Scripture, and Myth." Indiana
University,DA,28 (March, 1968), 3662A-3A.

409   Alley, Alvin D. "Coleridge and Existentialism." SHR, 2
(Fall, 1968), 451-61.

410   Anderson, Erland G. "Harmonious Madness: A Study of Musical Metaphors in the Poetry of Coleridge, Shelley, and Keats." University of Washington, DAI,34 (January, 1974), 4185A.

411   Anderson, Peter S. and Stroupe, John H. "Two Guests of The Mariner." EngR, 17 (October, 1966), 24-26.

412   Angus, Douglas. "The Theme of Love and Guilt in Coleridge's Three Major Poems." JEGP, 59 (October, 1960), 655-68.

413   Arias, Bogddy. "Sailors' Reveries." Costerus, 4 (1972), 1-8.

414   Ashbrook, Joseph. "Coleridge's 'Star Within the Moon'." ST, 28 (December, 1964), 335.

415   Baker, James V. "A Return to Xanadu." Forum (Houston), 2 (1957), 21-24.

416   Bald, R. C. "Coleridge and The Ancient Mariner: Addenda to The Road to Xanadu." NCS (1940), 1-45.

417   Barnett, Gail Z. "The Endless Journey: An Ontogenetic Study of Three Poets." University of Maryland, DAI, 33 (November, 1972), 2314A.

418   Beach, Joseph Warren. "The Rime of the Ancient Mariner." (In Joseph Warren Beach. A Romantic View of Poetry...Minneapolis: University of Minnesota Press, 1944), 8-22.

419   Beatty, Arthur. "The Borderers and The Ancient Mariner." TLS (February 29, 1936), 184.

420   Beatty, Frederika. "A By-Path Along The Road to Xanadu." CJ, 44 (December, 1948), 211-12.

       A passage in The Ancient Mariner echoes the Aeneid, II, 460-73.

421   Beer, J. B. "The Glorious Sun" Coleridge, the Visionary. London: Chatto & Windus, 1959, 133-74.

422   Begnal, M. H. "Lord Jim and The Rime of the Ancient Mariner." Conrad, 1 (Fall, 1968), 54.

423   Bellis, George. "The Fixed Crime of The Ancient Mariner." EIC, 24 (July, 1974), 243-60.

424   Benoit, R. "The Contrite Consciousness of The Ancient Mariner." (In Benoit, R. Single Nature's Double Name: The Collectedness of the Conflicting in British and American Romanticism. The Hague: Mouton, 1973), 23-29.

425   Beres, David. "A Dream, a Vision, and a Poem." IJP, 32
(1951), 97-116.

    A psychoanalytic study of the origins of The Rime of The
    Ancient Mariner.

426   Berkoben, Lawrence D. "Varieties of Evil Experience I:
The Ancient Mariner." (In Berkoben, Lawrence D. Coleridge's
Decline As a Poet, The Hague: Mouton, 1975), 73-92.

427   Bewley, Eugene M. "The Poetry of Coleridge." Scrut, 8
(March, 1940), 406-20.

428   Beyer, Werner W. "The Background of Coleridge's 'Cain,'
Precursor of The Ancient Mariner." N&Q, 3 (January, 1956), 32-34;
(February, 1956), 82-84.

429   _____. "Coleridge. Wieland's Oberon and The Ancient
Mariner." RES, 15 (October, 1939), 401-11.

    Parallels in imagery and expression between The Ancient
    Mariner and a work which we know Coleridge was reading in
    the original.

430   _____. "Coleridge. Wieland's Oberon and The Wanderings
of Cain." RES, 16 (July, 1940), 274-89.

    Continues his study of Wieland's influence on both The Cain
    and The Ancient Mariner, written at the time Coleridge was
    translating The Oberon.

431   _____. The Enchanted Forest. Oxford: Blackwell; New York:
Barnes & Noble, 1963.

    Wieland's Oberon and Coleridge.

432   Bishop, Morchard. "Captain James' Voyage and Ivor James."
TLS (January 16, 1959), 35.

    On the use of Captain James' Voyage as a source for The
    Ancient Mariner.

433   Boas, Louise S. "Coleridge's The Ancient Mariner, Part IV."
EXPL, 2 (May, 1944), Item 52.

434   Bogholm, N. "The Ancient Mariner." ANGL, 63 (January, 1939),
186-96.

435   Booth, Bradford A. "Renascense and The Ancient Mariner."
N&Q, 192 (October, 1947), 431-32.

436   Bostetter, Edward E. "The Nightmare World of The Ancient
Mariner." SIR, 1 (Summer, 1962), 241-54.

437   Boulger, James D. "Christian Skepticism in The Rime of the
Ancient Mariner." (In From Sensibility to Romanticism: Essays
Presented to Frederick A. Pottle. ed. by Frederick W. Hilles and
Harold Bloom, New York: Oxford University Press, 1965), 439-52.

438   _____. "Coleridge on Imagination Revisited." WC, 4
(Winter, 1973), 13-24.

439   _____. ed. Twentieth Century Interpretations of The
Rime of the Ancient Mariner: A Collection of Critical Essays.
Englewood Cliffs: Prentice-Hall, 1969.

440   Bowen, Hoyt E. "Coleridge's The Rime of the Ancient Mariner,
197." EXPL, 15 (November, 1956), Item 9.

441   Bowra, C. M. "The Ancient Mariner." (In Bowra, C. M. The
Romantic Imagination. New York: Oxford University Press, 1961),
51-75, passim.

442   Brett, R. L. Reason and Imagination: A Study of Form and
Meaning in Four Poems. New York: Oxford University Press for the
University of Hull, 1960, 78-107.

       Lycidas, An Essay on Man, The Ancient Mariner, and Four
       Quartets.

443   Brooks, Roger L. "A Second Possible Source for Mark Twain's
The Aged Pilot Man." RLC, 36 (July-September, 1962), 451-53.

444   Brown, Huntington. "The Gloss to The Rime of the Ancient
Mariner." MLQ, 6 (September, 1945), 319-24.

       Believes that the gloss "serves to emphasize the remoteness
       of the story and its teller," and is in effect, choric in
       its function.

445   Bryant, E. P. "The Rime of the Ancient Mariner: A Coleridgean
Reading." Standpunte, 18 (April, 1965), 15-30.

446   Buchan, A. M. "The Sad Wisdom of the Mariner." SP, 61
(October, 1964), 669-88.

447   Buckley, Vincent. "Coleridge: Vision and Actuality." MCR,
4 (1961), 3-17.

448   Burke, Kenneth. "The Ancient Mariner." (In Burke, Kenneth.
The Philosophy of Literary Form. Baton Rouge: Louisiana State
University Press, 1941), passim.

449   _____. "Towards Objective Criticism." Poetry, 70
(April, 1947), 42-47.

450   Campbell, Clare. "The Ancient Mariner." Crit Q, 7 (Spring,
1965), 93.

451   Campbell, Oscar James. "Wordsworth's Conception of the Esthetic Experience." (In Wordsworth and Coleridge: Studies in Honor of George McLean Harper. ed. by Earl L. Griggs, New York: Russell & Russell 1962), 26-46.

452   Carey, Glenn O. "Ethics in The Mariner." EngR, 17 (October, 1966), 18-20.

453   Chandler, Alice. "Structure and Symbol in The Rime of The Ancient Mariner. MLQ, 26 (September, 1965), 401-13.

454   Chayes, Irene H. "Coleridge, Metempsychosis, and 'Almost All the Followers of Fenelon'." ELH, 25 (December, 1958), 290-315.

455   _____. "A Coleridgean Reading of The Ancient Mariner." SIR, 4 (Winter, 1965), 81-103.

456   Christensen, Merton A. "Udolphe, Horrid Mysteries, and Coleridge's Machinery of the Imagination." WC, 2 (Autumn, 1971), 153-59.

457   Cierpial, Leo Joseph. "Degeneration and the Religion of Beauty: A Traditional Pattern in Coleridge's the Rime of The Ancient Mariner, Pater's The Renaissance, Maugham's Of Human Bondage, and Joyce's Ulysses." Wayne State University, DA, 23 (October, 1962), 1361-62.

458   Ciniglio, Ada V. "Two Gallants: Joyce's Wedding Guests." JJQ, 10 (Winter 1973), 264.

459   Coffin, Tristram P. "Coleridge's Use of the Ballad Stanza in The Rime of The Ancient Mariner." MLQ, 12 (December, 1951), 437-45.

460   Cooke, Michael G. "The Manipulation of Space in Coleridge's Petry." (In Hartman, Geoffrey H. ed. New Perspectives on Coleridge and Wordsworth. Selected Papers from the English Institute. New York: Columbia University Press, 1971), 165-94.

461   _____. "The Will in English Romanticism: The Will in Romantic Poetry." (In Cooke, Michael G. The Romantic Will. New Haven: Yale University Press, 1976), 29-51.

462   Creed, Howard. "The Rime of The Ancient Mariner: A Rereading." EJ, 49 (April, 1960), 215-22, 228.

463   D'Avanzo, Mario L. "Coleridge's Wedding-Guest and Marriage Feast: The Biblical Context." UWR, 8 (Fall, 1972), 62-66.

464   Day, Robert A. "The Rebirth of Leggatt." L&P, 13 (Summer, 1963), 74-80.

      Pattern of rebirth, as exhibited in The Ancient Mariner.

465   Delson, Abe. "A Search for Meaning: A Critical History of the Thematic Interpretations of The Rime of the Ancient Mariner, 1798-1965." New York University, DAI   (April, 1970), 4447A-48A.

466   _____. "The Symbolism of the Sun and the Moon in The Rime of The Ancient Mariner." TSLL, 15 (Winter 1974), 707-20.

467   Demarest, Anthony Kevin. "Coleridge and the Elder Edda: 1795-1798." Fordham University DAI   (September, 1975), 1521A.

468   Dendinger, Lloyd N. "Stephen Crane's Inverted Use of the Key Images of The Rime of The Ancient Mariner." SSF, 5 (Winter 1968), 192-94.

469   Dickson, Arthur. "Coleridge's The Ancient Mariner." EXPL, 6 (June, 1948), Item 52.

470   Dillingham, William B. "The Narrator of Moby Dick." ES, 49 (February, 1968), 20-29.

471   Duff, Gerald. "Speech as Theme in The Rime of The Ancient Mariner." HAB, 21 (Summer, 1970), 26-31.

472   Dyck, Sarah. "Perspective in The Rime of The Ancient Mariner." SEL, 13 (Autumn, 1973) 591-604.

473   Ebbatson, J. R. "Coleridge's Mariner and the Rights of Man." SIR, 11 (Summer, 1972), 171-206.

474   Ellis, Amanda M. Rebels and Conservatives: Dorothy and William Wordsworth and Their Circle. Bloomington: Indiana University Press, 1967.

475   Empson, William. "The Ancient Mariner." CritQ, 6 (Winter, 1964), 298-319.

476   _____ and David, eds. Coleridge's Verse: A Selection. London: Faber & Faber, 1972.

       Reviewed in TLS (December 15, 1972), 1524.

477   Enrico, Harold. "Shipwreck in Infinity: Leopardi, Coleridge, and Wordsworth in the Imagination." (In Baldner, Ralph W., ed. Proceedings: Pacific Northwest Conference on Foreign Languages. Twenty-First Annual Meeting, April 3-4, 1970. Victoria, B. C.: University of Victoria, 1970), 93-101.

478   Everett, Edwin M. "Lord Byron's Lakist Interlude." SP, 55 (January, 1958), 62-75.

479   Fields, Beverly Frankel. "Reality's Dark Dream: A Study of Dejection in Coleridge." Northwestern University, DA, 26 (December, 1965), 3333-34.

480   Fleissner, Robert F. "Shakespeare in Xanadu." Shakespeare Studies (University of Tokyo), 6 (1967-68), 94-102.

481   Fogle, Richard Harter. "The Genre of The Ancient Mariner."
TSE, 7 (1957), 111-24.

Stresses the "one life" theme.

482   _____. "The Genre of The Ancient Mariner." (In Fogle,
Richard Harter. The Permanent Pleasure: Essays on Classics of
Romanticism. Athens: University of Georgia Press, 1974), 27-42.

483   Ford, Newell F. "Kenneth Burke and Robert Penn Warren:
Criticism by Obsessive Metaphor." JEGP, 53 (April, 1954), 172-42.

An attack on the symbolic approach.

484   Forstner, Lorne J. "Coleridge's The Ancient Mariner and the
Case for Justifiable 'Mythocide': An Argument on Psychological,
Epistemological, and Formal Grounds." CRIT, 18 (Summer 1976),
211-29.

485   Freedman, R. "Eyesight and Vision: Forms of the Imagination
in Coleridge and Novalis." (In Cheuse, A. and Koffler, R. eds.
The Rarer Action: Essays in Honor of Francis Fergusson, New
Brunswick, N. J.: Rutgers University Press, 1970), 202-17.

486   Fulmer, O. Bryan. "The Ancient Mariner and The Wandering
Jew." SP, 66 (October, 1969), 797-815.

487   Gallup, Donald. "Eugene O'Neill's The Ancient Mariner."
YULG, 35 (October, 1960), 61-86.

Includes text of the play, 63-86.

488   Gardner, Martin, ed. The Annotated Ancient Mariner. New
York: C. N. Potter, Inc.; London: Blond, 1965.

The Rime of the Ancient Mariner, with an introduction and
notes by Martin Gardner. Illustrated by Gustave Doré
(1st ed.) Bibliography. 191-200.

489   Gardner, W. H. "The Poet and the Albatross (A Study in
Symbolic Suggestion)." ESA, 1 (1958), 102-25.

490   Gaskins, Avery F. "Real and Imaginary Time in The Rime of
The Ancient Mariner." NDQ, 37 (Autumn,1969), 43-47.

491   Gettman, Royal A., ed. The Rime of the Ancient Mariner: A
Handbook. San Francisco: Wadsworth Publishing Company, 1961.

492   Gibbons, Edward E. "Point of View and Moral in The Rime of
the Ancient Mariner." University Review-Kansas City, 35 (June,
1969), 257-61.

493   Gibson, Walker. "Coleridge: An Explanation by Literary Origins."
Poems in the Making. Boston: Houghton Mifflin, 1963, 93-151.

        "The Sleeping Images" from The Road to Xanadu by John
        Livingston Lowes, and "The Frontiers of Criticism" from
        On Poetry and Poets by T. S. Eliot.

494   Gose, Elliott B., Jr. "Coleridge and the Luminous Gloom:
An Analysis of the 'Symbolical Language' in The Rime of the Ancient
Mariner." PMLA, 75 (June, 1960), 238-44.

        Symbolic approach to the religious theme.

495   Green, Andrew J. "Essays in Miniature: The Resistless Eye."
CE 3 (May, 1942), 722-23.

496   Griggs, Earl L. "The Willing Suspension of Disbelief."
(In University of Colorado Studies Series B. Studies in the Humanities,
Vol. 2, No. 4. Boulder: University of Colorado Press, 1945), 272-85.

        The Rime of the Ancient Mariner and Christabel exemplify
        Coleridge's idea.

497   Grow, L. M. "The Rime of the Ancient Mariner: Multiple Veils
of Illusion." NDEJ, 9 (1973), 23-30.

498   Gunston, David. "A Second Look at the Albatross." DR, 40
(Summer, 1960), 206-11.

        The modern superstition of the evil consequences of killing
        an albatross is traced to Coleridge.

499   Hall, P. E. "A Latin Translation of In Memoriam." BC,
17 (Spring 1968), 78.

500   Handley, Graham. "Mrs. Gaskell's Reading: Some Notes on
Echoes and Epigraphs in Mary Barton." DUJ, 59 (June, 1967),
131-38.

501   Harding, D. C. W. "The Rime of the Ancient Mariner." (In
Bentley, Eric, ed. Importance of Scrutiny: Selections from Scrutiny:
A Quarterly Review, 1932-1948. New York: George W. Stewart, 1948),
174-81.

502   _____. "The Theme of The Ancient Mariner." Scrut,
9 (March, 1941), 334-42.

        Defends the religious theme. (Reprinted in Experience into
        Words. London: Chatto & Windus, Ltd., 1963.)

503   Harris, Lynn H. "Coleridge's The Ancient Mariner." EXPL,
6 (March, 1948), Item 32.

504   Hartley, A. J. "Frederick Denison Maurice, Disciple and
Interpreter of Coleridge: 'Constancy to an Ideal Object'." ARIEL
(April, 1972), 5-16.

505   Harvey, W. J. "Help!" EIC, 16 (April, 1966), 259-60.

506   Haven, Richard. "The Ancient Mariner in the Nineteenth
Century." SIR, 11 (Fall, 1972), 360-74.

507   Hopwood, V. G. "The Interpretation of Dream and Poetry."
UTQ, 21 (January, 1952), 128-39.

       Discusses The Ancient Mariner.

508   House, Humphry. "The Ancient Mariner." (In Abrams, M. H.
English Romantic Poets: Modern Essays in Criticism. London, New
York: Oxford University Press, 1960), 170-95.

509   Houston, Neal B. "Fletcher Christian and The Rime of the
Ancient Mariner." DR, 45 (Winter, 1965-66), 431-46.

510   Huang, Roderick. "William Cowper and The Rime of the Ancient
Mariner." UWR, 3 (Spring, 1968), 54-56.

511   Humo, Olga. "Kolridzov 'Stari Mornar' Kao Problem Kritickog
Metoda." (Coleridge's Ancient Mariner as a problem of the Critical
Method). Beograd, AFF, 8 (1968), 463-81.

512   Icaban-Castro, Rosalina. "The Crucifixion Story in Coleridge's
The Rime of the Ancient Mariner." DilR, 7 (July, 1959), 326-33.

513   Ishii, Hakusan. S. T. Coleridge: Ro Suifu No Uta--Skikei
Rhythm Chukai. Tokyo: Shinozaki Shorin, 1970.

       Commentary on Coleridge's Ancient Mariner, the form and
       rhythm.

514   Jacobus, Mary. "Peter Bell the First." EIC, 24 (July,
1974), 219-42.

515   _____. "William Huntington's Spiritual Sea-Voyage:
Another Source for the Ancient Mariner." N&Q, 16 (November,
1969), 409-12.

516   Jayne, Edward. "Up Against the Mending Wall: The Psycho-
analysis of a Poem by Frost." CE, 34 (April, 1973), 934-51.

517   Jeffrey, Lloyd N. "Human Interest and a Semblance of
Truth in the Slaying of Coleridge's Albatross." CEA, 30 (February,
1968), 3-5.

518   Jordan, John E. "The Hewing of Peter Bell." SEL, 7 (Autumn
1967), 559-603.

519   Justus, James H. "The Mariner and Robert Penn Warren."
SLL, 8 (Spring, 1966), 117-28.

520   Kaufman, R. J. "Bruising the Serpent: Milton As a Tragic
Poet." CentR, 11 (Summer, 1967), 371-86.

521   Kendle, Burton S. "Trilling's 'Of This Time, Of That Place'."
EXPL, 22 (April, 1964), Item 61.

      Many references to The Ancient Mariner and Kubla Khan.

522   Keppler, Carl Francis. "Symbolism in The Ancient Mariner:
A Study in Method." University of Michigan, DA, 17 (1957), 1338-39.

523   Kilby, Clyde S. "Tolkien and Coleridge." ORCRIST, 3
(January, 1970), 16-19.

524   Kirschbaum, Leo. "Coleridge's The Ancient Mariner." EXPL,
7 (October, 1948), Item 5.

525   Knight, G. Wilson. "Coleridge's Divine Comedy." (In
Abrams, M. H., ed. English Romantic Poets: Modern Essays in
Criticism. London, New York: Oxford University Press, (1960),
158-69.

526   _____. "The Rime of The Ancient Mariner." (In Knight,
G. Wilson. The Starlit Dome: Studies in the Poetry of Vision.
London, New York, Toronto: Oxford University Press, 1971), passim.

527   Kreuzer, James R. "Diction." (In Kreuzer, James R.
Elements of Poetry. New York: Macmillan, 1955), 18-21, et passim,
84-90 et passim.

528   Kroeber, Karl. "The Rime of The Ancient Mariner As Stylized
Epic." WASAL, 46 (1957), 179-87.

      Argues that the ballad is a guest epic similar to the
      Odyssey.

529   Larson, Charles R. "Coleridge's Ancient Mariner and the
Skinner Box." CEA, 37 (November, 1974), 21-2.

530   Lefebure, M. Samuel Taylor Coleridge: A Bondage of Opium.
New York: Stein & Day, 254-63; 481-85.

531   Leitz, Robert C. III. "Fletcher Christian and The Ancient
Mariner: A Refutation." DR, 50 (Spring, 1970), 62-70.

532   Lerner, Laurence. "Roads to Xanadu--And Back." EIC, 20
(January, 1970), 89-98.

533   Levy, Raphael. "Coleridge's The Rime of The Ancient Mariner,
193." EXPL, 22 (May, 1964), Item 74.

534   Lindberger, Orjan. "Les Differentes Interpretations de la
Rime of the Ancient Mariner. Un Apercu d'Ensemble de la Discussion."
OL, 19 (1964), 122-39.

535   Littman, Mark. "The Ancient Mariner and Initiation Rites."
PLL, 4 (Fall 1968), 370-89.

536   Lloyd, D. Tecwyn. "Reviews." Poetry of Wales, 8 (Winter, 1972),
85-92.

537   Lupton, Mary J. "The Rime of the Ancient Mariner: The Agony
of Thirst." AI, 27 (Summer, 1970), 140-59.

538   McDonald, Daniel. "Too Much Reality: A Discussion of The
Rime of the Ancient Mariner." SEL (Rice University) 4 (Autumn,
1964), 543-54.

539   McFarland, Thomas A., Jr. "Nine Fathoms Deep: The Background,
Imagery, and Symbolic Unity of Coleridge's Ancient Mariner." Yale
University. Unpublished Doctoral Dissertation, 1953.

540   McGann, Jerome, Jr. "Romanticism and the Embarrassments of
Critical Tradition." MP, 70 (February, 1973), 249-51.

541   Marsh, Florence. "The Ocean-Desert: The Ancient Mariner
and The Waste Land." EIC, 9 (April, 1959), 126-32.

542   Marshall, William H. "Coleridge, The Mariner, and Dramatic
Irony." Person, 42 (October, 1961), 524-32.

543   Martin, Bernard. The Ancient Mariner and the Authentic
Narrative. London: W. Heineman, 1949.

       Reviews: T. M. Raysor in PQ, 29 (1952), 116-17; R. D. Havens
       in MLN, 66 (January, 1951), 72.

544   Maxwell, J. C. "The Ancient Mariner and the Squire's Tale."
N&Q, 13 (June, 1966), 224.

545   _____. "Three Notes on Moby Dick." N&Q, 14 (February,
1967), 53.

546   May, Charles E. "Objectifying the Nightmare: Cain and the
Mariner." BSUF, 14 (Autumn, 1973), 45-48.

547   Mendilow, A. A. "Symbolism in Coleridge and the Dantesque
Element in The Ancient Mariner." SH, 2 (1955), 25-81.

       The influence of Dante is stressed.

548   Meier, Hans H. "Xanaduvian." ES, 48 (April, 1967), 145-55.

549   Monk, Samuel H. "Anna Seward and the Romantic Poets: A
Study in Taste." (In Wordsworth and Coleridge: Studies in Honor
of George McLean Harper, ed. by Earl L. Griggs, New York: Russell
& Russell, 1962), 118-34.

550   Moses, Edwin. "A Reading of The Ancient Mariner." Costerus,
8 (1973), 101-8.

551   Nelson, Carl. "The Ironic Allusive Texture of Lord Jim:
Coleridge, Crane, Milton, and Melville." Conrad, 4 (1972), 47-59.

552   Nelson, William. "A Coleridge 'Borrowing'." TLS (June 11,
1954), 377.

        A passage in The Ancient Mariner derives from a stanza in
        Sir John Davies' Orchestra.

553   Nemerov, Howard. "An Essay: The Difficulty of Difficult
Poetry." CM, 5 (Spring,1964), 35-51.

554   Newman, Paul B. "Joseph Conrad and The Ancient Mariner."
KM (1960), 79-83.

555   Ober, Warren U. "Heart of Darkness: The Ancient Mariner a
Hundred Years Later." DR, 45 (Autumn 1965), 333-7.

556   _____. "The Rime of The Ancient Mariner and Pinkard's
Notes on the West Indies." N&Q, 4 (September, 1957), 380-82.

557   O'Hear, Michael F. "The Constant Dream: Coleridge's Vision
of Woman and Love." University of Maryland, DAI, 31 (February,
1971), 4174A-5A.

558   Olson, Elder. "The Rime of The Ancient Mariner." MP, 45
(May, 1948), 275-9.

        With an essay by Robert Penn Warren.

559   Owen, Charles A., Jr. "Structure in The Ancient Mariner."
CE, 23 (January, 1962), 261-7.

560   Pafford, Ward. "Coleridge's Wedding-Guest." SP, 60 (October,
1963), 618-26.

561   _____. "Samuel Taylor Coleridge." EUQ, 21 (Spring,
1965), 3-14.

562   Parsons, Coleman O. "The Mariner and the Albatross."
VQR, 26 (Winter, 1950), 102-23.

        Defense of the religious theme.

563   Parsons, Howard. "Coleridge As the 'Wedding Guest' in The
Rime of The Ancient Mariner. N&Q, 195 (June 10, 1950), 251-52.

564   Pearce, Frank W. "Keats and The Ancient Mariner: Book III
of Endymion." KSJ, 24 (1975), 13-15.

565   Peckham, Morse. "Poet and Critic (or The Damage Coleridge
Has Done)." STwenC, 6 (Fall,1970), 1-11.

566   Pollin, Burton R.   "The Influence of The Ancient Mariner upon
The Ballad of Reading Gaol."   RLV, 40 (1974), 228-34.

567   Poston, Lawrence, III.   "The Ancient Mariner and a Minor
Religious Poem."   N&Q (April, 1958), 143.

      C. F. Alexander's "All Things Bright and Beautiful."

568   Prickett, Stephen.   "The Living Edicts of the Imagination:
Coleridge on Religious Language."   WC, 4 (Spring, 1973), 99-110.

569   Purser, J. W. R.   "Interpretation of The Ancient Mariner."
RES, 8 (August, 1957), 249-56.

      Defends the religious theme.

570   Quillen, Kathleen K.   "The Dimensions of the Sacred in Poetry:
Coleridge's The Rime of The Ancient Mariner and Poems of George
Macbeth."   Emory University, DAI, 36 (January, 1976), 4464A.

571   Raben, Joseph.   "Coleridge As the Prototype of the Poet in
Shelley's Alastor."   RES, 17 (August, 1966), 278-92.

      Commented on by Timothy Webb in "Coleridge and Shelley's
      Alastor: A Reply."   RES, 18 (November, 1967), 402-11.

572   Raysor, Thomas M.   "Coleridge's Comment on the Moral of
The Ancient Mariner."   PQ, 31 (January, 1952), 88-91.

      A comparison of Coleridge's two comments to Mrs. Barbauld.

573   Richards, I. A.   "Coleridge: The Vulnerable Poet."   YR, 48
(June, 1959), 491-504.

574   Ridge, George Ross and Davy, S.   "A Bird and a Motto: Source
for Benito Cereno."   MQ, 12 (Winter, 1959-60), 22-29.

575   Rostvig, Maren-Sofie.   "Another Source for Some Stanza of
The Rime of The Ancient Mariner?"   MLN, 66 (December, 1951), 543-46.

      Suggests that the source of "A sail, a sail." and "Hark,
      hark," in the ballad's first version may be a poem by Charles
      Cotton.

576   _____.   "The Rime of The Ancient Mariner and the Cosmic
System of Robert Fludd."   TSL, 12 (1967), 69-81.

577   Rowell, Charles H.   "Coleridge's Symbolic Albatross."   CLAJ,
6 (December, 1962), 133-35.

578   Sanders, Charles R.   "The Ancient Mariner and Coleridge's
Theory of Poetic Art."   (In Romantic and Victorian: Studies in
Memory of William H. Marshall.   Ed. by W. Paul Elledge and Richard
L. Hoffman.   Rutherford, N. J.: Fairleigh Dickinson University
Press, 1971), 110-28.

579   Scarfe, Francis. "Coleridge's Nightscapes." EA, 18 (January-March, 1965), 27-43.

580   Schanzer, Ernest. "Shakespeare, Lowes, and The Ancient Mariner." N&Q, 2 (June, 1955), 260-61.

581   Schulz, Max F. "The Ventriloquism Voice." (In Schulz, Max F. Voices of Coleridge. Detroit: Wayne State University Press, 1963), 51-71.

582   Schwegel, Douglas. "Joyce's Ulysses, Calypso Episode." EXPL, 27 (March, 1969), Item 49.

583   Scott, Thomas H. F. "The Ethics of The Ancient Mariner." DR, 18 (1938), 348-54.

584   Seely, Frederick F. "A Footnote to The Road to Xanadu." MLN, 59 (May, 1944), 333-4.

      Cites parallels between The Ancient Mariner and the Ballad of Chevy Chase.

585   Seronsy, Cecil C. "Dual Patterning in The Rime of The Ancient Mariner." N&Q, 3 (November, 1956), 497-9.

586   Smith, Bernard. "Coleridge's Ancient Mariner and Cook's Second Voyage." JWIC, 19 (January, 1956), 117-54.

587   Smith, Gayle S. "A Reappraisal of the Moral Stanza in The Rime of The Ancient Mariner." SIR, 3 (Autumn,1963), 42-52.

588   Spacks, Patricia M. "Horror--Personification in Late Eighteenth-Century Poetry." SP, 59 (July, 1962), 560-78.

589   Sparrow, John. "A Coleridge 'Borrowing'." TLS (July 16, 1954), 457.

590   Stebelman, Scott David. "The Theme of Betrayal in Coleridge's Poetry." University of Wisconsin, DAI, 34 (July, 1974), 418A.

591   Stevenson, Lionel. "The Ancient Mariner As a Dramatic Monologue." Person, 30 (Winter, 1949), 34-44.

      Argues against the religious theme; the poem is merely a dramatic story about a superstitious sailor who thinks that killing a bird has caused his woes.

592   Stoll, Elmer Dedgar. "Symbolism in Coleridge." PMLA, 63 (March, 1948), 214-33.

      An attack on Robert Penn Warren's symbolic approach.

593   Stuart, John A. "Augustine and The Ancient Mariner." MLN, 76 (February, 1961), 116-20.

594 _____. "The Augustinian Cause of Action in Coleridge's
The Rime of The Ancient Mariner." HTR, 60 (April, 1967), 177-211.

595 Suther, Marshall. The Dark Night of Samuel Taylor Coleridge.
New York: Columbia University Press; London: Oxford University Press,
1960.

   Reviews: J. V. Baker in CRIT, 3 (1961), 252-54; Patrick
   Cruttwell in HR, 14 (1961), 598-606; E. E. Bostetter in
   SR, 69 (1961), 490-500; E. E. Bostetter in TLS (June 2, 1961),
   339; E. L. Griggs in MP, 59 (May, 1962), 289-92; John Colmer
   in MLR, 57 (April, 1962), 306-7; W. J. B. Owen in RES, 13
   (August, 1962), 313-15.

596 _____. Visions of Xanadu. New York, London: Columbia
University Press, 1965.

   For Reviews, see section on Kubla Khan.

597 Teich, Nathaniel. "Correcting the Reference to the Monthly
Magazine in Fenwick's Note to Wordsworth's We Are Seven." WC,
1 (Spring, 1970), 55-6.

598 Teichman, Milton. "The Marriage Metaphor in The Rime of
The Ancient Mariner." BNYPL, 73 (January, 1969), 40-48.

599 Tillyard, E. M. W. "Coleridge: The Rime of The Ancient Mariner."
(In Tillyard, E. M. W. Poetry and Its Background: Illustrated by
Five Poems, 1470-1870. New York: Barnes and Noble, 1970), 66-86.

600 Twitchell, James B. "The Romantic Psychodrama: An Interpretation
of The Ancient Mariner, Manfred and Prometheus Unbound, Act IV."
University of North Carolina, Chapel Hill (March, 1972), 5204A-5A.

601 _____. "The World above The Ancient Mariner." TSLL,
17 (Spring, 1975), 103-17.

602 Visiak, E. H. "Two Voices in the Air. A Note on The Rime
of The Ancient Mariner." N&Q, 179 (August 10, 1940), 99.

603 Visweswariah, H. S. "Motive-Finding in The Rime of The Ancient
Mariner." LCrit, 8 (1969), 27-38.

604 Waldoff, Leon. "The Mythic Basis of Three Major Poems of
the Romantic Period." University of Michigan, DA, 28 (January,
1968), 2699A.

605 _____. "The Quest for Father and Identity in The Rime of
The Ancient Mariner." PsyR, 58 (Fall, 1971), 439-53.

606 Walters, Jennifer R. "Butor's Use of Literary Texts in
Degrees." PMLA, 88 (March, 1973), 311-20.

607   Waples, Dorothy. "David Hartley in The Ancient Mariner."
JEGP, 35 (July, 1936), 337-51.

      Traces the influence of Hartley's philosophy on the ballad.

608   Ware, J. Garth. "Coleridge's Great Poems Reflecting the
Mother Image." AI, 18 (Winter 1961), 331-52.

609   Ware, Malcolm. "Coleridge's 'Spectre-Bark': A Slave Ship?"
PQ, 40 (October, 1961), 589-93.

      Suggests that the poem's spectre ship may have been intended
      as a slave ship.

610   _____. "The Rime of The Ancient Mariner: A Discourse
on Prayer?" RES, 11 (August, 1960), 303-4.

      Defends the religious theme with special emphasis on the
      poem's references to prayer.

611   Warner, Oliver. "Coleridge's 'Naval Poetry' and Southey's
Life of Nelson." N&Q, 17 (May, 1970), 169-70.

612   Warren, Robert P. "A Poem of Pure Imagination: Reconsideration
6." KR, 8 (Summer, 1946), 391-427.

      A study of The Rime of The Ancient Mariner.

613   _____. The Rime of The Ancient Mariner, by Samuel Taylor
Coleridge. New York: Reynal and Hitchcock, 1946.

      Contains an extended interpretation and full annotation.
      Reviews: Harvey Breit in NYTBR (January 5, 1947), 5;
      R. P. Blackmur in NATION, 164 (1947), 307-9; Kenneth Burke
      in POETRY, 70 (1947), 42-47; Elder Olson in MP, 45 (May, 1948),
      275-79.

614   Watson, H. F. "The Borderers and The Ancient Mariner."
TLS (December 28, 1935), 899.

615   _____. "A Note on The Ancient Mariner." PQ, 13 (January,
1934), 83-4.

616   Watson, Melvin R. "The Redemption of Peter Bell." SEL,
4 (Autumn, 1964), 519-30.

617   Webb, Timothy. "Coleridge and Shelley's Alastor: A Reply."
RES, 18 (November, 1967), 402-11.

618   Wells, Evelyn Kendrick. "The Literary Ballad." The Ballad
Tree. New York: Ronald Press, 1950, 313-6.

619 Whalley, George. "The Mariner and the Albatross." UTQ, 16 (July, 1947), 381-98.

On The Rime of the Ancient Mariner as a revelation of Coleridge's inner life; the albatross is a symbol of the creative imagination.

620 White, Alison. "Coleridge's The Rime of the Ancient Mariner, 198." EXPL, 13 (November, 1954), Item 11.

Life-in-Death may whistle trice to confound the Trinity.

621 Whitesell, J. Edwin. "The Rime of the Ancient Mariner, Line 142." N&Q, 3 (January, 1956), 34-35.

"The albatross hung around the mariner's neck."

622 Wilcox, Stewart C. "The Arguments and Motto of The Ancient Mariner." NLQ, 22 (September, 1961), 264-68.

623 _____. "Coleridge's The Ancient Mariner." EXPL, 7 (February, 1949), Item 28.

624 _____. "The Water Imagery of The Ancient Mariner." Person, 35 (July, 1954), 285-92.

625 Wolman, Kenneth. "The Ancient Mariner's Unethical World." EngR, 23 (Spring, 1973), 34-39.

626 Woodring, Carl. "The Mariner's Return." SIR, 11 (Fall, 1972), 375-80.

627 Wormhoudt, Arthur. "The Rime of the Ancient Mariner." (In Wormhoudt, Arthur. The Demon Lover: A Psychoanalytical Approach to Literature. New York: Exposition Press, 1949), 29-42.

628 Yonce, Margaret J. "The Spiritual Descent into the Maelstrom: A Debt to The Rime of the Ancient Mariner." PoeN, 2 (1969), 26-29.

629 Yura, Kimiyashi. "The Ancient Mariner: Intentional Fallacy." SEL-Japan, 39 (1962).

630 _____. "The Moral of the Ancient Mariner." SEL-Japan, 38 (1961), 219-35.

THIS LIME-TREE BOWER MY PRISON

631 Boulger, James D. "Coleridge on Imagination Revisited." WC, 4 (Winter, 1973), 13-24.

632 _____. "Imagination and Speculation in Coleridge's Conversation Poems." JEGP, 64 (October, 1965), 691-711.

633   Campbell, Oscar James. "Wordsworth's Conception of the
Esthetic Experience." (In Wordsworth and Coleridge: Studies in
Honor of George McLean Harper. ed. by Earl Leslie Griggs. New
York: Russell, 1962), 26-46.

634   D'Avanzo, Mario L. "Coleridge's This Lime-Tree Bower My
Prison and The Tempest." WC, 1 (Spring 1970), 66-8.

635   Durr, R. A. "This Lime-Tree Bower My Prison and a Recurrent
Action in Coleridge." ELH, 26 (December, 1959), 514-30.

636   Frese, John J. "Four Voices: Studies in Consciousness and
the Romantic Ode." University of Iowa, DAI, 33 (October, 1972),
1681A.

637   Gaskins, Avery H. "Coleridge: Nature, the Conversation Poems,
and the Structure of Meditation." NEOPHIL, 59 (1975), 629-35.

638   Harper, George McLean. "Coleridge's Conversation Poems."
(In Abrams, M. H. English Romantic Poets, New York: Oxford University
Press, 1960), 144-57.

639   Henry, William Harley. "Coleridge's Meditative Poems and
Early Religious Thought: The Theology of The Eolian Harp, This
Lime-Tree Bower My Prison, and Frost at Midnight." The John Hopkins
University, DAI, 31 (November, 1970), 2345A.

640   Magnuson, Paul A. "The Dead Calm in the Conversation Poems."
WC, 3 (Spring,1972), 53-60.

641   Rubenstein, Jill. "Sound and Silence in Coleridge's
Conversation Poems." ENGLISH, 21 (Summer, 1972), 54-60.

642   Rudrum, A. W. "Coleridge's This Lime-Tree Bower My Prison."
SoR, 1 (1964), 30-42.

643   Schmidt, Michael. "Coleridge: This Lime-Tree Bower My
Prison." CS, 6 (1973), 44-47.

644   Taylor, Anya. "Magic in Coleridge's Poetry." WC, 3 (Spring,
1972), 76-84.

645   Ward, Patricia. "Coleridge's Critical Theory of the Symbol."
TSLL, 8 (Spring,1966), 15-32.

646   Wendling, Ronald C. "Dramatic Reconciliation in Coleridge's
Conversation Poems." PLL, 9 (Spring,1973), 145-60.

THE WATCHMAN

647   Beer, J. B. "Coleridge's Watchman." N&Q, 8 (June 1961), 217.

649   Davis, Bertram R. "The Coleridge Canon." TLS (September 10, 1938), 584.

650   Gibbs, Warren E. "An Autobiographical Note of Coleridge's in the Watchman." N&Q, 160 (February 7, 1931), 99–100.

651   Johnson, S. F. "Coleridge's The Watchman: Decline and Fall." RES, 4 n.s. (April, 1953), 147–48.

652   _____. "An Uncollected Early Poem by Coleridge." BNYPL, 61 (October, 1957), 505–07.

       Also, in Evidence for Authorship, ed. by David V. Erdman
       and Ephim G. Fogel, New York: Cornell University Press,
       1966, 344–47.

       The poem is "Lines on the Portrait of a Lady"

653   Patton, Lewis. "Coleridge and the 'Enquirer' Series." RES, 14 (April, 1940), 188–89.

       Evidence that Enfield was the author of this series in the
       Monthly Magazine. Notes other borrowings by Coleridge in
       The Watchman.

654   _____. "The Coleridge Canon." TLS (September 3, 1938), 570.

       Rejects from the Canon several pieces which first appeared
       in The Watchman.

655   Priestley, Mary E. "English Syntax in the Early Prose of Samuel Taylor Coleridge: A New Reading of The Watchman, 1976." University of Alabama, DA, 28 (February, 1968), 3195A–96A.

General Criticism

PERIODICALS

656   Abel, Darrel. "Coleridge's 'Life-in-Death' and Poe's 'Death-in-Life'." N&Q, 2 (May, 1955), 218-20.

657   Abrams, M. H. "Archetypal Analogies in the Language of Criticism." UTQ, 18 (July, 1949), 313-27.

  Chiefly concerned with biological concepts used metaphorically to describe creative processes.

658   _____. Coleridge's 'A Light in Sound': Science, Metascience, and Poetic Imagination." PAPS, 116 (1972), 458-76.

659   _____. "Wordsworth and Coleridge on Diction and Figures." EIE, (1952), 171-201.

660   Adams, Maurianne S. and Haven, Richard. "Coleridge in Victorian Journalism." VPN, 2 (June, 1968), 20-2.

661   Adelman, Clifford. "The Dehumanization of William Blake." CamR, 89A (June 7, 1968), 549-50.

662   Adlard, John. "Coleridge and Enmore." N&Q, 17 (1970), 117-18.

663   _____. "John Clare: The Long Walk Home." ENGLISH, 19 (Autumn, 1970), 85-89.

664   Ahmad, Munir. "Coleridge and the Brahman Creed." IJES, 1 (1960), 18-37.

665   _____. "A Probable Indian Source of a Coleridge Verse Fragment." N&Q, 8 (June, 1961), 217-18.

666   Aldrich, Ruth I. "The Wordsworths and Coleridge: 'Three Persons' but <u>not</u> 'One Soul'." SIR, 2 (Autumn, 1962), 61-3.

667   Alkon, Paul K. "Critical and Logical Concepts of Method from Addison to Coleridge." ECS, 5 (Fall, 1971), 97-121.

668   _____. "Structuring Coleridge's Ideas." MLQ, 32 (June, 1971), 206-13.

669   Armour, Richard W. "A Poet's Heights and Depths," SatR (July 7, 1956), 14.

670   _____ and Raymond F. Howes. "Addenda to <u>Coleridge the Talker</u>." QJS, 32 (October, 1946), 298-303.

671   Arntson, Herbert E. "A Probable Borrowing by Coleridge from <u>The Seasons</u>." RS, 15 (September, 1947), 201-02.

672   Ashbrook, Joseph. "Coleridge's 'Star Within the Moon'." ST, 28 (December, 1964), 335.

673   Ashe, Dora J. "Byron's Alleged Part in the Production of Coleridge's <u>Remorse</u>." N&Q, 198 (January, 1953), 33-6.

674   _____. "Coleridge, Byron, and Schiller's <u>Der Geisterseher</u>." N&Q, 3 (October, 1956), 436-38.

675   Atherton, J. S. "A Few More Books at the Wake." JJQ, 2 (Spring, 1965), 142-49.

676   "At Home on Highgate Hill." TLS (March 31, 1972), 354.

677   Audet, Ronald A. "<u>Frost at Midnight</u>: The Other Coleridge." EJ, 59 (November, 1970), 1080-85.

678   Badawi, M. M. "Coleridge's Formal Criticism of Shakespeare's Plays." EIC, 10 (April, 1960), 148-62.

679   _____. "A Note on Coleridge and the Acting of Shakespear's Plays." BFA (Alexandria University), 14 (1960), 89-96.

680   Bagley, Carol L. "Early American Views of Coleridge as Poet." RS, 32 (December, 1964), 292-307.

681   Baker, Carlos. "The Infinite Sea: The Development and Decline of Wordsworth and Coleridge: An Account of Professor Harper's Unfinished Book." PULC, 11 (Winter, 1950), 62-75.

682   _____. "A Poet Whose Gift Survived the Man." NYT (July 22, 1956), 1.

683   Baker, James V. "Catching Up with Coleridge." FORUM (University of Houston), 4 (Spring and Summer, 1964), 31-6.

684   Bald, R. C. "Lives of the Poets." YR, 28 (June, 1939),
855-59.

685   Bandy, W. T. "Coleridge's Friend Joseph Hardman: A Bibliographical Note." JEGP, 47 (October, 1948), 395-97.

       His relationship with the author of the first appearance of
       Coleridge's translation of "Kennst du das Land."

686   Banerji, Jibon. "The Role of Godwinian Ideas in The Borderers."
Calcutta Rev. 1 (January-March, 1970), 419-22.

687   Barfield, Owen. "Abysses of Incomprehension." Nation,
214 (June 12, 1972), 764-65.

688   _____. "Coleridge Collected." Encounter, 35 (November,
1970), 74-83.

689   Barnes, Sam G. "Was Theory of Life Coleridge's 'Opus
Maximum'?" SP, 55 (July, 1958), 494-514.

690   Barnet, Sylvan. "Coleridge on Puns: A Note to His Shakespeare
Criticism." JEGP, 56 (October, 1957), 602-09.

691   _____. "Coleridge on Shakespeare's Villains." SQ, 7
(Winter, 1956), 9-20.

692   _____. "Coleridge's Marginalia in Stockdale's Shakespeare of 1784." HLB, 12 (Spring,1958), 210-19.

693   Barth, J. Robert. "A Newer Criticism in America: The Religious
Dimension." Mon/HES, No. 4 (1973), 67-82.

694   _____. "Symbol as Sacrament in Coleridge's Thought."
SIR, 11 (Fall, 1972), 320-31.

       Coleridge's view compared to formal theological doctrine.

695   Bassett, T. D. Seymour and Duffy, John J. "The Library
of James Marsh." ESQ, 63 (Spring,1971), 2-10.

696   Bates, R. "Donner Un Sens Plus Pur Aux Mots D Ela Tribu."
N&Q, 198 (November, 1953), 493-94.

697   Beach, Joseph W. "Coleridge's Borrowing from the German."
ELH, 9 (March, 1942), 36-58.

       Coleridge's reluctance to acknowledge his borrowings.

698   Beaty, Frederick L. "Dorothy Wordsworth and the Coleridges:
A New Letter." MLR, 51 (July, 1956), 411-13.

699   _____. "Mrs. Radcliffe's Fading Gleam." PQ, 42 (January,
1963), 126-29.

700 _____. "Two Manuscript Poems of Coleridge." RES, 7
(1956), 185-87.

The poems are "The Knight's Tomb" and a portion of "Youth
and Age".

701 _____. "Coleridge and Lamb: The Central Themes." ChLB
14 (1976), 109-23.

702 _____. "Coleridge at School." N&Q, 5 (March, 1958),
114-16.

703 _____. "Coleridge, the Wordsworths, and the State of
Trance." WC, 8 (Spring, 1977), 121-38.

704 _____. "Coleridge's 'Great Circulating Library'."
N&Q, 3 (June, 1956), 264.

705 _____. "Revolutionary Youth of Wordsworth and Coleridge:
Another View." CritQ, 19 (Summer, 1977), 79-87.

706 Benziger, James. "Organic Unity: Leibniz to Coleridge."
PMLA, 66 (March, 1951), 24-48.

707 Beres, Davis. "The Notebooks of Samuel Taylor Coleridge."
PsyQ, 28 (1959), 267-70.

708 Berkoben, Lawrence D. "Coleridge on Wit." HAB (Canada),
15 (Spring, 1964), 24-30.

709 _____. "The Composition of Coleridge's Hymn Before Sunrise:
Some Mitigating Circumstances." ELN, 4 (September, 1966), 32-7.

710 Bernhardt-Kabisch, Ernest. "The Epitaph and the Romantic
Poets: A Survey." HLQ, 30 (February, 1967), 113-46.

711 Betz, Paul F. "After the Lyrical Ballads: Wordsworth and
Coleridge in 1801-1802." SIR, 12 (Spring, 1973), 580-89.

712 _____. "T. J. Wise and Gordon Wordsworth." BNYPL,
74 (November, 1970), 577-86.

713 Beyer, Werner W. "Coleridge's Early Knowledge of German."
MP, 52 (February, 1955), 192-200.

714 _____. "A Cryptic Entry in Coleridge's Gutch Notebook,
fol. 20b." N&Q, 197 (December 20, 1952), 556.

715 Bhattacharya, Biswanath. "Mismanaged Sensibility." LCrit,
9 (1970), 81-3.

716 Bilsland, John W. "DeQuincey on Poetic Genius." DR, 48
(Summer, 1968), 200-14.

717 Bishop, Morchard. "A Coleridge Footnote." TLS (August 20,
1964), 747.

718 _____. "Notes of Two Coleridges." BNYPL, 63 (October, 1959), 531-3.

719   Blackwell, Louise. "Song of Myself and the Organic Theory of Poetry." WWR, 12 (June, 1966), 35-41.

720   "Bliss Was It in That Dawn: The Matter of Coleridge's Revolutionary Youth and How It Became Obscured." TLS (August 6, 1971), 929-32.

721   Blocker, H. Gene. "Another Look at Aesthetic Imagination." JAAC, 30 (Summer, 1972), 529-36.

722   Bloom, Harold. "Work in Progress. Coleridge: The Anxiety of Influence." DIAC, 2 (Spring, 1972), 36-41.

723   Blunden, Edmund. "Coleridge's Notebooks." REL, 7 (January, 1966), 25-31.

724   _____. "Lives of the Poets: If Dr. Johnson Had Lived Rather Longer. I. William Wordsworth, II. Samuel Taylor Coleridge." TLS (May 20, 1955), 276.

   Reviews: David C. Ruther in TLS (May 27, 1955), 285; (May 27, 1955), 292: R. W. King in TLS (June 3, 1955), 301; Gordon W. Dennis TLS (June 10, 1955), 323.

725   _____. "The Poet Hood." REL, 1 (January, 1960), 26-34.

726   Blunden, Edmund, and Jacques L. LeClaire. "Poéme inédit de Hartley Coleridge." EA, 19 (July-September, 1966), 234-38.

   Text with essay by each.

727   Boas, Louise S. "Coleridge's Ode on the Departing Year, 149-161." EXPL, 9 (November, 1950), Item 15.

728   Bonnard, G. "The Invasion of Switzerland and English Public Opinion (January to April, 1798): The Background to S. T. Coleridge's France: An Ode:" ES, 22 (1940), 1-26.

729   Booth, Karen Marshall. "Two Unreported Watermarks." PBSA, 64 (1970), 338-39.

730   Bonnerot, Louis. "The Two Worlds of Coleridge: Some Aspects of His Attitude to Nature." EDH, 28 (1956), 93-105.

731   Bostetter, E. E. "Coleridge's Manuscript Essay: On the Passions." JHI, 31 (January-March, 1970), 99-108.

732   _____. "The Man Behind the Curtain." WR, 23 (Autumn, 1958), 90-6.

733   _____. "The New Romantic Criticism." SR, 69 (1961), 490-500.

734   Boulger, James D. "Coleridge: The Marginalia, Myth-Making, and the Later Poetry." SIR, 11 (Fall, 1972), 304-19.

735   _____. "Reader's Queries: Coleridge's Simile of a Watch." N&Q, 18 (September, 1971), 344-45.

736   _____. "The Sad Ghost of Coleridge." PS, 33 (1959), 187-90.

737   Boulton, James T. "Arbitrary Power: An Eighteenth-Century Obsession." Studies in Burke and His Time. 9 (Spring, 1968), 905-26.

738   Bouslog, Charles S. "Coleridge and Mithraic Symbolism." N&Q, 1 (October, 1954), 66-7.

739   _____. "Coleridge, Bruce, and Ode to the West Wind." N&Q, 1 (October, 1954), 4444.

740   _____. "The Symbol of the Sod-Seat in Coleridge," PMLA, 60 (September, 1945), 802-10.

        The sod-seat "became and remained a symbol of love," associated with Sara Hutchinson.

741   Boyd, John D. "Texture and Form in Theodore Roethke's Greenhouse Poems." MLQ, 32 (December, 1971), 409-24.

742   Boyle, Robert S. J. "Hopkins' Use of 'Fancy'." VP, 10 (Spring, 1972), 17-27.

743   Braekman, W. "An Imitation by Samuel Taylor Coleridge of a Medieval German Love Song." NEOPHIL, 56 (1972), 100-06.

744   _____. "The Influence of William Collins on Coleridge in 1793." RLV, 31 (1965), 228-39.

745   _____. "Letters by Robert Southey to Sir John Taylor Coleridge." SGG, 6 (1964), 103-230.

        Contains an index of Names.

746   _____. "A Reconsideration of the Genesis of S. T. Coleridge's Poem On Taking Leave of-----." N&Q, 11 (January, 1964), 21-4.

747   _____. "Two Hitherto Unpublished Letters of Charles and Mary Lamb to the Morgans." ES, 44 (April, 1963), 108-18.

        Mentions Coleridge's Sibylline Leaves.

748   _____. "An Unpublished Poem by S. T. Coleridge." N&Q, 10 (May, 1963), 181-82.

749   Braekman, W. and A. Devolder. "Three Hitherto Unpublished Letters of S. T. Coleridge to J. J. Morgan." SGG, 4 (1962), 203-23.

750   Brantlinger, Patrick. "Bluebooks, the Social Organism, and
the Victorian Novel." CRIT, 14 (Fall, 1972), 328-44.

751   Breit, Harvey. "Coleridge's Strange Hierarchy of the Damned."
NYTBR (January 5, 1947), 5.

752   Breitkreuz, Hartmut. "Coleridge at Gottingen in 1799."
AN&Q, 12 (December, 1973), 56-59.

753   _____. "S. T. Coleridge's German Vocabulary." N&Q,
20 (February, 1973), 44-45.

754   Bremer, Heather. "Coleridge and the Rhinoceros." TLS (July
29, 1960), 481.

       An anticipation of Ionesco.

755   Brett, R. L. "Coleridge's Theory of the Imagination."
ES, Ser. 2 (1949), 75-90.

756   Breyer, B. R. "Wordsworth's Pleasure: An Approach to his
Poetic Theory." SHR, 6 (Spring, 1972), 123-31.

757   Brier, Peter. "On Teaching Coleridge." PCP, 9 (April,
1974), 20-24.

758   Brinkley, R. Florence. "Coleridge on John Petvin and John
Locke." HLQ, 8 (May, 1945), 277-92.

       Prints Coleridge's marginalia from a copy of Petvin's
       Letters Concerning Mind.

759   _____. "Coleridge on Locke." SP, 46 (October, 1949),
521-43.

       Describes four unpublished letters undertaking to prove that
       Locke's philosophy derives from Descartes and examines the
       ramifications of Coleridge's interest in the matter.

760   _____. "Coleridge's Criticism of Jeremy Taylor." HLQ,
13 (May, 1950), 313-23.

761   _____. "Coleridge Transcribed." RES, 24 (July, 1948),
219-26.

762   _____. "Some Coleridge Notes on Richter and Reimarus."
PULC, 5 (November, 1943), 1-13.

763   _____. "Some Notes Concerning Coleridge Material at the
Huntington Library." HLQ, 8 (May, 1945), 312-20.

764 _____. "Some Unpublished Coleridge Marginalia: Richter and Reimarus." JEGP, 44 (April, 1945), 113-30.

   Prints Coleridge's marginal notes to Richter's Das Kampaner Thal (1797) and Reimarus' Ueber Die Grunde Der Menschlichen Religion (1787). The two works, bound in one volume, are now in the Library of Princeton University.

765 Brisman, Leslie. "Coleridge and the Ancestral Voices." GR, 29 (1975), 163-67.

766 _____. English Book, 1808-1812. Poems by S. T. Coleridge, Esq." PBSA, 39 (1945), 163-67.

   Demonstrates that this sixteen-page pamphlet was printed between 1808-1812.

767 Broderick, John C. "The Date and Source of Emerson's Grace." MLN, 73 (February, 1958), 91-95.

768 Brogan, Howard O. "Coleridge's Theory and Use of the Praeter-Supernatural." Bulletin of the Citadel, 7 (1943), 3-17.

769 Brooks, Nicholas. Coleridge's True and Original Realism." DUJ, 53 (March, 1961), 58-59.

770 Brooks, Cleanth. "Religion and Literature." SR, 82 (January-March, 1974), 93-107.

771 Brooks, E. L. "Coleridge's Second Packet for Blackwood's Magazine." PQ, 30 (October, 1951), 426-30.

   On Coleridge's authorship of certain articles in the London Magazine, 1821-1822.

772 Broughton, Leslie N. "Some Early Nineteenth-Century Letters Hitherto Unpublished." NCS, (1940), 47-48.

   Letters of Colerdige, Southey, etc.

773 Brown, Daniel R. "A Look at Archetypal Criticism." JAAC, 28 (Summer, 1970), 465-72.

774 Bruns, Gerald L. "Poetry as Reality: The Orpheus Myth and Its Modern Counterparts." ELH, 37 (June, 1970), 263-86.

775 Buchan, A. M. "The Influence of Wordsworth on Colerdige." (1795-1800). UTQ, 32 (July, 1963), 346-66.

776 Buckley, Vincent. "Coleridge: Vision and Actuality." MCR, 4 (1961), 3-17.

777 Bunn, James. "Circle and Sequence in the Conjectural Lyric." NLH, 3 (1972), 511-26.

778 Burke, Carol. "Riddle of the Rider." Coronet, 33 (March, 1953), 150-52.

779   Burke, Charles B. "Coleridge and Milton." N&Q, 176 (January 21, 1939), 42.

780   _____. "Coleridge and Shelley." N&Q, 176 (February 11, 1939), 98-9.

       Compares a passage in Coleridge's France: An Ode with one in Shelley's Alastor.

781   Bush, Douglas. "Pure Serene." TLS (November 18, 1944), 559.

782   Butler, James A. "Wordsworth's Tuft of Primroses: An Un-relenting Doom." SIR, 14 (1975), 237-48.

783   Butterfield, L. H. "Coleridge as a Critic." SRL, 15 (January 30, 1937), 16.

784   Byers, John R., Jr. "Coleridge's Time, Real and Imaginary." EXPL, 19 (April, 1961), Item 46.

785   _____. "The Turn of the Screw: A Hellish Point of View." Markham Review, 2 (May, 1971), 101-04.

786   Calleo, David. "Coleridge on Napoleon." YFS, 26 (1960), 83-93.

787   Cam, W. H. and E. Blunden. "A Coleridge Portrait." TLS (February 14, 1935), 92.

788   Cambon, Glauco. "The Wasteland as Work in Progress." Mosiac, 6 (Fall,1972), 191-200.

789   Cameron, Kenneth Neill. "Shelley and the Conciones Ad Populum." MLN, 57 (December, 1942), 673-74.

       On the indebtedness of Swellfoot the Tyrant to Coleridge's work.

790   Cameron, Kenneth W. "Coleridge and the Genesis of Emerson's Uriel." PQ, 30 (April, 1951), 212-17.

791   _____. "Did Whittier Plagiarize The Barefoot Boy?" ESQ, 47: 2nd Q (1967), 112-13.

792   _____. "Emerson and the Motif That 'Spirits Associate'." ESQ, 12: 3rd Q (1958), 45-46.

793   _____. "Emerson's Capital Print of Coleridge." ESQ, 2: 1st Q (1956), 8-9.

794   _____. "Schiller's Die Ideale and Odes of Coleridge and Wordsworth." ESQ, 19: 2nd Q (1960), 36-37.

795   _____. "Young Emerson's Transcendental Vision." ESQ, 64-65 (Summer-Fall,1971), 1-584.

796   Carver, P. L.   "Coleridge and the Theory of Imagination."
UTQ, 9 (July, 1940), 452-65.

797   Cawley, A. C.   "Love's Fool Paradise."   Meanjin, 23 (June,
1964), 179-85.

798   Cevasco, G. A.   "Slings and Arrows: A Consideration of
Captious Literary Criticism."   ABC, 20 (May, 1970), 8-10.

799   Chadwick, Elizabeth.   "Coleridge's Headlong Horsemen:
Insinuating the Supernatural."   WC, 8 (Winter,1977), 47-55.

800   Chaffee, Alan J.   "The Rendezvous of Mind."   WC, 3 (Autumn,
1972), 196-203.

801   Chamberlain, John.   "The Common Sense of Bahehot."   NR, 7
(May 9, 1959), 58-59.

802   Chambers, E. K.   "Some Dates in Coleridge's Annus Mirabilis."
E&S, 19 (1933), 85-111.

803   Chayes, Irene H.   "Coleridge, Metempsychosis, and 'Almost
All the Followers of Fenelon'."   ELH, 25 (December, 1958), 290-315.

804   _____.   "Little Girls Lost: Problems of a Romantic
Archetype."   BNYPL, 67 (November, 1963), 579-92.

805   Chevigny, Bell Gale.   "Instress and Devotion in the Poetry
of Gerard Manley Hopkins."   VS, 9 (December, 1965), 151-53.

806   Chinol, Elio.   "Poe's Essays on Poetry."   SR, 68 (July, 1960),
390-97.

807   Christensen, Morton A.   "Udolpho, Horrid Mysteries, and
Coleridge's Machinery of the Imagination."   WC, 2 (Autumn,1971),
153-59.

808   Cinglio, Ada V.   "Two Gallants: Joyce's Wedding Guests."
JJQ, 10 (1973), 264.

809   Coanada, Richard.   "Hawthorne's Scarlet Letter."   REN, 19
(Spring,1967), 161-66.

810   Coburn, Kathleen.   "Coleridge and Restraint."   UTQ, 38
(April, 1969), 233-47.

811   _____.   "Coleridge and Wordsworth on the 'Supernatural'."
UTQ, 25 (January, 1956), 121-30.

812   _____.   "Coleridge Queries."   N&Q, 199 (August, 1954), 360.

813   _____.   "Coleridge's Quest for Self-Knowledge."   Listen,
42 (September 8, 1949), 395-96.

814 _____. "Critics Who Have Influenced Taste-XVI: S. T. Coleridge." LT, (July 18, 1963), 13.

815 _____. "The Interpenetrations of Man and Nature." PBA, 49 (1963), 95-113.

816 _____. "Original Versions of Two Coleridge Couplets." N&Q, 5 (May, 1958), 225-26.

817 _____. "Poet into Public Servant." PTRSC, 54 (1960), 1-11.

818 _____. Reader's Queries: Quotations in Coleridge's Notebooks." N&Q, 18 (December, 1971), 461-62.

819 _____. "Research on the Coleridge Notebooks." ChLB, 142 (1958), 199-200.

820 _____. "S. T. C. in His Letters." MP, 57 (May, 1960), 264-68.

821 Cochrane, Resmond C. "Francis Bacon in Early Eighteenth Century English Literature." PQ, 37 (January, 1958), 58-79.

822 Cohen, Ralph. "S. T. Coleridge and William Sotheby's Orestes." MLR, 52 (January, 1957), 19-27.

    Coleridge's marginalia on the play.

823 Coldicutt, Dorothy. "Was Coleridge the Author of the Enquirer Series in the Monthly Magazine, 1796-9?" RES, 15 (January, 1939), 45-60.

824 "Coleridge at the British Museum." TLS (July 21, 1972), 852.

825 "Coleridge on Politics. The Ideas of Church and State. A Frightened Philosopher." TLS (July 9, 1938), 464.

826 "Coleridge: The I and the World." TLS (August, 1939), 412-14.

827 "Coleridge to a Young Clergyman." MB, 14 (November, 1939), 412-14.

    Text of a hitherto unpublished letter, dated November 9,
    1832, and addressed to the Rev. James Gillman.

828 Coleridge, Nicholas, F. D. "Coleridge and Wordsworth." TLS (July 3, 1948), 373.

829 Coleridge, Samuel Taylor. "Prospectus of Coleridge's Lectures on Shakespeare." ShQ, 9 (Winter, 1958), frontispiece.

830 Colmer, John A. "Coleridge: A Library Cormorant." ALJ, 16 (February, 1967), 6-12.

831 _____. "Coleridge and the Communication of Political Truth."
ESA, 1 (September, 1958), 126-33.

832 _____. "Coleridge and the Life of Hope." SIR, 2 (Fall,
1972), 332-41.

833 _____. "Coleridge on Addington's Adminstration." MLR,
54 (January, 1959), 69-72.

        (Also in Evidence for Authorship. Ed. by David V. Erdman
        and Ephim G. Fogel, New York: Cornell University Press,
        1966, 338-43.)

834 _____. "An Unpublished Sermon by S. T. Coleridge."
N&Q, 5 (April, 1958), 150-52.

835 Cooke, Michael. "DeQuincey, Coleridge, and the Formal Uses
of Intoxication." YFS, 50 (1975), 26-40.

836 Cottle, Basil. "Damaged." EIC, 23 (October, 1973), 413-19.

837 Cox, R. G. "Coleridge As a Dual Personality." Scrut, 4
(1935), 205-07.

838 Crane, R. S. "Cleanth Brooks; or, The Bankruptcy of Critical
Monism." MP, 45 (May, 1948), 226-45.

839 Cranston, Maurice. "The Young S. T. C." Listen, 55 (June
14, 1956), 811.

840 Crawford, Walter B. and Lauterbach, Edward S. "Coleridge
in Narrative and Drama, Part I." WC, 3 (Spring, 1972), 117-22.

841 _____. "Coleridge in Narrative and Drama, Part II."
WC, 4 (Winter, 1973), 36-40.

842 _____. "Recent Coleridge Scholarship." WC, 3 (Winter,
1972), 41-48.

843 _____. "Recent Coleridge Scholarship: A Survey." WC,
3 (Summer, 1972), 186-92.

844 Creed, Howard H. "Coleridge as Critic." Vanderbilt University
Summaries of Theses. (1945), 109-32.

845 _____. "Coleridge as Critic." Bulletin of Vanderbilt
University. 43 (1943), 5-6.

846 _____. "Coleridge on Taste." ELH, 13 (June, 1946)
143-55.

        Brings together Coleridge's comments on taste as the basis
        of critical theory.

847 _____. "Coleridge's Metacriticism." PMLA, 69 (December, 1954), 1160-80.

848 Crow, Charles R. "Chiding the Plays: Then Till Now." ShS, 18 (1965), 1-10.

849 Cruttwell, Patrick. "The Eighteenth Century: A Classical Age?" ARION, 7 (Spring, 1968), 110-32.

850 Curry, Kenneth. "A Note on Coleridge's Copy of Malthus." PMLA, 54 (June, 1939), 613-15.

Comment upon G. R. Potter's article in PMLA, 51 (December, 1936), 1061-68, establishing the circumstances under which certain marginalia of Coleridge were made.

851 Curtis, Jared R. "The Best Philosopher: New Variants for Wordsworth's Immortality Ode." YULG, 44 (January, 1970), 139-47.

852 D. A. E. "Zapolya and Merope." N&Q, 183 (September 12, 1942), 164-65.

853 Dameron, John L. "Emerson and the Edinburgh Review of Statesman's Manual." ESQ, 8 (1957), 31.

854 Daniel, Robert W. "The Publication of Lyrical Ballads." MLR, 33 (July, 1938), 406-10.

Reason for thinking that Cottle may never actually have published the book, and that Arch's London issue is the first trade edition.

855 Darcy, C. P. "Coleridge and the Italian Artist, Migliarini." N&Q, 23 n.s. (March, 1976), 104-05.

856 D'Avanzo, Mario L. "The Literary Sources of 'My Kinsmen, Major Molineux': Shakespeare, Coleridge, Milton." SSF, 10 (Spring, 1973), 121-36.

857 Davidson, Clifford. "Organic Unity and Shakespearian Tragedy." JAAC, 30 (Winter, 1971), 171-76.

858 Davies, David. Coleridge's Marginalia in Mather's Magnalia. HLQ, 2 (January, 1939), 233-40.

Records "anti-Puritan and anti-Mather Notes by Coleridge in the Huntington Library Copy.

859 Davis, Bartram R. "The Coleridge Canon." TLS, (September 10, 1938), 584.

860 Davis, H. Francis. "Was Newman a Disciple of Coleridge?" DuR, 217 (1945), 165-73.

861   Davis, Kay. "Unpublished Coleridge Marginalia in a Volume of
John Donne's Poetry." N&Q, 10 (May, 1963), 187-89.

862   Day, Robert A. "The Rebirth of Leggatt." L&P, 13 (Summer,
1963), 74-80.

863   Deen, Leonard W. "Coleridge and the Radicalism of Religious
Dissent." JEGP, 61 (July, 1962), 496-510.

864   _____. "Coleridge and the Sources of Pantisocracy:
Godwin, the Bible, and Hartley." BUSE, 5 (Winter, 1961), 232-45.

865   Degroot, H. B. "The Ouroboras and the Romantic Poets: A
Renaissance Emblem in Blake, Coleridge, and Shelley." ES, 50
(December, 1969), 553-74.

      Includes eight plates.

866   DeLaura, David J. "Coleridge, Hamlet, and Arnold's Empedocles."
PLL, 8 (Fall,1972), 17-25.

867   Dendurent, H. O. "The Coleridge Collection in Victoria
University Library, Toronto." WC, 5 (Autumn,1974), 225-86.

868   Deneau, Daniel P. "Coleridge's Limbo: A 'Riddling Tale'?"
WC, 3 (Spring,1972), 97-105.

869   Dennis, Carl. "Emerson's Poetry of Mind and Nature." ESQ,
58, 1st. Q (1970), 139-53.

870   De Selincourt, Ernest. "Lewti." TLS (December 20, 1941), 643.

871   Deutsch, Babette. "Coleridge on Himself." Poetry, 102
(May, 1963), 128-30.

872   _____. "Intimate Glimpses of the Myriad Minded." Poetry,
91 (March, 1958), 385-89.

873   Dewey, John. "James Marsh and American Philosophy." JHI,
2 (April, 1941), 131-50.

874   Dickson, Arthur. "Coleridge's Ode on the Departing Year, 149-
161." EXPL, 9 (November, 1950), Item 15.

875   Dickstein, Morris. "Coleridge, Wordsworth, and the 'Conversation
Poems'." CentR, (Fall,1972), 367-83.

876   Dilworth, E. N. "Fielding and Coleridge: Poetic Faith." N&Q,
5 (January, 1958), 35-37.

      Reexamination of parallel noted by Nettie S. Tillett, SP,
      43 (1946), 675-81. Argues that "Fielding wishes to satisfy
      a taste for what is reasonable--Coleridge," a desire to
      dream.

877   Dipasquale, Pasquale, Jr. "Coleridge's Framework of Objectivity
and Eliot's Objective Correlative." JAAC, 26 (Summer, 1968),
489-500.

878   Donoghue, Denis. "The Purer Eye." Art I, 15 (June 6, 1971),
22-24, 69.

879   Dorenkamp, Angela G. "Hope at Highgate: The Late Poetry of
S. T. Coleridge." Barat R, 6 (Spring-Summer, 1971), 59-67.

880   Doughty, Oswald. "Coleridge and a Poet's Poet: William Lisle
Bowles." EM, 14 (1963), 95-114.

881   _____. "Coleridge and The Gothic Novel, or Tales of Terror."
EM, 23 (1972), 125-48.

882   _____. "Coleridge as Statesman." EM, 20 (1969), 241-55.

883   Dove, John Roland and Gamble, Peter. "'Our Darker Purpose'-
The Division Scene in Lear." NM, 70 (1969) 306-18.

884   Dudley, O. H. T. "Pure Serene." TLS (September 23, 1944),
463.

885   Duff, Gerald. "William Cobbett and the Prose of Revelation."
TSLL, 11 (Winter, 1970), 1349-65.

886   Duffy, Edward. "The Cunning Spontaneities of Romanticism."
WC, 3 (Autumn, 1972), 232-40.

887   Duffy, John T. "From Hanover to Burlington: James Marsh's
Search for Unity." VH, 38 (Winter, 1970), 27-48.

      The first American edition of Coleridge.

888   _____. "Problems in Publishing Coleridge: James Marsh's
First American Edition of Aids to Reflection." NEQ, 43 (June,
1970), 193-208.

889   _____. "Transcendental Letters from George Ripley to
James Marsh." ESQ, 50, 1st Q (1968), 20-4.   Supp.

890   Dumbleton, William A. "Coleridge and Gerald Manley Hopkins."
ARIEL, 3 (April, 1972), 17-31.

891   Duncan-Jones, E. E. "Mrs. Gould and Fairy Blackstick."
N&Q, 14 (July, 1967), 245.

892   Dunlap, Rhodes. "Verses by Coleridge." PQ, 42 (April,
1963), 282-84.

893   Dunn, John J. "Coleridge's Debt to Macpherson's Ossian."
SSL, 7 (July-October, 1969), 76-89.

      Coleridge incorporated Ossianic imagery into his early poetry,
      and... continued to do so in passages of his greatest work.

894   Edelstein, J. M. "America's First Native Botantists."
QJCA, 15 (1958), 51-59.

895   Ehrenpreis, Irvin. "Southey to Coleridge, 1799." N&Q,
195 (March 18, 1950), 124-26.

      Prints a letter dated 15 December from the original in the
      Bodleian Library.

896   Ehrstine, John W. "The Drama and Romantic Theory: The Cloudy
Symbols of High Romance." RS, 34 (June, 1966), 85-106.

897   Eiseley, Loren. "Darwin, Coleridge, and the Theory of
Unconscious Creation." LC, 31 (Winter, 1965), 7-22.

898   _____. "Darwin, Coleridge, and the Theory of Unconscious
Creation." DAEDALUS, 94 (Summer, 1965), 588-602.

899   Elliott, John S., Jr. "History Play as Drama." RORD,
11 (1968), 21-28.

900   Elmen, Paul. "Editorial Revisions of Coleridge's Marginalia."
MLN, 67 (January, 1952), 32-37.

      Suggests various considerations which induced Henry Nelson
      Coleridge to amend or expunge passages.

901   _____. "The Fame of Jeremy Taylor." ATR (October, 1962),
389-403.

902   Emerson, Donald. "Henry James on the Role of the Imagination
in Criticism." WASAL, 51 (1962), 287-94.

903   Emery, Clark. "Remorse: Coleridge's Venture in Tragedy."
CARRELL, 5 (December, 1964), 5-11.

904   Emmett, Dorothy. "Coleridge on the Growth of the Mind."
Vol. 34 BJRL 34 (March, 1952), 276-95.

905   Endicott, N. J. "Sir Thomas Browne's Letter to a Friend."
UTQ, 36 (October, 1966), 68-86.

906   England, Martha Winburn. "Garrick and Stratford, Part II."
BNYPL, 66 (March, 1962), 178-204.

907   Epstein, Arthur D. "Coleridgean Reconciliation in Euripide's
Bacchae." CentR, 15 (Spring, 1971), 162-73.

908   Erdman, David V. "The Case for Internal Evidence (6):
The Signature of Style." BNYPL, 63 (February, 1959), 88-109.

       As evidenced by Coleridge.

909   _____. "Coleridge as Nehemiah Higginbottom." MLN,
73 (December, 1958), 569-80.

910   _____. "Coleridge in Lilliput: The Quality of Parliamentary
Reporting in 1800." SM, 27 (March, 1960), 33-62.

911   _____. "Coleridge and the 'Review Business': An Account
of His Adventures with The Edinburgh, The Quarterly, and Maga."
WC, 6 (Winter 1975), 3-50.

912   _____. "Coleridge in All His 'Own Ebullient' Unreservedness."
SR, 65 (1957), 166-70.

913   _____. "Coleridge on Coleridge: The Context (and Text) of
His Review of Mr. Coleridge's Second Lay Sermon." SIR, 1 (Autumn
1961), 47-64.

914   _____. "Coleridge on George Washington: Newly Discovered
Essays of 1800." BNYPL, 61 (February, 1957), 81-97.

       (Also, in Evidence for Authorship, ed. by David V. Erdman
       and Ephim G. Vogel. New York: Cornell University Press,
       1966, 321-37.)

915   _____. "Coleridge, Wordsworth and the Wedgwood Fund,
Part I, Tom Wedgwood's 'Master Stroke'." BNYPL, 60 (September,
1956), 425-43; Part II, 487-507.

916   _____. "A Glass Bee-Hive Before You." SR, 68 (1960),
331-35.

917   _____. "Immoral Acts of a Library Cormorant: The Extent
of Coleridge's Contributions to the Critical Review." Part I.
BNYPL, 63 (September, 1959), 433-54. Part II, (October, 1959),
515-530; Part III, (November, 1959), 575-87.

918   _____. "Intricacy with Unity: Colerige's Notebooks
Edited." SR, 66 (1958), 685-88.

919   _____. "Lost Poem Found: The Cooperative Pursuit and
Recapture of an Escaped Coleridge 'Sonnet' of 72 Lines." BNYPL,
65 (April, 1961), 249-68.

       The "Snow Drop" poem.

920   _____. "Newspaper Sonnets Put to the Concordance Test:
Can They Be Attributed to Coleridge?" BNYPL, 62 (January, 1958),
46-49,

921 _____. "Reliques of the Contemporaries of William Upcott, 'Emperor of Autographs'." BNYPL, 64 (November, 1960), 581-87.

    William Blake issue.

922 _____. "Unrecorded Coleridge Variants." SB, 11 (1958), 143-62.

923 _____, Werkmeister, Lucyle, and Woof, R. S. "Unrecorded Coleridge Variants: Additions and Corrections." SB, 14 (1961), 236-45.

    This list of variants supplements the original one in SB, 11 (1958), 143-62, and sets forth 26 new items.

924 _____ and Zall, Paul M. "Coleridge and Jeffrey in Controversy." SIR, 14 (Winter, 1975), 75-83.

925 Evans, B. Ifor. "Coleridge on Slang." TLS (May 29, 1937), 412.

926 _____. "Coleridge's Copy of Fears in Solitude." TLS (April 18, 1935), 255.

927 Everett, Edwin M. "Lord Byron's Lakist Interlude." SP, 55 (January, 1958), 62-75.

928 Ewen, Frederic. "Coleridge and Wordsworth." SS, 23 (Fall, 1959), 368-74.

929 Fairbanks, A. Harris. "Coleridge's Opinion of France: An Ode." RES, 26 (1975), 181-82.

930 _____. "Dear Native Brook'! Coleridge, Bowles, and Thomas Warton, the Younger." WC, 6 (Autumn, 1975), 313-15.

931 Fairchild, Hoxie N. "Hartley, Pistorius, and Coleridge." PMLA, 62 (December, 1947), 1010-21.

    On the relation of the Religious Musings to Hartley's religious ideas and the annotations of H. A. Pistorius, the German translator of Hartley.

932 "Feeling Mind." TLS (July 1, 1960), 417.

933 Fenner, Theodore L. "The Traveler Reports on Coleridge's 1811 Lectures." N&Q, 21 (September, 1974), 330-31.

934 Ferry, David. "Patterns of Consciousness in Coleridge." MR, 11 (Autumn, 1970), 837-40.

935 Finch, Jeremiah S. "Charles Lamb's Copy of The History of Philip De Commines with Autograph Notes by Lamb and Coleridge." PULC, 9 (November, 1947), 30-37.

936   Finch, John A.   "The Ruined Cottage Restored: Three Stages of Composition, 1795-1798." JEGP, 66 (April, 1967), 179-99.

937   Fisch, M. H.   "The Coleridges, Dr. Prati, and Vico." MP, 41 (November, 1943), 111-22.

    On Coleridge's interest in and debt to Giambattista Vico, with whose writings he became acquainted through Prati.

938   Fiske, Roger.   "The Macbeth Music." ML, 45 (April, 1964), 114-25.

939   Fleissner, R. F.   "A Comment and Correspondence on Robert Frost." L Crit, 10 (Summer, 1973), 67-72.

940   _____.   "'Pot Luck': Drugs and Romanticism." EAOB, 2 (1970), 9-11.

941   Foakes, R. A.   "Repairing The Damaged Archangel." EIC, 24 (October, 1974), 423-27.

942   _____.   "The Text of Coleridge's 1811-12 Shakespeare Lectures." ShS, 23 (1970), 101-11.

943   Fogle, Ephim G.   "Salmons in Both or Some Caveats for Canonical Scholars." BNYPL, 63 (May, 1959), 223-36; (June, 1959), 292-308.

944   Fogle, Richard H.   "Coleridge, Hilda, and The Marble Faun." ESQ, 19 (1973), 105-11.

945   _____.   "Coleridge in the Dock." VQR, 48 (Summer 1972), 477-80.

946   _____.   "Coleridge on Dramatic Illusions." TDR, 4 (May, 1960), 33-44.

947   _____.   "Coleridge's Conversation Poems." TSE, 5 (1955), 103-10.

948   _____.   "Coleridge's Critical Principles." TSE, 6 (1956), 57-69.

949   _____.   "Hawthorne and Coleridge on Credibility." CRIT, 13 (Summer, 1971), 234-41.

950   _____.   "Hawthorne's Pictorial Unity." ESQ, 55 (2nd Q) (1969), 71-76.

951   _____.   "Johnson and Coleridge on Milton." BuR, 14 (March, 1966), 26-32.

952   _____.   "Nathaniel Hawthorne and the Great English Romantic Poets." KSJ, 22 (1973), 219-35.

953 _____. "Romanticism Revisited." SR, 82 (April-June, 1974), 383-92.

954 Ford, George H. "Shelley or Schiller? A Note on D. H. Lawrence at Work." TSLL, 4 (Summer, 1962), 154-56.

955 Forstman, H. Jackson. "Samuel Taylor Coleridge's Notes Toward the Understanding of Doctrine." JR, 44 (October, 1964), 310-27.

956 Fox, Arnold B. "Political and Biographical Background of Coleridge's Osario." JEGP, 61 (April, 1962), 258-67.

957 French, Richard. "Sir Walter Scott and His Literary Contemporaries." CLAJ, 11 (March, 1968), 248-54.

958 Fricke, Douglas C. "Ride on a Time Machine: A Study of the Romantic Imagination in To the Cuckoo and Frost at Midnight." NASSAU REVIEW, 2 (1971), 18-25.

959 Fricker, Robert. "Shakespeare und das Englische Romantische Drama." Shakespeare Jahrbuch, 95 (1959), 63-81.

960 Fruman, Norman. "Coleridge and the Opium Mystique." QQ, 82 (August, 1975), 440-44.

961 Fynmore, A. H. W. "Coleridge MSS." N&Q, 3 (March, 1956), 134.

962 Garber, Frederick. "The Hedging Consciousness in Coleridge's Conversation Poems." WC, 4 (Spring,1973), 124-38.

963 Gardner, Joseph H. "The 'Realist' as Dickensian." MFS, 16 (Autumn,1970), 323-44.

964 Garrett, Clard. "Coleridge's Utopia Revisited." Soundings, 55 (Spring,1972), 121-37.

965 Gaskins, Avery F. "Coleridge: Nature, the Conversation Poems, and the Structure of Meditation." NEOPHIL, 59 (1975), 629-35.

966 Gatta, John, Jr. "Coleridge and Allegory." MLQ, 31 (1977), 62-77.

967 Gaull, Marilyn. "On The Notebooks of Samuel Taylor Coleridge, III, ed. Kathleen Coburn." WC, 7 (Winter, 1976), 63-64.

    Concerning Norman Fruman's review in WC, 6 (1975), 165-71.

968 Geckle, George L. "Poetic Justice and Measure for Measure." Costerus 1 N.S. (1974), 95-111.

969 Gegenheimer, Albert F. "They Might Have Been Americans." SAQ, 46 (October, 1947), 520-23.

970   Gerard, Albert. "Clevedon Revisited: Further Reflections on
Coleridge's Reflections on Having Left a Place of Retirement. N&Q,
7 (March, 1960), 101-02.

971   _____. "Coleridge, Keats. and the Modern Mind." EIC,
1 (July, 1951), 249-61.

972   _____. "Le Romantisme Anglais." RLV, 25 (1959), 192-202.

973   _____. "Le Romantisme Anglais: Orientations Recentes de
L' Historie it de la Critique II." RLV, 25 (1959), 397-401.

974   _____. "The Systolic Rhythm: The Structure of Coleridge's
Conversation Poems." EIC, 10 (July, 1960), 307-19.

975   Gerber, Gerald E. "The Coleridgean Context of Poe's Blackwood
Satires." ESQ, 60 (Fall, 1970), 87-91.

976   Gerus, Tarnawecky, Iraida. "Literary Onomastics." Names,
16 (December, 1968), 312-24.

977   Gierasch, Walter. "Coleridge's Ode on the Departing Year,
141-161." EXPL, 8 (March, 1950), Item 34.

978   Gilpin, George H. "Coleridge and the Spirit of Poetic Thought."
SEL, 12 (Autumn, 1972), 639-52.

979   _____. "Coleridge: The Pleasure of Truth." SCB, 30
(Winter, 1970), 191-94.

980   Glickfield, Charlotte W. "Coleridge's Prose Contributions
to the Morning Post." PMLA, 69 (June, 1954), 681-85.

981   Godfrey, D. R. "Imagination and Truth -- Some Romantic
Contradictions." ES, 44 (August, 1963), 254-67.

982   Gold, V. F. R. S. "Samuel Taylor Coleridge and the Appointment
of J. F. Daniell, F. R. S. as Professor of Chemistry at King's
College, London." NRRSL, 28 (1973), 25-9.

983   Golden, Morris. "The Time of Writing of the Vicar of
Wakefield." BNYPL, 65 (September, 1961), 442-50.

984   Goodwin, George. "The Comic as a Critique of Reason:
Tristram Shandy." CE, 29 (December, 1967), 206-23.

985   Gordon, I. A. "The Case-History of Coleridge's Monody
on the Death of Chatterton." RES, 18 (January, 1942), 49-71.

986   Greiner, Walter. "Deutsche Einflusse aüf die Dichtungs
Theorie von Samuel Taylor Coleridge." NS, 9 (February, 1960),
57-65. (In German)

987   Griffin, Robert J. "'These Contraries Such Unity Do Hold':
Patterned Imagery in Shakespeare's Narrative Poems." SEL, 4
(Winter, 1964), 43-55.

988   Griggs, Earl Leslie. "Coleridge and His Friends." ChLB,
132 (September, 1956), 119-21.

       Coleridge's friendships with Southey, Poole, Wordsworth, and
       Lamb.

989   _____. "Coleridge's Letters." TLS (July 19, 1947), 369.

990   _____. "Diadeste, a Fragment of an Unpublished Play by
Samuel Taylor Coleridge." MP, 34 (May, 1937), 377-85.

991   _____. "Ludwig Tieck and Samuel Taylor Coleridge." JEGP,
54 (April, 1955), 262-68.

       Prints a previously unpublished letter from Tieck to Coleridge.

992   _____. "A Note on Wordsworth's A Character." RES, 4
(January, 1953), 57-63.

993   _____. "Notes Concerning Certain Poems by Samuel Taylor
Coleridge." MLN, 69 (January, 1954), 27-31.

994   _____. "Robert Southey's Estimate of Samuel Taylor
Coleridge: A study in Human Relations." HLQ, 9 (November, 1945),
61-94.

       A Study of Southey's letters reflects his changing attitudes
       toward Coleridge.

995   _____. "Samuel Taylor Coleridge and Opium." HLQ, 17
(August, 1954), 357-78.

       Traces the record of Coleridge's addiction and prints the
       text of "Notes Respecting the Late S. T. Coleridge" by S. T.
       Porter, who was an apprentice to a Highgate chemist.

996   _____. "Unflattering Imitation." SR, 49 (April-June,
1941), 285-88.

997   _____. "Wordsworth Through Coleridge's Eyes." WCS (1951),
45-90.

998   Grigson, Geoffrey. "A Bottle of Brandy in Spitzbergen."
NSta, (March 17, 1972), 359-60.

999   _____. "Coleridge in Extenso." NSta, (September 26, 1969),
418-20.

1000   Grindea, Moron. "Coleridge and Rimbaud." Adam, (1972), 52-54.

1001 Grubb, Gerald C. "Coleridge the Metaphysician." R&E, 42 (1945), 3-23.

1002 Gutteridge, J. D. "Coleridge and Descarte's Meditations." N&Q, 20 (February, 1973), 45-46.

1003 Haeger, Jack H. "Coleridge's Speculations on Race." SIR, 13 (1974), 333-57.

1004 Hale, J. R. "Samuel Rogers, the Perfectionist." HLQ, 25 (November, 1961), 61-67.

1005 Hall, P. E. "A Latin Translation of In Memoriam." BC, 17 (Spring, 1968), 78.

1006 Hall, Thomas. "A Check List of Coleridge Criticism." BB, 25 (January-April, 1968), 124-31.

This is an alphabetical list of secondary material ranging from 1790-1965.

1007 _____. "Coleridge Criticism, Part 2." BB, 25 (May-August, 1968), 153-56.

This covers letters G-M of the alphabetical listing begun in January-April, 1968.

1008 _____. "Coleridge Criticism, Part 3." BB, 24 (September-August, 1968), 175-82.

This covers letters M-Z of the alphabetical listing begun in January-April, 1968.

1009 Hamilton, Richard. "Derwent Coleridge." TLS (September 13, 1947), 465.

1010 Hardy, Barbara. "Coleridge's Marginalia in Fuller's Pisgah-Sight of Palestine." MLR, 47 (April, 1952), 203-08.

1011 _____. "Distinction Without Difference: Coleridge's Fancy and Imagination." EIC, 1 (October, 1951), 336-44.

1012 _____. "'I Have a Smack of Hamlet': Coleridge and Shakespeare's Characters." EIC, 8 (July, 1958), 238-55.

1013 _____. "Imagination and Fancy." EIC, 2 (July, 1952), 347-49.

1014 _____. "Keats, Coleridge and Negative Capability." N&Q, 197 (July 5, 1952), 299-300.

1015 _____. "The Natural Man." EIC, 9 (July, 1959), 309-15.

1016 Harper, George McLean. "A Factual Account of Coleridge's Life." SRL, 19 (March 11, 1939), 11.

1017 _____. "Poor Coleridge." SRL, 18 (October 1, 1938), 10.

1018 Harris, John. "Coleridge's Reading in Medicine." WC, 3 (Spring, 1972), 85-95.

1019 Harris, Wendell, V. "The Shape of Coleridge's 'Public' System." MP, 68 (August, 1970), 46-61.

1020 Harrison, Thomas P. "Bird of Paradise: Phoenix Redivisou." ISIS, 51 (1960), 173-80.

   History of the Phoenix with reference to Du Bartas, Coleridge, and Wordsworth.

1021 Hart, Alfred. "A Criticism by Coleridge." TLS (May 9, 1935), 301.

1022 Hartley, A. J. "Frederick Denison Maurice, Disciple and Interpreter of Coleridge: 'Constancy to an Ideal Object'." ARIEL, 3 (April, 1972), 5-16.

1023 Hartman, Herbert. "A Letter of Hartley Coleridge." Colophon, 3 (1938), 113-19.

1024 _____. "The Mad Monk." TLS (November 2, 1940), 555.

1025 Hassan, M. A. "Coleridge's Letter to Peter Morris, M. D." N&Q, 19 (August, 1972), 286-87.

1026 Haven, Richard. "Coleridge and the Greek Mysteries." MLN, 70 (June, 1955), 405-07.

   Coleridge's use of Schelling seems to obscure rather than illuminate Coleridge's argument.

1027 _____. "Coleridge and Jacob Boehme: A Further Comment." N&Q, 13 (May, 1966), 176-78.

1028 _____. "Coleridge, Hartley, and the Mystics." JHI, 29 (October-December, 1959), 477-94.

1029 _____. "Coleridge on Milton: A Lost Lecture." WC, 3 (Winter, 1972), 21-22.

1030 _____. "Dr. De' Prati: A Note and A Query." VPN, 16 (June, 1972), 47-50.

1031 _____. "The Romantic Art of Charles Lamb." ELH, 30 (June, 1963), 137-46.

1032 Hayden, John O. "Coleridge, the Reviewers, and Wordsworth." SP, 68 (January, 1971), 105-19.

1033 Heath, William. "Review: <u>A Voyage in Vain: Coleridge's</u>
<u>Journey to Malta in 1804</u> by Alethea Hayter." WC, 5 (Summer,
1974), 161-64.

1034 Heidbrink, F. H. "Coleridge's Ode to The Departing Year'."
EXPL, 2 (December, 1943), Item 21.

1035 _____. "Coleridge's <u>Time, Real and Imaginary</u>." EXPL,
3 (October, 1944), Item 4.

1036 Heilman, Robert B. "Bardolatry." YR, 50 (December, 1960),
257-70.

1037 Heller, Erich. "The Artist's Journey into the Interior:
From Hegel to Hamlet." TRI-Q, (Winter, 1965), 37-49.

1038 Hellman, George S. "Coleridge on Trial Marriages." SRL,
25 (August 29, 1942), 17-18.

1039 Henderson, Arnold. "Some Constants of Charles Lamb's
Criticism." SIR, 7 (Winter, 1968), 104-16.

1040 Henkle, Roger B. "Pynchon's Tapestries on the Western
Wall." MFS, 17 (Summer, 1971), 207-20.

1041 Hewlett, Dorothy. "On the Romantic Movement in English
Poetry." AP, 35 (November, 1964), 498-501.

1042 _____. "Pure Serene." TLS, (September 30, 1944), 475.

      "Highgate Grove." TLS (May 1, 1953), 285.

1043 Hill, John S. "Eugene Gant and the Ghost of Ben." MFS,
11 (Autumn, 1965), 245-49.

1044 Hobsbaum, Philip. "Coleridge, the Ice Skater." <u>Listen</u>,
87 (March 30, 1972), 417-19.

1045 Hocks, Richard A. "Thoreau, Coleridge, and Barfield:
Reflectionson the Imagination and the Law of Polarity." Cent R,
17 (Spring, 1973), 175-98.

1046 Hoggart, Richard. "Imagination and Society." NSN, 59
(January 2, 1960), 16-17.

1047 Hoheisel, Peter. "Coleridge on Shakespeare: Method Amid
the Rhetoric." SIR, 13 (Winter, 1974), 15-23.

1048 Honig, Edwin. "In Defense of Allegory." KR, 20 (Winter,
1958), 1-19.

1049 Hopkins, R. H. "Coleridge's Parody of Melancholy Poetry
in The Nightingale: A Conversation Poem." ES, 49 (October,
1968), 436–41.

1050 Hough, Graham. "The Occasional Philosopher." TLS (July 11,
1975), 756.

1051 _____. "Some Coleridge Marginalia." MLN, 66 (June,
1951), 361–65.

       In a copy of William Hone's Apocryphal New Testament.

1052 Houston, Robert W. "Coleridge's Psychometaphysics." THOTH,
9 (Winter, 1968), 14–24.

1053 Howard, Ben. "Fancy, Imagination, and Northrop Frye."
THOTH, 9 (Winter 1968), 25–36.

1054 Howarth, R. G. "Coleridge: A Misattribution." N&Q, 186
(June 17, 1944), 290–91.

1055 Hughes, Daniel J. "Helping People Live Their Lives."
VOICES, 174 (January–April, 1961), 54–55.

1056 Hughes, Peter. "Language, History and Vision: An Approach
to 18th Century Literature." Mon/PMUA, 1 (1971), 77–96.

1057 Hume, Robert D. "Coleridge's Retention of Primary Imagination."
N&Q, 16 (February, 1969), 55–56.

1058 _____. "Gothic Versus Romantic: A Revaluation of the
Gothic Novel." PMLA, 84 (March, 1969), 282–90.

1059 _____. "Kant and Coleridge on Imagination." JAAC, 28
(Summer, 1970), 485–96.

1060 Hunt, Bishop C., Jr. "Coleridge and the Endeavor of Philosophy."
PMLA, 91 (October, 1976), 829–39.

1061 Hunt, Everett E. "Two Cambridge Critics." SR, 44 (January–
March, 1936), 103–07.

1062 Hunter, Doreen. "America's First Romantics: Richard Henry
Dana, Sr., and Washington Allston." N&Q, 45 (March, 1972), 3–30.

       Coleridge's psychological explorations were a major influence
       on Dana's and Allston's early works.

1063 Hussain, Imdad. "Orientalism and Coleridge." Ven, 1
(December, 1960), 336–46.

1064 _____. "Orientalism and Coleridge." Ven, 2 (March, 1961),
44–55.

1065 Hutchinson, Percy. "Coleridge and the Wordsworths." NYTBR
(September 25, 1938), 5, 18.

1066 _____. "A Poet in Boyhood and Youth." NYTBR (June 25,
1939), 2, 16.

1067 Inglis-Jones, Elisabeth. "A Pembrokeshire County Family in
the Eighteenth Century." NLWJ, 17 (Winter, 1971), 136-60.

1068 Isaacs, J. "Coleridge's Critical Terminology." E & S
21 (1935), 86-104.

1069 Isoda, Koichi. "The Preface to Lyrical Ballads." SEL-Japan,
(1962).

1070 Jackson, Jr. R. De J. "Coleridge on Dramatic Illusions and
Spectacle in the Performance of Shakespeare's Plays." MP, 62
(August, 1964), 13-21.

1071 _____. "Coleridge on Shakespeare's Preparation." REL,
7 (January, 1966), 53-62.

1072 _____. "Free Will in Coleridge's Shakespeare." UTQ,
38 (October, 1968), 34-50.

1073 Jacobus, Mary. "Southey's Debt to Lyrical Ballads, 1798."
RES, 22 (February, 1971), 20-36.

1074 James, D. J. "Kant's Influence on Wordsworth and Coleridge."
Listen, 44 (August 31, 1950), 311-12.

1075 Jenkins, Harold. "Hamlet Then Till Now." ShS, 18 (1965),
34-45.

1076 Jofen, Jean. "Polonius the Fishmonger." N&Q, 19 (April,
1972), 126-27.

1077 Johnson, Edith C. "Lamb and Coleridge." ASch, 6 (Spring
1937), 153-69.

     An account of their friendship.

1078 Johnson, S. F. "Reflections on the Consistency of Coleridge's
Political Views." HLB, 3 (Winter 1949), 131-39.

     Examines the development and alterations in the text of the
     "Introductory Address" in Conciones Ad Populum.

1079 _____. "An Uncollected Early Poem by Coleridge." BNYPL,
61 (October, 1957), 505-07.

     The poem is "Lines on the Portrait of a Lady."

1080 Jones, Alun R. "The Compassionate World: Some Observations
on Wordsworth's Lyrical Ballads of 1798." English, 19 (1970), 7-12.

1081 Jones, John. "The Middle Years." NSN, 58 (October 24, 1959),
552.

1082 _____. "A New Delve at Coleridge." NSN, 58 (July 11,
1959), 56.

1083 Joost, Nicholas. "A View of Coleridge: The Sensibility and
the Art in His Early Notebooks (1794-1804)." DESB, 5 (1960), 53-64.

1084 "Joseph Henry Green: Eminent Surgeon and Literary Executor
of Samuel Taylor Coleridge." Annals of Medical History, MS,
9 (1937), 91-92.

1085 Josephs, Lois. "Shakespeare and a Coleridgean Synthesis:
Cleopatra, Leontes, and Falstaff." ShQ, 18 (Winter, 1967), 17-21.

1086 Joughin, G. Louis. "Coleridge's Lewti: The Biography of a
Poem." SE (Texas), (1943), 66-93.

1087 Kahn, Sholom J. "Psychology in Coleridge's Poetry." JAAC,
9 (March, 1951), 208-26.

1088 Kaiser, Rudolf. "Ver Sonette Thomas Wharton, 'to the River
London'; W. L. Bowles, 'to the River Itchin'; S. T. Coleridge, 'to
the River Otter'; W. Wordsworth, 'to the River Duddon'." NS, 12
(June, 1963), 252-62.

1089 Kamijima, Kentichi. "The Explorers of the Inane: Part V,
Shelley." ESELL, 17 (December, 1963), 11-34.

1090 Katsurada, Rikichi. "Coleridge no Shi ni suite." EIGO S,
116 (1970), 69-70.

     On Coleridge's poetry.

1091 Kaufman, Paul. "Coleridge's Use of Cathedral Libraries."
MLN, 75 (May, 1960), 295-99.

1092 _____. "James Losh." N&Q, 7 (May, 1960), 190.

1093 _____. "New Light on Coleridge as Undergraduate." REL,
7 (January, 1966), 63-70.

     Information on Coleridge from 1791-1794 is Henry Gunning's
     Reminiscences. Another source is Robert Owen's The Life of
     Robert Owen by Himself.

1094 _____. "Reading Vogues of the Eighteenth Century."
BNYPL, 67 (December, 1963), 643-72.

1095 _____. "Wordsworth's 'Candid and Enlightened Friend'."
N&Q, 9 (November, 1962), 403-08.

1096 Kauvar, Gerald B. "Coleridge, Hawkesworth, and the Willing
Suspension of Disbelief." PLL, 5 (Winter, 1969), 91-94.

1097 Kegel, Charles H. "William Cobbett and Malthusianism."
JHI, 19 (June, 1958), 348-62.

1098 Kelly, Michael J. "Coleridge and Dram Phenomenology."
MSE, 1 (1967), 1-7.

1099 Kermode, Frank. "Coleridge Casebooks." NSN, 63 (May 25,
1962), 762.

1100 Klingender, F. D. "Coleridge on Robinson Crusoe." TLS
(February 1, 1936), 96.

1101 Knieger, Bernard. "Wordsworth and Coleridge as Playwrights."
CLAJ, 6 (September, 1962), 57-63.

1102 Kohli, Devindra. "Coleridge, Hazlitt, and Keats' Negative
Capability." LCrit, 8 (1967), 21-26.

1103 Kreutz, Christian. "Hartley Coleridge's Prometheusbild."
ANGL, 88 (1970), 197-221.

1104 Kurtz, Benjamin P. "Coleridge on Swedenborg, with Unpublished
Marginalia on the Prodromus." UCPE, 14 (1943), 199-214.

1105 LaMoine, Georges. "Thomas Chatterton Bicentenaire." Caliban,
8 (1971), 13-37.

      Includes an early version of Coleridge's Monody, first printed
      in 1794.

1106 Land, Stephen K. "Coleridge, Freud, and the Tribe of Asra."
L&P, 22 (1972), 49-50.

1107 Landon, Carol. "Wordsworth, Coleridge, and The Morning Post:
An Early Version of The Seven Sisters." RES, 11 (November, 1960),
392-402.

1108 Landow, George P. "Hartley Coleridge on the Death of His
Father: A New Letter." N&Q, 20 (August, 1973), 289.

1109 Lang, D. B. "Point Counterpoint: The Emergence of Fancy and
Imagination in Coleridge." JAAC, 16 (March, 1958), 384-97.

1110 Larsen, Joan. "S. T. Coleridge: His Theory of Knowledge."
WASAL, 48 (1959), 221-32.

1111 Lauterback, Edward S. and Crawford, Walter B. "Coleridge
in Narrative and Drama. Part II." WC, 4 (Winter, 1973), 36-40.

1112 Leavis, F. R. "Coleridge in Criticism." Scrut, 9 (June,
1940), 57-69.

1113 _____. "Dr. Richards, Bentham, and Coleridge." Scrut,
3 (1935), 382-402.

1114   Lees-Milne, James. "Coleridge's Cottage at Nether Stowey."
TLS (May 20, 1944), 250.

1115   Lefcowitz, Barbara F. "Omnipotence of Thought and the Poetic
Imagination: Blake, Coleridge, and Rilke." PsyR, 59 (1972), 417-32.

1116   Lengler, Rainer. "Thomas Wolfe and S. T. Coleridge." N&Q,
20 (September, 1973), 332-33.

1117   Lentricchia, Frank. "Coleridge and Emerson: Prophets of
Silence, Prophets of Language." JAAC, 32 (Fall, 1973), 37-46.

1118   Levich, Marvin. "Form and Content in Poetry." JP, 56
(June 18, 1959), 586-95.

1119   Lindsay, Jack. "The Sunset Ship: Keats, Coleridge and
Turner." LL, 54 (September, 1947), 199-211.

1120   Lindsay, Julian I. "Coleridge Marginalia in Jacobi's Werke."
MLN, 50 (April, 1935), 216-24.

1121   _____. "A Note on the Marginalia." HLQ, 1 (October,
1937), 95-99.

        Offers an explanation of the surprising fact that the
        Coleridge marginalia reported by Miss Shearer are in
        Wordsworth's hand, considering his well-known aversion to
        using a pen.

1122   Link, Arthur S. "Samuel Taylor Coleridge and the Economic
and Political Crisis in Great Britain, 1816-1820." JHI, 9 (June,
1948), 323-38.

        "His...was a voice crying in an age of commercialism for a
        return to idealistic, non-materialistic Christian values."

1123   Little, Geoffrey. "Hartley, Coleridge, Wordsworth, and
Oxford." N&Q, 6 (September, 1959), 324-28.

1124   _____. "James Losh." N&Q, 8 (December, 1961), 474-75.

1125   _____. "Lines Written at Shurton Bars: Coleridge's First
Conversation Poem." SoR, 2 (1966), 137-49.

1126   Logan, Sister Eugenia. "An Indebtedness of Coleridge to
Crashaw." MLN, 59 (December, 1944), 551-53.

        In the poem "Coeli Enarrant" Coleridge seems to have borrowed
        from Crashaw.

1127   Lovejoy, Arthur O. "Coleridge and Kant's Two Worlds."
ELH, 7 (December, 1940), 341-62.

1128   Lyon, Judson S. "Romantic Psychology and the Inner Senses:
Coleridge." PMLA, 81 (June, 1966), 246-60.

GENERAL CRITICISM   81

1129 McAleer, John J. "William Hazlitt-Shakespeare's 'Advocate and Herald'." ShN, 22 (February, 1972), 4.

1130 McArthur, Herbert. "Romeo's Loquacious Friend." ShQ, 11 (Winter, 1959), 35-44.

1131 McDonald, W. U., Jr. "Notes to Hazlitt's Writings Against the Phrenologists." N&Q, 7 (July, 1960), 263-64.

> Annotates five references by Coleridge to 19th Century Edinburgh phrenologists or statements by them.

1132 McElderry, B. R., Jr. "Coleridge on Blake's Songs." MLQ, 9 (September, 1948), 298-302.

> On Coleridge's 'grades' for the poem as indicated in a letter to C. A. Tulk.

1133 _____. "Walton's Lives and Gillman's Life of Coleridge." PMLA, 52 (June, 1937), 412-22.

> Accounts for the character of Gillman's Life important for its influence upon subsequent biographies of Coleridge, as due to the author's acceptance of Walton as his mode.

1134 McFarland, G. F. "The Early Literary Career of Julius Charles Hare." BJRL, 46 (September, 1963), 42-83.

> Early influential disciple of Coleridge.

1135 _____. "Julius Charles Hare: Coleridge, DeQuincey, and German Literature." BJRL, 47 (September, 1964), 165-97.

1136 McFarland, Thomas. "Coleridge and Wordsworth." YR, 59 (Spring, 1970), 439-48.

1137 _____. "Coleridge's Plagiarisms Once More: A Review Essay." YR, 63 (December, 1973), 252-86.

1138 _____. "The Symbiosis of Coleridge and Wordsworth." SIR, 11 (Fall, 1972), 263-303.

1139 MacGillivray, J. R. "A New and Early Poem by Coleridge." BNYPL, 63 (March, 1959), 153-54.

> "The Abode of Love."

1140 McKenzie, Gordon. "Organic Unity in Coleridge." Publications in English, Berkeley: University of California, 7 (1939), 1-107.

> Reviewed by A. D. Snyder in MLN, 55 (1940), 227-29.

1141 McLaughlin, Elizabeth T. "Coleridge and Milton." SP, 61 (July, 1964), 545-72.

1142 McMaster, R. D. "Dickens, Jung, and Coleridge." DR, 38
(Winter,1959), 512-16.

1143 Mabbott, Thomas O. "Coleridge MSS." N&Q, 160 (May 2, 1931),
317.

       An unpublished letter.

1144 _____. "Coleridge's Ballad of the Dark Ladie." N&Q,
150 (January 2, 1926), 8.

1145 _____. "Coleridge's Wanderings of Cain and Blake's Death
of Abel." N&Q, 181 (August 23, 1941), 111.

1146 Madden, Richard. "The Old Familiar Faces: An Essay in the
Light of Some Recently Discovered Documents of Charles Valentine
LeGrice Referring to Lamb, Coleridge, and Wordsworth." ChLB, 6
(1974), 113-21.

1147 Madeda, Masahiko. "Coleridge on Hihyo Genri." Eigo S,
118 (1972), 496-97.

1148 Maeda, Yoshihiko. "The Idea of Duration in Coleridge."
SEL-Japan, (1974), 43-61.

1149 Magnuson, Paul A. "The Dead Calm in the Conversation Poems."
WC, 3 (Spring,1972), 53-60.

1150 _____. "A New Coleridge Text." WC, 6 (Summer,1975), 172.

1151 Mahoney, John L. "Some Antiquarian and Literary Influences
of Percy's Reliques." CLAJ, 7 (March, 1964), 240-46.

       Points out influences on Wordsworth, Coleridge, and Scott.

1152 _____. "'The Reptiles Lot': Theme and Image in Coleridge's
Later Poetry." WC, 8 (Autumn,1977), 349-60.

1153 Male, Roy R., Jr. "The Background of Coleridge's Theory
of Life." SE (Texas), 33 (1954), 60-8.

1154 Maniquis, Robert M. "The Puzzling Mimosa: Sensitivity and
Plant Symbols in Romanticism." SIR, 8 (Spring,1969), 129-55.

1155 Mann, Peter. "Coleridge, Joseph Gerrald, and the Slave Trade."
WC, 8 (Winter,1977), 38-46.

1156 _____. "Two Autograph Letters of S. T. Coleridge." RES,
25 (1974), 312-17.

       One letter to Joseph Cottle and one to George Bartley.

1157 Marcucci, Silvestro. "Il 'platonisml' filosofico ed estetico
di Samuel Taylor Coleridge." Rd E, 17 (1972), 289-322.

1158 Marcus, Leah Sinanoglou. "Baughan, Wordsworth, Coleridge and the Encomium Asini." ELH, 42 (Summer, 1975), 224-41.

1159 Margoliouth, H. M. "Wordsworth and Coleridge: Dates in May and June 1798." N&Q, 198 (August, 1953), 352-54.

1160 Marks, Emerson R. "The Achive of the Master..." JAAC, 16 (1957), 103-11.

       Aesthetic values in Coleridge, new critics, and others.

1161 _____. "Means and Ends in Coleridge's Critical Method." ELH, 26 (September, 1959), 387-401.

1162 _____. "T. S. Eliot and the Ghost of S. T. C." SR, 72 (April-June, 1964), 262-80.

1163 Marcovitz, Sanford E. "Othello Unmasked: A Black Man's Conscience and a White Man's Fool." SoR, 6 (June, 1973), 108-37.

1164 Marsh, Florence G. "Coleridge: 'A Mountain-Birth'." N&Q, 2 (June, 1955), 261-62.

1165 _____. "Resolution and Independence, Stanza XVIII." MLN, 70 (November, 1955), 488-90.

1166 Marshall, William H. "A Coleridgean Borrowing from Plato." CJ, 55 (May, 1960), 371-72.

1167 _____. "The Structure of Coleridge's Reflections on Having Left a Place of Retirement." N&Q, 6 (September, 1959), 319-21.

1168 Martin, C. G. "Coleridge and William Crowe's Lewisdon Hill." MLR, 62 (July, 1967), 400-06.

1169 _____. "Coleridge, Edward Rushton, and the Cancelled Note to the Monody on the Death of Chatterton." RES, 17 (November, 1966), 391-402.

1170 _____. "Coleridge Reminiscence in Yeats' A Prayer For My Daughter." N&Q, 12 (July, 1965), 258-60.

1171 _____. "Coleridge's Lines to Thelwall: A Corrected Text and a First Version." SB, 20 (1967), 254-57.

1172 _____. "The Dating of S. T. Coleridge's Fire, Famine, and Slaughter." N&Q, 19 (August, 1972), 289-90.

1173 _____. "Sara Coleridge: An Unpublished Letter." N&Q, 14 (February, 1967), 51-52.

1174 _____. "An Unpublished Coleridge Letter." N&Q, 14
(January, 1967), 18-19.

1175 Martin, John S. "Peter Bayley and the Lyrical Ballads."
ES, 48 (December, 1967), 533-37.

1176 Martin, Richard T. "Coleridge's Use of sermoni propriora."
WC, 3 (Spring, 1972), 71-75.

1177 Matsinger, Jane. "Coleridge Scholarship: An Annual Register."
WC, 5 (Summer, 1974), 165-68; WC, 6 (Summer, 1975), 162-64; WC, 7
(Summer, 1976), 244-46.

1178 Maxwell, J. C. "Coleridge: A False Attribution." N&Q,
10 (May, 1963), 182.

1179 _____. "Coleridge Queries." N&Q, 199 (November, 1954), 501.

1180 _____. "Goodyness." N&Q, 8 (June, 1961), 222.

1181 _____. S. T. C. and Priestley," TLS (January 5, 1946), 7.

1182 Mayo, Robert. "The Contemporaneity of the Lyrical Ballads."
PMLA, 69 (June, 1954), 486-522.

1183 _____. "Two Early Coleridge Poems." BLR, 5 (October, 1956),
311-18.

     Absence, An Ode and Absence, A Poem.

1184 Mayoux, Jean Jacques. "At the Sources of Symbolism." CRIT,
1 (Fall, 1959), 279-97.

1185 Mehrotra, R. R. "Coleridge's Hobby-Horse: Psychology."
IJES, 12 (December, 1971), 22-32.

1186 Metzger, Lore. "Coleridge: The Legacy of an Adventurous
Conservative." MLQ, 30 (March, 1969), 121-31.

1187 _____. "Coleridge's Vindication of Spinoza: An Unpublished
Note." JHI, 21 (April-June, 1960), 279-93.

     Coleridge's text edited with introduction.

1188 _____. "The Workshop of Productive Eclecticism." JHI,
24 (January-March, 1963), 143-49.

1189 Meyer, George W. "Wordsworth: An Appreciation." TSE, 3
(1952), 5-31.

1190 _____. "A Note of the Sources and Symbolism of the
Intimations Ode." TSE, 3 (1952), 33-45.

1191 Meyerstein, E. H. W. "Chatterton, Coleridge, and Bristol:
'The Sacred River'." TLS (August 21, 1937), 606.

1192 _____. "Coleridge and 'Sir Eglamour'." TLS (April 6, 1933), 248.

1193 _____. "Lewti." TLS (December 6, 1941), 611.

1194 _____. "The Mad Monk." TLS (November 9, 1940), 567.

1195 _____. "Wordsworth and Coleridge." TLS (November 29, 1941), 596.

   Coleridge's Lewti or the Circassian's Love Chant.

1196 Miller, Craig W. "Coleridge's Concept of Nature." JHI, 25 (January-March, 1964), 77-96.

1197 Miller, Joyce. "Volpone: A Study of Dramatic Ambiguity." SH, 17 (1966), 35-95.

1198 Milne, Fred. "Pantisocracy: A Reflection of Coleridge's Opium Use?" ELN, 9 (March, 1972), 177-82.

1199 Milner, R. H. "Coleridge's Sacred River." TLS (May 18, 1951), 309.

1200 Milton, John R. "The Literary Challenge of the West." WAL, 1 (Winter, 1967), 267-84.

1201 Minton, Arthur. "Other Words and Usages: The Protean Basson." AS, 33 (May, 1958), 100-03.

1202 Monteiro, George. "Edgar Poe and the New Knowledge." SLJ, 4 (Spring, 1972), 34-40.

1203 Moore, Nancy. "Deism and Samuel Taylor Coleridge." Person, 21 (Spring, 1940), 147-58.

1204 Moorman, Mary. "Wordsworth and Coleridge." TLS (April 30, 1971), 504.

   Relationship between Dorothy and William Wordsworth.

1205 _____. "Wordsworth's Commonplace Book." N&Q, 4 (September, 1957), 400-05.

1206 Morgan, Bayard Q. "What Happened to Coleridge's Wallenstein?" MLJ, 43 (April, 1959), 195-201.

1207 Morgan, Roberta. "The Philosophic Basis of Coleridge's Hamlet Criticism." ELH, 6 (December, 1939), 256-70.

1208 Mossner, Ernest C. "Coleridge and Bishop Butler." PhR, 45 (March, 1936), 206-08.

1209 Mother Mary Eleanor. "Strange Voyages: Coleridge and Rimbaud." Ren, 8 (Winter, 1955), 64-70, 87.

1210   Mounts, Charles E. "Coleridge's Self-Identification with Spenserian Characters." SP, 47 (June, 1950), 522-33.

1211   Muir, Kenneth. "The Mad Monk." TLS, (October 12, 1940), 522.

1212   Munday, Michael. "John Wilson and the Distinction Between Fancy and Imagination." SIR, 13 (Fall, 1974), 313-22.

1213   Munro, H. "Coleridge and Shelley." KSMB, 21 (1970), 35-38.

1214   Nelson, Carl. "The Ironic Allusive Texture of Lord Jim: Coleridge, Crane, Milton, and Melville." Conrad, 4 (1972), 47-59.

1215   Nelson, William. "A Coleridge 'Borrowing'." TLS, (June 11, 1954), 377.

1216   Nemerov, Howard. "An Essay: The Difficulty of Difficult Poetry." CM, 5 (Spring, 1964), 35-51.

1217   Nethercot, Arthur H. "Coleridge's Ode on the Departing Year." EXPL, 1 (June, 1943), 64.

1218   Nethery, Wallace. "Coleridge's Use of Judgment in Shakespearean Criticism." Person, 33 (October, 1952), 411-15.

1219   Neumann, Joshua H. "Coleridge on the English Language." PMLA, 63 (June, 1948), 642-61.

1220   Newell, I. "Coleridge and J. G. E. Maass." N&Q, 8 (June, 1961), 218-19.

1221   Norman, Sylva. "The Two Selves of Coleridge." TQ, 7 (Winter, 1964), 145-55.

1222   Norwood, W. D. "Tolkien's Intention in the Lord of the Rings." MSCS, 2 (February, 1967), 18-24.

1223   Nosworthy, J. M. "Coleridge on a Distant Prospect of Faust." E&S, 10 (1957), 69-90.

1224   Noyes, Russell. "The Oscar L. Watkins Wordsworth-Coleridge Collection." Indiana Quarterly for Bookmen, 1 (1945), 18-26.

1225   _____. "The Penalties of Freedom: A Review of William Heath, Wordsworth and Coleridge: A Study of Their Literary Relations in 1801-1802." WC, 2 (Summer, 1971), 101-03.

1226   Ober, Warren U. "Mohammed: The Outline of a Proposed Poem by Coleridge and Southey." N&Q, 5 (October, 1958), 448.

1227   _____. "Original Versions of Two Coleridge Couplets." N&Q, 4 (October, 1957), 454-55.

1228   Ogden, Terry. "Report from the Wordsworth-Coleridge Association." WC, 8 (Summer, 1977), 216.

1229 Okamoto, Akio. "Coleridge to Marco Polo." EIGO-S, 114 (1968), 580-81.

In Japanese.

1230 Oras, Ants. "Kathleen Raine, the Ancient Springs, and Blake." SR, 80 (Winter, 1972), 200-11.

1231 Ormsby-Lennon, Hugh. "The Case Against a Genius." ASch, 41 (Summer, 1972), 468-72.

1232 Orsini, G. N. G. "Coleridge and Schlegel Reconsidered." CL, 16 (Spring, 1964), 97-118.

1233 _____. "Philosophy." TLS, (August 20, 1971), 999.

1234 Osborn, Robert. "Memorabilia." N&Q, 19 (March, 1972), 82.

1235 Ostle, Robin C. "Three Egyptian Poets of 'Westernization,' and 'Abd al-Rahman Shukri,' Ibrahim 'Abd al-Qadir al-Mazini,' and Mahmur 'Abbas al-Aqqad'." CLS, 7 (September, 1970), 354-73.

1236 Owen, H. Parry. "The Theology of Coleridge." CritQ, 4 (Spring, 1962), 59-67.

1237 Owen, W. J. B. "Wordsworth in the Light of Science." Mosaic, 4 (1971), 111-17.

1238 Packer, Lona Mosk. "The Protestant Existentialism of Christina Rossetti." N&Q, 6 (June, 1959), 213-15.

1239 Padwick, G. Joyce. "A Tour in Scotland, 1803." Literia, 6 (1959), 9-17.

Dorothy Wordsworth's and Coleridge's accounts compared.

1240 Pafford, Ward. "Samuel Taylor Coleridge." EUQ, 21 (Spring, 1965), 3-14.

1241 Park, Roy. "Coleridge and Kant: Poetic Imagination and Practical Reason." BJA, 8 (1968), 335-46.

1242 _____. "Coleridge: Philosopher and Theologian As Literary Critic." UTQ, 38 (October, 1968), 17-33.

1243 _____. "Coleridge's Two Voices as a Critic of Wordsworth." ELH, 36 (June, 1969), 361-81.

1244 Parker, Patricia. "The Progress of Phaedria's Bower: Spenser to Coleridge." ELH, 49 (Fall, 1973), 372-97.

1245 Parker, W. M. "Coleridge Again in His Letters." QR, 294 (October, 1956), 70-78.

1246 _____. "Samuel Taylor Coleridge in His Letters." QR, 294 (October, 1956), 488-98.

1247 Parrish, Stephen Maxfield. "Dramatic Technique in the Lyrical Ballads." PMLA, 74 (March, 1959), 85-97.

1248 _____. "Wordsworth and Coleridge on Meter." JEGP, 59 (January, 1960), 41-49.

1249 _____ and Erdman, David V. "Who Wrote The Mad Monk: A Debate." BNYPL, 64 (April, 1960), 209-37.

1250 Partridge, Monica. "Romanticism and the Concept of Communication in a Slavonic and a Non-Slavonic Literature." RMS, 17 (1973), 62-82.

1251 _____. "Slavonic Themes in English Poetry of the 19th Century." SEER, 41 (June, 1963), 420-41.

1252 Patrick, John M. "Ammianus and Alpheus: The Sacred River." MLN, 72 (May, 1957), 335-37.

1253 Patterson, Charles I. "The Authenticity of Coleridge's Reviews of Gothic Romances." JEGP, 50 (October, 1951), 517-21.

     Casts doubt upon the attribution to Coleridge of four reviews first assigned to him in 1927 and included in Raysor's Coleridge's Miscellaneous Criticism.

1254 _____. "Coleridge's Conception of Dramatic Illusion in the Novel." ELH, 18 (June, 1951), 123-37.

1255 Patton, Lewis. "Coleridge and the Soldier." TLS, (August 21, 1937), 608.

     Describes marginalia by Coleridge in the Duke University copy of Brig. Gen. Stewart's Outlines of a Plan for the General Reform of the British Land Forces, 1806.

1256 Paul-Emile, Barbara T. "Samuel Taylor Coleridge as Abolitionist." ARIEL, 5 (April, 1974), 59-75.

1257 Peacock, Markham, Jr. "Variants to the Preface to Lyrical Ballads." MLN, 61 (March, 1946), 175-77.

     Describes the variants to be found in the Longman MSS, and suggests that Coleridge contributed the note on Chaucer in the Preface of 1800.

1258 Peckham, Morse. "Poet and Critic, or the Damage Coleridge Has Done." STC, 6 (Fall, 1960), 1-11.

1259 Peter, John. "Symbol and Implication: Notes Apropos of a Dictum of Coleridge's." EIC, 4 (April, 1954), 145-67.

     Considers the applicability of Coleridge's dictum that through symbolism the writer makes "the external internal, the internal external."

1260 Peters, Robert L. "Swinburne's Idea of Form." CRIT, 5 (Winter, 1963), 45-63.

1261 Pfeiler, William K. "Coleridge's and Schelling's Treatise in the Samothracian Deities." MLN, 52 (March, 1937), 162-65.

 Further considerations of Coleridge's indebtedness to Schelling.

1262 Phelps, William L. "Coleridge." YR, 23 (December, 1933), 397-99.

1263 Pienar, W. J. B. "Coleridge's Pantheistic Hymn." TLS, (February 23, 1928), 131.

1264 _____. "A Poem by Coleridge." TLS (November 15, 1928), 859.

1265 Pierce, Frederick E. "Coleridge and Sir John Davis." MLN, 45 (June, 1930), 395.

1266 Pike, Barry A. "The Coleridge Cottage Museum, Nether Stowey." WC, 3 (Summer, 1972), 167-68.

1267 Piper, Herbert. "The Pantheistic Sources of Coleridge's Early Poetry." JHI, 20 (January, 1959), 47-59.

1268 Pithey, Wensley. "A Coleridge Portrait." TLS (February 7, 1935), 76.

1269 Pizzo, Enrico. "Coleridge als Kritiker." ANGL, 40 (1916), 201-55.

1270 "The Plagiarisms of S. T. Coleridge." BMag, 47 (March, 1840), 287-99.

1271 Porter, Noah. "Coleridge and His American Disciples." BS, 4 (1847), 117-71.

1272 Potter, George R. "Coleridge and the Idea of Evolution." PMLA, 40 (June, 1925), 3179-97.

 Tempers some of the estimates of the extent to which he anticipated the doctrine.

1273 _____. "Unpublished Marginalia in Coleridge's Copy of Malthus 'Essay on Population'.' PMLA, 51 (December, 1936), 1061-68.

1274 Pottle, Frederick A. "An Important Addition to Yale's Wordsworth-Coleridge Collection." YULG, 41 (October, 1966), 45-59.

 Lyrical Ballads.

1275 Potts, L. J. "Imagination and Fancy." EIC, 2 (July, 1952),
345-47.

    Comments on the article by Barbara Hardy in EIC (October,
1951). Miss Hardy adds a rejoinder, pp. 347-49.

1276 Powell, Grosvenor. "Coleridge's Imagination and the Infinite
Regress of Consciousness." ELH, 39 (June, 1972), 266-78.

1277 Pradham, S. V. "Fancy and Imagination: Coleridge Versus
Wordsworth." PQ, 54 (1975), 604-23.

1278 Preyer, Robert O. "Julius Hare and Coleridgean Criticism."
JAAC, 15 (1957), 449-60.

1279 Price, Frances. "Coleridge's Eyes." N&Q, 185 (July 31,
1943), 31.

1280 Quennell, Peter. "An Eagle at Bay." NYTBR, 64 (December 13,
1959), 5.

1281 Raben, Joseph. "Coleridge as the Prototype of the Poet in
Shelley's Alastor." RES, 17 (August, 1966), 278-92.

    Commented on by Timothy Webb in Coleridge and Shelley's
Alastor. "A Reply." RES, 18 (November, 1967), 402-11.

1282 Rahme, Mary. "Coleridge's Concept of Symbolism." SEL,
9 (August, 1969), 619-32.

1283 Raine, Craig. "No French Polish." NSta, 87 (February 8,
1974), 191-92.

1284 _____. "A Giant Prone." NSN, 51 (June 23, 1956), 736-37.

1285 _____. "Great Pan Is Dead." NSN, 54 (December 7,
1957), 781-82.

1286 _____. "The Use of the Beautiful." SoR, 11 (Spring,
1966), 245-63.

1287 Rainsberry, Frederick B. "Coleridge and the Paradox of the
Poetic Imperative." ELH, 21 (June, 1954), 114-45.

1288 Raleigh, John Henry. "The New Criticism as an Historical
Phenomenon." CL, 11 (Winter, 1959), 21-28.

1289 Raven, A. A. "Coleridge's Time, Real and Imaginary." EXPL,
3 (February, 1945), Item 33.

1290 Rawson, C. J. "Pope Echoes in Byron's To Romance and Don
Juan IV, 3." N&Q, 13 (May, 1966), 179.

1291 Raymond, Ernest. "Coleridge's Tomb." TLS (March 28, 1958),
169.

   Comment by Kathleen Coburn (May 2, 1958), 241.

1292 Raysor, Thomas M. "Coleridge's Criticism." TLS (February 6,
1937), 92.

   Corrects an error in his edition of Coleridge's Shakespearean
   criticism.

1293 _____. "Coleridge's Criticism of Wordsworth." PMLA,
54 (June, 1939), 496-510.

   Defends Coleridge's criticism of Wordsworth in the Biographia
   Literaria, which the author considers "the finest critical
   essay in English literature, by demonstrating the justice
   of Coleridge's contention that Wordsworth did not mean to
   attack merely the vocabulary of poetry but the figurative use
   of words and style in its most general sense.

1294 _____. "Notes on Coleridge's Lewti." PQ, 32 (April,
1953), 207-10.

1295 Rea, John D. "Coleridge as Critic." SR, 56 (Autumn, 1948),
597-624.

1296 _____. "The Intangibility of Poetic Style." Style, 1
(Winter, 1967), 15-28.

1297 _____. "Originality." SR, 61 (1953), 533-56.

1298 _____. "Two Kinds of Poetry." AGENDA, 7 (Spring, 1969),
39-40.

1299 Reed, Mark L. "Wordsworth, Coleridge, and the 'Plan' of the
Lyrical Ballads." UTQ, 34 (April, 1965), 238-53.

1300 Reid, S. W. "The Composition and Revision of Coleridge's
Essay on Aeschylus' 'Prometheus'." SB, 24 (1971), 176-83.

1301 Reily, S. W. "Tolkien and the Fairy Story." Thought, 148
(Spring, 1963), 89-106.

   Historians might trace this fairy story to Coleridge.

1302 Renz, Marl F. "A Coleridge Unpublished Letter and Some
Remarks Concerning the Poet's Interest in the Sound of Words."
N&Q, 198 (April, 1953), 163-65.

1303 Rexroth, Kenneth. "The Evolution of Anglo-Catholicism."
CONT, 7 (Summer, 1969), 345-60.

1304 Rhys, Keidrych. "Coleridge and Wales." TLS (August 16,
1947), 415.

1305 Richards, I. A. "Coleridge: The Vulnerable Poet." YR,
48 (June, 1959), 491-504.

1306 _____. "Coleridge's Tiger Cats." NYTBR (January 13,
1952), 6.

1307 _____. "Friends of Coleridge." UTQ, 40 (Fall, 1970),
102-93.

1308 Ricks, Christopher. "The Moral Imbecility of a Would-Be
Wunderkind." Sat R, 55 (January 15, 1972), 31-3, 49.

1309 Ridenour, George M. "Source and Allusion in Some Poems of
Coleridge." SP, 60 (January, 1963), 73-95.

1310 Robbins, Derek. "Coleridge." TLS (September 18, 1969),
1026.

1311 Roberts, Michael. "The Two Coleridges." Merc 32 (1935),
292-93.

1312 Robinson, A. M. Lewin. "A Coleridge Poem." TLS (July 31,
1959), 447.

   A version of Coleridge's poem "My Maker! Of Thy Power the
   Trace," published in The Cape of Good Hope Literary Gazette,
   1832.

1313 Robinson, Fred C. "Coleridge, Personfication, and the
Personal Genitive." NS, 17 (November, 1968), 564-66.

1314 Rochlin, S. A. "Coleridge's A Hymn." TLS (January 17,
1935), 33.

1315 Rogers, David. "The Function of Form in Poetry." REN,
19 (Spring, 1967), 151-55, 167.

1316 Rogers, Venille. "The Poetic Process: Notes on Some
Observations by Keats, Rilke, and Others." KSMB, 18 (1967),
26-35.

1317 Roper, Derek. "Coleridge and The Critical Review." MLR,
55 (January, 1960), 11-16.

   Opposes Charles I. Patterson's "The Authenticity of Coleridge's
   Reviews of Gothic Romances." JEGP, 50 (October, 1951),
   517-21.

1318 _____. "Coleridge, Dyer, and The Mysteries of Udolpho."
N&Q, 19 (August, 1972), 287-89.

1319 Rose, Edgar Smith. "The Anatomy of Imagination." CE, 27
(February, 1966), 346-54.

1320 Rossiter, A. P. "Coleridge's Hymn Before Sunrise." TLS (September 28, 1951), 613; (October 26, 1951), 677.

1321 _____. "Coleridge's Soother in Absence." TLS (May 8, 1953), 301.

1322 Rowland, Beryl. "The Other Father in Yeats' A Prayer for My Daughter." OL, 26 (1971), 284-90.

1323 Rubenstein, Jill. "Sound and Silence in Coleridge's Conversation Poems." English, 21 (Summer, 1972), 54-60.

1324 Rule, Philip C., S. J. "Coleridge's Reputation as a Religious Thinker, 1816-1972." HTR, 67 (July, 1974), 289-320.

1325 _____. "S. T. Coleridge: A Christian in Search of an Aesthetic." Christianity and Literature, 24 (1974), 7-24.

1326 St. George, Priscilla P. "The Styles of Good and Evil in The Sensitive Plant." JEGP, 64 (July, 1965), 479-88.

1327 Salle, J. C. "Identification of Three Allusions in Hazlitt's Essays." N&Q, 19 (March, 1972), 99-100.

1328 Sanders, Charles R. "Coleridge as a Champion of Liberty." SP, 32 (October, 1935), 618-31.

1329 _____. "Coleridge, F. D. Maurice, and the Distinction Between the Reason and the Understanding." PMLA, 51 (June, 1936), 459-75.

1330 _____. "Coleridge, Maurice, and the Church Universal." JR, 21 (January, 1941), 31-45.

1331 _____. "Maurice as a Commentator on Coleridge." PMLA, 53 (March, 1938), 230-43.

1332 _____. "Sir Leslie Stephen, Coleridge, and Two Coleridgeans." PMLA, 55 (September, 1940), 795-801.

    Gathers Leslie Stephen's various utterances on Coleridge,
    F. D. Maurice, and J. Dykes Campbell.

1333 Sanders, C. Richard. "The Background of Carlyle's Portrait of Coleridge in the Life of John Sterling." BJRL, 55 (1973), 434-58.

1334 Sanderson, David R. "Coleridge's Political Sermons: Discursive Language and the Voice of God." MP, 70 (May, 1973), 319-30.

1335 Sankey, Benjamin. "Coleridge and the Visible World." TSLL, 6 (Spring, 1964), 59-67.

1336 Sastri, P. S. "The Moon in Coleridge's Poetry." IJES, 2 (1961), 59-77.

1337 Savage, Basil. "Another 'Lost Manuscript'." WC, 3 (Winter, 1972), 49.

1338 Schiff, Hilda. "Nature and Art in Oscar Wilde's The Decay of Living." E&S, 18 (1965), 83-102.

1339 Schneider, Duane B. "Coleridge's Light-Sound Theory." N&Q, 10 (May, 1963), 182-83.

      Based on passages in Boehme.

1340 _____. "A Note on Coleridge's Notebooks." N&Q, 8 (June, 1961), 219-21.

1341 Schnier, Jacques. "Free Association and Ego Function in Creativity: A Study of Content and Form in Art." AI, 17 (Spring, 1960), 61-74.

1342 Schreiber, Carl F. "Coleridge to Boosey--Boosey to Coleridge." YULG, 22 (July, 1947), 6-10.

      Prints two unpublished letters.

1343 Schrickx, W. "Coleridge and the Cambridge Platonists." REL, 7 (January, 1966), 71-91.

1344 _____. "Coleridge and Friedrich Heinrich Jacobi." RBPH, 36 (1958), 812-50.

      New light on the Coleridge-Jacobi relationship.

1345 _____. "Coleridge, Ernst Platner, and the Imagination." ES, 40 (June, 1959), 157-62.

1346 _____. "Coleridge Marginalia in Kant's Metaphysische Anfangsgrunde Der Naturwissenchaft." SGG, 1 (1959), 161-87.

1347 _____. "An Unnoticed Note of Coleridge's in Kant." NEOPHIL, 42 (1958), 147-51.

1348 _____. "Unpublished Coleridge Marginalia on Fichte." SGG, 3 (1961), 171-208.

1349 Schulz, Max F. "Coleridge's Agonistes." JEGP, 61 (April, 1962), 268-77.

1350 _____. "Coleridge's Apologetic Prefaces." TSE, 11 (1961), 53-64.

1351 _____. "Coleridge, Milton, and Lost Paradise." N&Q, 6 (April, 1959), 143-44.

1352 _____. "Coleridge's 'Debt' to Dryden and Johnson." N&Q, 10 (May, 1963), 189-91.

1353 _____. "Coleridge's Ode on the Departing Year and the
Sacred Theory of Earth: A Case for Analogical Criticism." CP,
1 (Spring, 1968), 45-54.

1354 _____. "The New Coleridge." MP, 69 (November, 1971),
142-51.

1355 _____. "Oneness and Multieity in Coleridge's Poems."
TSE, 9 (1959), 53-60.

1356 _____. "The Soother of Absence: An Unwritten Work by S. T.
Coleridge." SoR, 2 (1967), 289-98.

1357 _____. "S. T. Coleridge and the Poem as Improvisation."
TSE, 10 (1960), 83-99.

        A critique of The Improvisatore and other poems.

1358 Scott-James, R. A. "Science and Imagination." Merc., 31
(February, 1935), 385-86.

1359 Seaton, Ethel. "S. T. C. and Priestley." TLS (January 26,
1946), 43.

        The words "picture of Hymen" may be traced to Chapman's
        continuation of Marlowe's Hero and Leander.

1360 Selander, Glenn E. "Coleridge and the Existential Imagination."
Proceedings of the Utah Academy of Sciences, Arts, and Letters.
43 (1966), 13-23.

1361 Sells, A. Lytton. "Zanella, Coleridge, and Shelley." CL,
2 (Winter, 1950), 16-30.

1362 Sen, Ramendra Kumar. "Imagination in Coleridge and Abhinavagupta:
A Critical Analysis of Christian and Saiva Standpoints." JAAC, 24
(Fall, 1965), 97-107.

1363 Seronsy, Cecil C. "Coleridge's Marginalia in Lamb's Copy of
Daniel's Poetical Works." HLB, 7 (Winter, 1953), 105-12.

1364 _____. "Marginalia by Coleridge in Three Copies of His
Published Works." SP, 51 (July, 1954), 470-81.

1365 _____. "More Coleridge Marginalia." SP, 52 (July, 1955),
497-501.

1366 Sewell, Elizabeth. "Coleridge on Revolution." SIR, 11 (Fall,
1972), 342-59.

1367 Shaffer, Elinor S. "Coleridge's Revolution in the Standard of
Taste." JAAC, 28 (Winter, 1969), 213-21.

1368 _____. "Coleridge's Theory of Aesthetic Interest." JAAC,
27 (Summer, 1969), 399-408.

1369 _____. "Iago's Malignity Motivated: Coleridge's Unpublished
Opus Magnum." ShQ, 19 (Summer, 1968), 195–203.

1370 _____. "Metaphysics of Culture: Kent and Coleridge's Aid
to Reflection." JHI, 31 (April–June, 1970), 199–218.

1371 Sharratt, Bernard. "Coleridge: Friend or Partizan?" NB, 51
(1970), 175-83, 235–42.

1372 Shearer, Edna A. "Wordsworth and Coleridge Marginalia in a
Copy of Richard Payne Knight's Analytical Inquiry into the Principles
of Taste." HLQ, 1 (October, 1937), 63–94.

     The notes are in Wordsworth's hand.

1373 Sheraw, C. Darrel. "Coleridge, Shelley, Byron, and the Devil."
KSMB, 23 (1972), 6-9.

1374 Shipps, Anthony W. "A Charade Attributed to Coleridge." N&Q,
13 (November, 1966), 423-24.

1375 _____. "Coleridge's Notebooks." N&Q, 17 (October, 1970),
385.

1376 _____. "Quotations in Coleridge Notebooks." N&Q, 19
(March, 1972), 109.

1377 _____. "Quotations in Coleridge Notebooks." N&Q, 22
(January, 1975), 412-13.

1378 Siegel, Paul N. "Change and Continuity in Shakespearean
Criticism." ShN, 14 (April–May, 1964), 21.

1379 Sinclair, Nora Rea. "Coleridge and Education." QQ, 74
(Autumn, 1967), 413-26.

1380 Skeat, T. C. "Letters of Charles and Mary Lamb and Coleridge."
BMQ, 26 (September, 1962), 17-21.

1381 _____. "Notebooks and Marginalia of S. T. Coleridge." BMQ,
16 (1952), 91-93.

1382 Slakey, Roger L. "At Zero: A Reading of Wordsworth's 'She
Dwelt Among the Untrodden Ways'." SEL, 12 (Autumn, 1972), 629-38.

1383 Smith, Charles J. "Wordsworth and Coleridge: The Growth of a
Theme." SP, 54 (January, 1957), 53-64.

1384 Smith, D. J. "Pitt and Coleridge." TQ, 10 (Winter, 1967,
211-19.

1385 Smith, Nowell. "Dorothy Wordsworth: A Correction." N&Q,
184 (January 16, 1943), 42.

1386 Smyser, Jane W. "Coleridge's Use of Wordsworth's Juvenila."
PMLA, 65 (June, 1950), 419-26.

      Attributes to Wordsworth four poems usually included in the
      works of Coleridge.

1387 Snyder, Alice D. "Coleridge and the Encyclopedists." MP,
38 (November, 1940), 173-91.

      Prints with suitable commentary the minutes of a meeting of
      April 7, 1817, containing plans for the Encyclopedia Metro-
      politana, and the newly discovered quarto of the Prospectus
      in the Library of Congress.

1388 _____. "Coleridge Documents." TLS, (November 26, 1938),
760.

      Additional material concerning Coleridge's part in the
      publication of the Encyclopedia Metropolitana.

1389 Souffrin, Eileen. "Coup d'Oeil sur la Bibliotheque Anglaise
de Mallarme." RLC, 32 (Juillett-Septembre, 1958), 390-96.

1390 Spacks, Patricia Meyer. "Collins' Imagery." SP, 62
(October, 1965), 719-36.

1391 _____. "Horror-Personification in Late Eighteenth Century
Poetry." SP, 59 (July, 1962), 560-78.

1392 Sparrow, John. "Jortin and Coleridge." TLS, (April 3,
1943), 163.

      A Wish Written in Jesus Wood. Feb. 10, 1792 is not an
      original poem but a translation of a Latin ode Votum by
      Jortin.

1393 Speck, J. "Samuel Taylor Coleridge." ARCHIV, 170 (1936),
44-67.

1394 Spencer, Benjamin T. "'Beautiful Blood and Beautiful Brain':
Whitman and Poe." ESQ, 34, (1964), 45-49.

      The influence of Coleridge on Poe.

1395 Spencer, T. J. B. "Shakespeare and the Noble Woman."
Deutsche Shakespeare - Gesellschaft West Jahrbuch, (1966), 49-62.

1396 _____. "Shakespeare vs. the Rest: The Old Controversy."
ShS, 14 (1961), 76-89.

1397 Stanford, Derek. "Coleridge as Poet and Philosopher of
Love." English, 13 (Spring, 1960), 3-7.

1398 _____. "Coleridge: The Pathological Sage." Month, 28
(November, 1962), 276-80.

1399 _____. "Middleton Murry as a Literary Critic." EIC, 8
(January, 1958), 60-67.

1400 Starr, Nathan C. "Coleridge's Sir Leioline." PMLA, 61 (March,
1946), 147-62.

1401 Steiner, George. "Imagining Science." Listen, 86 (November 18,
1971), 686-88.

1402 _____. "On Reading Kenneth Burke." CamR, 89A (November 4,
1967), 69-70.

1403 Steinmann, Martin, Jr. "Coleridge, T. S. Eliot, and Organicism."
MLN, 71 (May, 1956), 339-40.

1404 Stempel, Daniel. "Coleridge and Organic Form: The English
Tradition." SIR, 6 (Winter, 1967), 89-97.

1405 _____. "Revelation on Mount Snowdon: Wordworth, Coleridge,
and the Fichtean Imagination." JAAC, 29 (Spring, 1971), 371-84.

1406 Stephens, Fran C. "The Coleridge Collection: A Sample." LCUT,
1 (March, 1970), 33-38.

1407 _____. "Cottle Wise and the MS Ashley 408." PBSA, 68
(1974), 391-403.

1408 Stevenson, John. "Arcadia Resettled: Pastoral Poetry and
Romantic Theory." SEL, 7 (Autumn, 1967), 629-38.

1409 Stevenson, Warren. "Lamia: A Stab at the Gordian Knot." SIR,
11 (Summer, 1972), 241-52.

1410 _____. "The Myth and the Mind: Towards a Theory of
Creativity." Person, 46 (July, 1965), 299-319.

1411 Stewart, Jack F. "Romantic Theories of Humor Relating to
Sterne." Person, 49 (Autumn, 1968), 459-73.

      Discusses the notions of humor presented by Coleridge,
      Hunt, Hazlitt, and Carlyle as they applied them to Sterne.

1412 Stock, Noel. "Fragmentation and Uncertainty." POET A, 31
(December, 1969), 41-44.

1413 Stoll, Elmer Edgar. "Symbolism in Coleridge." PMLA, 63
(March, 1948), 214-33.

1414 Stone, Edward. "Melville's 'Pip' and Coleridge's 'Servant Girl'."
AL, 25 (1953), 358-60.

1415 Stout, George D. "Leigh Hunt on Wordsworth and Coleridge." KSJ,
6 (Winter, 1957), 59-73.

1417 Strout, Alan L. "William Maginn as Gossip." N&Q, 2 (June,
1955), 263-65.

1418 Sugimoto, Ryutaro. "Coleridge on Metaphysical Poetry: A Note." SEL - Japan, 38 (1961).

1419 _____. "Coleridge." TLS (September 11, 1969), 1003; (October 2, 1969), 1131.

1420 Sultana, Donald. "Coleridge Autographs." TLS (February 15, 1963), 116.

1421 _____. "Coleridge's Diplomatic Jaunt." TLS (July 10, 1969), 755.

1422 Sundell, Michael G. "The Theme of Self-Realization in Frost at Midnight." SIR, 7 (Autumn, 1967), 34-39.

1423 Super, R. H. "Landor's Letters to Wordsworth and Coleridge." MP, 55 (November, 1957), 73-83.

1424 Sutherland, James R. "Lewti." TLS (December 6, 1941), 611.

1425 Svaglic, Martin J. "Two Ways of Talking About Prose Texts." Mon/ESP, 2 (1972), 43-68.

1426 Swanson, Donald R. "Carlyle on the English Romantic Poets." LHR, 2 (1969), 25-32.

1427 Sypher, F. Wylie. "Chatterton, Coleridge, and Bristol." TLS (August 28, 1937), 624.

      Replies to a communication by E. H. W. Meyerstein in TLS (August 21, 1937), 606.

1428 Takahashi, Yasunari. "Coleridge and the Stream." SEL-Japan, 42 (1965), 33-53.

1429 Taube, Edward. "German Influence on the English Vocabulary in the Nineteenth Century." JEGP (October, 1939), 486-93.

1430 Taylor, Anya. "Magic in Coleridge's Poetry." WC, 3 (Spring, 1972), 76-84.

1431 Ten, C. L. "Mill's Stable Society." MILLN, 7 (Fall, 1971), 2-6.

1432 Thayer, Mary R. "Keats and Coleridge: 'La Belle Dame Sans Merci'." MLN, 60 (April, 1945), 270-72.

      Suggests Coleridge's Love as a possible influence on Keats' poem.

1433 Thorpe, Clarence D. "Coleridge as Aesthetician and Critic." JHI, 5 (October, 1944), 387-414.

      An analysis of Coleridge's critical ideas as a partial answer to Coleridge's anti-Romantic detractors.

1434 _____. "The Imagination: Coleridge Versus Wordsworth."
PQ, 18 (January, 1939), 1-18.

Traces the genesis of Coleridge's differences with Wordsworth's
view and analyzes their respective positions.

1435 Thorpe, James. "A Note on Coleridge's Gutch Commonplace
Book." MLN, 63 (February, 1948), 130-31.

A passage on Milton is copied from Jonathan Richardson's
Explanatory Notes and Remarks in Milton's Paradise Lost
(1734).

1436 Tillett, Nettle S. "Is Coleridge Indebted to Fielding?"
SP, 43 (October, 1946), 675-81.

Finds anticipations of some of Coleridge's critical ideas
in Tom Jones, Book VIII.

1437 Tillotson, Geoffrey. "Ars Celare Artem?" Style, 1 (Winter,
1967), 65-68.

1438 _____. "Eighteenth-Century Poetic Diction." E&S, 25
(1939), 59-80.

1439 Tinker, Chauncey B. "Coleridge's Ballad of the Dark Ladie."
YULG, 25 (July, 1949), 17-20.

1440 Van Patten, Nathan. "A Presentation Copy of Coleridge's
Sibylline Leaves, with Manuscript Notes, Altered Readings and
Deletions by the Author." LIBRARY, 4th Ser., 17 (September,
1936), 221-24.

1441 Varma, R. S. "Symbolism in Coleridge's Poetry in Relation
to His Principal Ideas." The Gorakhpur Magazine, 3 (June, 1960),
8-18.

1442 Viebrock, Helmut. "A Note on Coleridge and Memory: Coleridge
ä la Recherche du Mot Perdu." ARCHIV, 200 (June, 1963), 118-19.

1443 Visiak, E. H. "Some Coleridge Parallels." N&Q, 178 (June 15,
1940), 422.

1444 Wagenblass, John H. "Coleridge in Dubious Battle." HLQ,
13 (August, 1950), 406-08.

1445 Wagner, Lydia E. "Coleridge's Use of Laudanum and Opium,
As Connected with His Interest in Contemporary Investigations
Concerning Stimulation and Sensation." PsyR, 25 (1938), 309-34.

1446 Walsh, William. "Coleridge's 'Self-Unraveling Clue': Its
Meaning for Education." WHR, 9 (Summer, 1955), 209-18.

1447 _____. "Coleridge's Vision of Childhood." Listen, 53
(February 24, 1955), 336-37, 340.

1448 Walton, Eda L. "I. A. Richards' Study of Coleridge's Critical
Theory." NYTBR (March 3, 1935), 2.

1449 Ward, Patricia. "Coleridge's Critical Theory of the Symbol."
TSLL, 8 (Spring, 1966), 15-32.

1450 Ware, J. Garth. "Coleridge's Great Poems Reflecting the
Mother Image." AI, 18 (Winter, 1961), 331-52.

1451 Wasserman, Earl R. "Coleridge's 'Metrical Experiments'."
MLN, 63 (November, 1948), 491-92.

    No. 10 of these poems from the Notebook seems to have
    been borrowed from William Cartwright.

1452 _____. "Coleridge's 'Metrical Experiments'." MLN,
55 (June, 1940), 432-33.

    Identifies two of the poems as seventeenth-century pieces
    and casts doubt on Coleridge's authorship of some of the
    others.

1453 _____. "The English Romantics: The Grounds of Knowledge."
SIR, 4 (Autumn, 1964), 17-34.

1454 _____. "The Inherent Values of Eighteenth-Century
Personification." PMLA, 65 (June, 1950), 435-63.

1455 Watson, George. "Abstractions." EIC, 12 (October, 1962),
424-26.

1456 _____. "On Patronizing Coleridge." Listen, 58 (October 24,
1957), 633-57.

1457 Watson, Vera. "Coleridge's Army Service." TLS (July 7,
1950), 428.

1458 Weather, Winston. "Coleridge and the Epic Experience."
Mon/Tu MS, 4 (1968), 63-75.

1459 Webb, William. "The Rumford Grate." N&Q, 12 (November,
1965), 425.

1460 Weintraub, Wiktor. "The Problem of Improvisation in Romantic
Literature." CL, 16 (Spring, 1964), 119-37.

1461 Weitz, Morris. "Reasons in Criticism." JAAC, 20 (Spring,
1962), 429-37.

    Considers assessments of Shakespeare by Dryden, Pope,
    Johnson, and Coleridge.

1462 Wellek, René. "The Concept of 'Romanticism' in Literary
History." CL, 1 (Winter, 1949), 1-23; 2 (Spring, 1949), 147-72.

1463 _____. "German and English Romanticism: A Confrontation."
SIR, 4 (Autumn, 1964), 35-56.

1464 Wells, G. A. "Herder's and Coleridge's Evaluation of the
Historical Approach." MLR, 48 (April, 1953), 167-75.

1465 _____. "Man and Nature: An Elucidation of Coleridge's
Rejection of Herder's Thought." JEGP, 51 (1952), 314-25.

1466 Wells, John E. "Lyrical Ballads, 1800: A Paste-in." Library,
4th Series, 19 (March, 1939), 486-91.

     Describes two specimens of a paste-in supplying the fifteenth
     lines of Michael omitted from the lower half of p. 210 of
     the edition of 1800.

1467 _____. "Lyrical Ballads, 1800: Cancel Leaves." PMLA,
53 (March, 1938), 207-29.

1468 _____. "Lyrical Ballads, 1798." TLS (January 17, 1942),
36.

1469 Welsh, John R. "An Anglo-American Friendship: Allston and
Coleridge." JAS, 5 (April, 1971), 81-91.

1470 Werkmeister, Lucyle. "Coleridge and Godwin on the Communication
of Truth." MP, 55 (February, 1958), 170-77.

     Borrowings from Godwin's Enquiry Concerning Political Justice
     in Coleridge's Essay On the Communication of Truth, included
     in the first edition of The Friend, 1809.

1471 _____. "Coleridge and The Work for Which Poor Pam Was
Murdered." JEGP, 53 (1954), 347-51.

     On Coleridge's translation of Arndt's Geist Der Zeit.

1472 _____. "Coleridge, Bowles, and Feelings of the Heart."
ANGL, 78 (1960), 55-73.

1473 _____. "Coleridge on Science, Philosophy, and Poetry:
Their Relation to Religion." HTR, 52 (April, 1959), 85-118.

1474 _____. "Coleridge's Anthem: Another Debt to Bowles."
JEGP, 58 (April, 1959), 270-75.

1475 _____. "Coleridge's 'Mathematical Problem'." MLN,
74 (December, 1959), 691-93.

1476 _____. "Coleridge's The Plot Discovered: Some Facts and
a Speculation." MP, 56 (May, 1959), 254-63.

1477 _____. "The Early Coleridge: His 'Rage for Metaphysics'."
HTR, 54 (April, 1961), 99-123.

1478 _____. "'High Jinks' at Highgate." PQ, 40 (January, 1961), 104-11.

1479 _____. "Jerdan on Coleridge." N&Q, 7 (February, 1959), 74-76.

1480 _____. "Some Whys and Wherefores of Coleridge's Lines Composed in a Concert-Room." MP, 60 (February, 1963), 201-05.

1481 _____ and Zall, P. M. "Coleridge's The Complaint of Ninathoma." N&Q, 16 (November, 1969), 412-14.

1482 _____. "Possible Additions to Coleridge's Sonnets on Eminent Characters." SIR, 8 (Winter 1969), 121-27.

1483 West, Anthony. "Triumphant." NSta, (October 20, 1972), 566-67.

1484 West, Geoffrey. "The Power of Coleridge." YR, 25 (June, 1936), 850-52.

1485 West, Herbert F. "Flashes of Poetic Vision." NYT (July 20, 1952), 6.

1486 Whalley, George. "The Aristotle-Coleridge Axis." UTQ, 42 (Winter, 1973), 93-109.

1487 _____. "The Bristol Library Borrowings of Southey and Coleridge, 1793-8." Library, 4 (September, 1949), 114-31.

1488 _____. "Coleridge and Southey, Bristol, 1795." RES, 1 (October, 1950), 324-40.

1489 _____. "Coleridge and the Royal Society of Literature." EDH, 35 (1969), 147-51.

1490 _____. "Coleridge as Philosopher." QQ, 57 (Spring, 1950), 69-78.

1491 _____. "Coleridge on Classical Prosody: An Unidentified Review of 1797." RES, 2 (July, 1951), 238-47.

1492 _____. "Coleridge on the Prometheus of Aeschylus." PTRSC, 54 (June, 1960), 13-24.

1493 _____. "Coleridge's Debt to Charles Lamb." E&S, (1958), 68-85.

1494 _____. "Coleridge's Marginalia Lost." BC, 17 (Winter, 1968), 428-42.

1495 _____. "Coleridge's Marginalia Lost." BC, 18 (Summer, 1969), 223.

1496 _____. "Coleridge's Poetical Canon: Selection and Arrangement." REL, 7 (January, 1966), 9-24.

1497 _____. "Coleridge, Southey, and Joan of Arc." N&Q,
1 (February, 1954), 67-69.

1498 _____. "Coleridge Unlabyrinthed." UTQ, 32 (July, 1963),
325-45.

1499 _____. "Coleridge's Sheet of Sonnets, 1796." TLS,
(November 23, 1956), 679.

1500 _____. "The Date of Two Letters from Coleridge to George
Dyer, 1795." N&Q, 194 (October 15, 1949), 454-55.

1501 _____. "The Harvest on the Ground: Coleridge Marginalia."
UTQ, 38 (April, 1969), 248-76.

1502 _____. "Late Autumn's Amaranth: Coleridge's Late Poems."
PTRSC, 2 (June, 1964), 159-79.

1503 _____. "A Library Cormorant." Listen, 52 (September 9,
1954), 396-97, 400.

1504 _____. "Portrait of a Bibliophile VII: Samuel Taylor
Coleridge, 1772-1834." BC, 10 (Autumn, 1961), 275-90.

1505 _____. "Preface to Lyrical Ballads: A Portent." UTQ,
25 (July, 1956), 467-83.

1506 _____. "The Publication of Coleridge's Prometheus
Essay." N&Q, 16 (February, 1969), 52-55.

1507 _____. "Recent Wordsworth and Coleridge Studies." QQ,
76 (Spring, 1969), 118-30.

1508 _____. "Romantic Chasms." TLS (June 21, 1947), 309.

1509 _____. "Some Studies of Wordsworth and Coleridge." QQ,
81 (1974), 265-77.

1510 Wheeler, Charles B. "The People Versus Art: Coleridge's
Testimony Re-Examined." SAQ, 67 (Winter, 1968), 40-52.

1511 _____. "Unpublished Letters." TLS (September 10, 1938),
584.

1512 White, Robert L. "Washington Allston: Banditti in Arcadia."
AQ, 13 (Fall, 1961), 387-401.

1513 Whitehill, Joseph. "Samuel Taylor Coleridge: Prisoner and
Prophet of System." ASch, 37 (Winter, 1967-68), 145-58.

1514 Wiley, Margaret L. "Coleridge and the Wheels of Intellect."
PMLA, 67 (March, 1952), 101-12.

1515 Will, Frederic. "Cousin and Coleridge: The Aesthetic Ideal."
CL, 8 (Winter, 1956), 63-77.

1516 Willey, Basil. "At Home on Highgate Hill." TLS (March 31, 1972), 354.

1517 _____. "Charles Lamb and S. T. Coleridge." ChLB, 1 (1973), 1-19.

1518 _____. "Coleridge on Imagination and Fancy." PBA (1946), 173-87.

1519 Williams, Franklin B., Jr. "Tracking Down STC Authors." TLS (January 7, 1955), 9.

1520 Williams, Ralph M. "Coleridge's Parody of Dyer's Gronger Hill." MLR, 41 (January, 1946), 61-62.

1521 Willoughby, L. A. "Coleridge As a Philologist." MLR, 31 (April, 1936), 176-201.

1522 Wilson, Douglas B. "Coleridge: Dreams and Poetry." UDQ, 3 (Autumn, 1968), 114-16.

1523 Wilson, James D. "A Note on Coleridge and The Quarterly Review." WC, 6 (Winter, 1975), 51-53.

1524 Winwar, Frances. "A Coleridge Study." NYTBR (February 26, 1939), 22.

1525 Wittreich, Joseph Anthony, Jr. "Milton's Romantic Audience." AN&Q, 10 (June, 1972), 147-50.

1526 Wojcik, Manfred. "Coleridge and the Problem of Transcendentalism." ZAA, 18 (1970), 30-58.

1527 _____. "Coleridge: Symbolization, Expression, and Artistic Creativity." ZAA, 19 (1971), 117-54.

1528 _____. "Coleridge: Symbol, Organic Unity, and Modern Aesthetic Subjectivism." ZAA, 18 (1970), 355-90.

1529 _____. "The Mimetic Orientation of Coleridge's Aesthetic Thought." ZAA, 17 (1969), 344-91.

1530 Wojcik, S. J. "Tolkien and Coleridge: Remaking of the Green Earth." REN, 20 (Spring, 1968), 134-39, 146.

1531 Wood, Barry. "The Growth of the Soul: Coleridge's Dialectical Method and the Strategy of Emerson's Nature." PMLA, 91 (May, 1976), 385-97.

1532 Woodridge, Homer E. "Coleridge and The Nightingale." SRL, (September 28, 1935), 9.

1533 Woodring, Carl R. "Coleridge and Mary Hutchinson." N&Q, 4 (May, 1957), 213-14.

1534 _____. "Two Prompt Copies of Coleridge's Remorse."
BNYPL, 65 (April, 1961), 229-35.

1535 Woof, R. S. "Coleridge and Thomasina Dennis." UTQ, 32
(October, 1962), 37-54.

1536 _____. "A Coleridge-Wordsworth Manuscript and Sarah
Hutchinson's Poets." SB, 19 (1966), 226-31.

1537 _____. "John Stoddart, Michael and Lyrical Ballads."
ARIEL, 1 (April, 1970), 7-22.

1538 Wordsworth, Jonathan. "Letters of the Coleridge Circle."
TLS (February 15, 1968), 164.

1539 Wright, G. W. "Coleridge and Dr. Hartley." N&Q, 177
(September 2, 1939), 179.

1540 _____. "Talfourd on Coleridge." N&Q, 180 (March 22,
1941), 211.

1541 Yura, Kimiyoshi. "Coleridge's Terror Corporeus Sive
Materialism." EIGO S, 114 (1968), 505-57.

1542 _____. "The Involuntary Memory as Discovered by S. T.
Coleridge." SEL-Japan, 42 (1966), 133-43.

1543 Zall, P. M. "Coleridge and Sonnets From Various Authors."
CLJ, 2 (1967), 49-67.

1544 _____. "A Coleridge Inscription." TLS (May 22, 1953),
333.

      On a page from a copy of Mary Lamb's Mrs. Leicester's
      School.

1545 _____. "Coleridge in the Huntington Library." WC, 2
(Winter, 1971), 1-16.

      This checklist is a supplement to Florence Brinkley's Some
      Notes Concerning Coleridge Material at the Huntington Library,
      HLQ, 8 (May, 1945), 312-320.

1546 _____. "Coleridge's Unpublished Revisions to Osorio."
BNYPL, 71 (October, 1967), 516-23.

1547 _____. "The Cool World of Samuel Taylor Coleridge: The
American Connection: Dr. Richard Price, 1723-91." WC, 7 (Spring,
1976), 95-100.

1548 _____. "The Cool World of Samuel Taylor Coleridge: Bawdy
Books and Obscene Ballads." WC, 5 (Winter, 1974), 59-64.

1549 _____. "The Cool World of Samuel Taylor Coleridge:
Citizen John Up Against the Wall." WC, 3 (Spring,1972), 111-16.

1550 _____. "The Cool World of Samuel Taylor Coleridge: Do
Ye Ken Tom Poole?" WC, 8 (Winter,1977), 56-61.

1551 _____. "The Cool World of Samuel Taylor Coleridge: Dr.
Beddoes the Bristol Brunonian." WC, 2 (Spring,1971), 67-73.

1552 _____. "The Cool World of Samuel Taylor Coleridge: George
Canning, Comical Poet/Politician." WC, 8 (Autumn,1977), 306-10.

1553 _____. "The Cool World of Samuel Taylor Coleridge:
Implacable Christian." WC, 5 (Summer,1974), 169-73.

1554 _____. "The Cool World of Samuel Taylor Coleridge:
James Perry, VOX POP." WC, 6 (Winter,1975), 59-64.

1555 _____. "The Cool World of Samuel Taylor Coleridge: More
for the Millions." WC, 4 (Spring,1973), 152-57.

1556 _____. "The Cool World of Samuel Taylor Coleridge: Mrs.
Barbauld's Crew and the Building of a Mass Reading Class." WC,
2 (Summer,1971), 74-79.

1557 _____. "The Cool World of Samuel Taylor Coleridge:
Richard Brothers--The Law and the Prophet." WC, 4 (Winter,1973),
24-30.

1558 _____. "The Cool World of Samuel Taylor Coleridge:
Richard Parson, Don or Devil." WC, 6 (Autumn,1975), 255-60.

1559 _____. "The Cool World of Samuel Taylor Coleridge:
The Trials of William Frend." WC, 2 (Winter,1971), 26-31.

1560 _____. "The Cool World of Samuel Taylor Coleridge:
Up Loyal Sock Creek." WC, 3 (Summer,1972), 161-67.

1561 _____. "Sam Spitfire: or Coleridge in The Satirist."
BNYPL, 71 (April, 1967), 239-44.

1562 Zimmerman, Lester. "Walt Whitman and the Tradition of the
Organic." Mon/TuMs, 11 (1970), 44-55.

BOOKS

1563 Abercrombie, Lascelles. Romanticism. New York: Barnes &
Noble, 1963.

1564 Abrams, Meyer H. English Romantic Poets: Modern Essays in
Criticism. London, New York: Oxford University Press, 1960.

1565 _____. The Mirror and the Lamp: Romantic Theory and the
Critical Tradition. New York: Oxford University Press, 1953.

    Review: E. D. H. Johnson in YR, 43 (December, 1953), 298-301.

1566 Adair, Patricia M. The Waking Dream: A Study of Coleridge's
Poetry. London: E. Arnold, 1967; New York: Barnes & Noble, 1968.

    Reviews: D. B. Wilson, UDQ 3 (Autumn 1968), 114-16; D. B.
Wilson, TLS (August 29, 1968), 914.

1567 Akatmo, Masao. Wordsworth and Coleridge. Tokyo: Kenkyusha,
1956.

1568 Appleyard, J. A. Coleridge's Philosophy of Literature: The
Development of a Concept of Poetry, 1791-1819. Cambridge, Mass.:
Harvard University Press; London: Oxford University Press, 1965.

    Reviews: Harold Lancour, LJ, 91 (January 1, 1966), 110-11;
L. C. Knights in NYRB, 6 (May 26, 1966), 12-14; J. R. de J.
Jackson in QQ, 73 (1966), 297-98:   L. Werkmeister in CE,
28 (November, 1966), 184-85; L. Werkmeister in TLS (June 9,
1966), 512; Carl Woodring in ELN 4 (March, 1967), 219-21;
R. H. Fogle in MLQ 28 (March, 1967), 113-14; John L. Mahoney
in THOUGHT, 42 (Spring 1967), 129-31; John Colmer in MLR,
62 (July, 1967), 514-15; R. L. Brett in CritQ, 9 (1967),
188-89; W. H. Werkmeister in Person, 48 (Spring 1967), 266-67;
P. M. Zall in CL, 20 (Winter 1968), 69-71; Nicholas Brooke
in N&Q, 17 (May, 1970), 193-94; Hans-Peter Breuerin in
California English Journal, 7 (February, 1971), 49-51.

1569 Arens, Hans. Sprachwissenschaft. Freiburg: K. Alber, 1955.

1570 Armour, Richard W. and Howes, Raymond F., ed. Coleridge the
Talker: A Series of Contemporary Descriptions and Comments. Ithaca,
N.Y.: Cornell University Press; London: Oxford University Press,
1940.

    Reviews: F. A. Pottle in SRL, 22 (May 11, 1940), 18;
H. Read in Spect, 164 (June 21, 1940), 840; H. Read in N&Q,
178 (1940), 305-06; H. Read in NYHTBR, 16 (February 4, 1940),
18; E. Hunt in QJS, 26 (1940), 324-25; E. L. Griggs in YR,
29 (1940), 835-37; J. J. R. in CW, 151 (1940), 118-19;
J. J. R. in Atlantic Monthly Bookshelf, 165 (April, 1940);
T. M. Raysor in MLN, 56 (June, 1941), 310-11; H. S. V. Jones
in JEGP, 49 (1941), 310-11; R. W. King in RES, 17 (January,
1941), 112-16; E. C. Batho in MLR, 36 (1941), 127-29;
Friedrich Brie in Ang. BB1, 53 (1942), 23-25; René Wellek
in PQ, 22 (1943), 383-84.

1571 Badawi, Muhammad M. Coleridge: Critic of Shakespeare.
London: Cambridge University Press, 1973.

    Reviews: Elinor S. Shaffer in WC, 6 (Summer 1975), 151-54;
W. J. B. Owen in RES, 25 (1974), 218-20; R. A. Foakes in WLN,
23 (March, 1975), 206-08; J. C. Maxwell in N&Q, 23 ns (March,
1976), 127-28; Brian Vickers in YES, 5 (1975), 302-04.

1572 Baker, Carlos, ed. Coleridge: Poetry and Prose. New York:
Bantam, 1965.

1573 Baker, James V. The Sacred River: Coleridge's Theory of the
Imagination. Baton Rouge: Louisiana State University Press, 1957.

> Reviews: L. Marchand in SatR (February 8, 1958), 22; A. H.
> Roper in DR, 38 (Spring 1958), 129-33; A. H. Roper in TLS
> (May 23, 1958), 284; M. Price in YR, 47 (June, 1958), 619-21;
> C. R. Sanders in SAQ, 57 (Summer 1958), 397-99; M. H. Abrams
> in MP, 56 (November, 1958), 139-41; T. McFarland in CE, 20
> (March, 1959), 329-30; J. M. Raines in BA, 33 (Winter 1959),
> 87; E. E. Bostetter in PS, 33 (1959), 187-90.

1574 Ball, Patricia M. The Science of Aspects: The Changing Role
of Fact in the Work of Coleridge, Ruskin, and Hopkins. London:
Athlone Press; New York: Oxford University Press, 1971.

> Reviews: in TSL (October 15, 1971), 1280; Robert Ackerman
> in VS, 16 (September, 1972), 117; Rachel Trickett in NQ,
> 20 (August, 1973), 307-08.

1575 Barfield, Owen. What Coleridge Thought. 1st ed. Middletown:
Wesleyan Press, 1971; New York: Oxford University Press, 1972.

> Reviews: M. H. Abrams in The Ohio Review, 13 (Spring 1972),
> 84-89; G. A. Cevasco in DR, 52 (Spring 1972), 153-54; G. A.
> Cevasco in SIR, 11 (Spring 1972), 148-61; in TLS (August 11,
> 1972), 943-44: Barbara Lupini in English, 21, (1972),
> 111-12; Douglas Wilson in UDQ, 7 (1972), 61-71; J. Robert
> Barth in ELN, 11 (September, 1973), 61-64; W. J. B. Owen
> in RES, 24 (1972), 222-25; Thomas McFarland in WC 4 (Summer
> 1973), 165-70; E. D. Mackerness in N&Q, 21 (September,
> 1974), 348-49; Rodger K. Meiners in CRIT, 15 (1973), 174-82;
> George Whalley in QQ, 81 (1974), 265-77.

1576 Barrell, John ed. Samuel Taylor Coleridge: On the Constitution
of the Church and State. London: Dent, 1972.

1577 Barth, J. Robert. Coleridge and Christian Doctrine. Cambridge,
Mass: Harvard University Press, London: Oxford University Press,
1969.

> Reviews: James D. Boulger in JEGP, 60 (1970), 533-58;
> Thomas Hall in MSch, 44 (1970), 624-49; J. A. Appleyard in
> MLQ, 32 (June, 1971), 206-13; Max F. Schulz in MP, 69,
> (November, 1961), 142-51; John Colmer in YES, 2 (1972),
> 296-98.

1578 Bate, Walter Jackson. Coleridge. New York: Macmillan, 1968.

> Reveiws: Burton Feldman in UDQ, 3 (Spring 1968), 94-99;
> Frederic E. Faverty in BW (June 30, 1968), 8; L. C. Knights
> in NYRB, 11 (December 19, 1968), 25-28; Lore Metzger in MLQ,
> 30 (March, 1969), 121-31; in TLS (April 17, 1969), 411.

1579 _____. "Coleridge on the Function of Art." (In Harry
Levin, ed. Perspectives of Criticism. Cambridge: Harvard University
Press; London: Cumberlege, 1950), 125-59.

1580 _____. Criticism: The Major Texts. New York: Harcourt,
Brace, 1953.

    Forty-two pages are occupied by Coleridge under the heading
    of "Romantic Transcendentalism and the Organic View of Nature."

1581 Bayley, John. The Romantic Survival: A Study in Poetic
Evolution. London: Constable, 1957.

1582 Beaty, Frederick L. Light from Heaven: Love in British Romantic
Literature. DeKalb: Northern Illinois University Press, 1957.

    Review: George Bornstein, WC, 4 (Summer, 1973), 185-86.

1583 Beer, J. B. Coleridge the Visionary. London: Chatto &
Windus, 1959.

    Reviews: J. Jones in NSN (July 11, 1959), 56; in TLS
    (July 17, 1959), 424; F. Kermode in Spect. (September 11,
    1959), 339; John Bayley in NER (September, 1959), 82-83;
    R. L. Brett in Crit. Q, 1 (1959), 269-71; in QR, 297,
    (October, 1959), 478-79; H. Read in Listen, 62 (July 16,
    1959), 107; J. I. M. Stewart in LM, 7 (January, 1960),
    76-78; F. T. Wood in ES, 41 (December, 1960), 299-400;
    W. Stevenson in QQ, 67 (Spring, 1960), 135-36.

1584 _____. Coleridge: Poems. London: Dent; New York: Dutton,
1963.

1585 _____. Coleridge's Variety, Bicentenary Studies. London:
Macmillan, 1974; Pittsburgh: University of Pittsburgh Press, 1975.

    Reviews: J. R. Alexander in YES, 6 (1976), 290-93; R. J.
    Barth in WC, 7 (Summer, 1976), 239-43; G. Hough in TLS (July
    11, 1957), 756; J. D. Gutteridge in N&Q, 23 ns (March, 1976),
    125-26.

1586 Benet, Laura. Coleridge, Poet of Wild Enchantment. New
York, Toronto: Dodd, Mead, 1952.

1587 Berkoben, Lawrence D. Coleridge's Decline as a Poet.
Mouton: The Hague, 1975.

    Review: Joseph in WC, 7 (Summer, 1976), 191-92.

1588 Bernbaum, Ernest. "Samuel Taylor Coleridge." Guide Through
the Romantic Movement. New York: Ronald Press, 1949, 53-78.

1589 Beyer, Werner W. The Enchanted Forest. Oxford: Blackwell;
New York: Barnes & Noble, 1963.

   Reviews: in TLS (December 5, 1963), 1015; W. J. B. Owen
   in RES, 16 (February, 1965), 86-88; Horst Oppel in ANGL,
   83 (1965), 248-50.

1590 Bishop, Morchard, ed. The Complete Poems of Samuel Taylor
Coleridge. London: McDonald, 1954.

   Review: in TLS (January 8, 1955), 63.

1591 Bonjour, Adrien. Coleridge's "Hymn Before Sunrise." A
Study of Facts and Problems Connected with the Poem. Lausanne:
Imprimerie La Concorde, 1942.

   Reviews: A. H. Nethercot in MLN, 59 (May, 1944), 358-59;
   R. C. Bald in JEGP, 43 (1944), 135-37; R. W. King in RES,
   21 (January, 1945), 75-76; J. M. S. Tompkins, MLR, 39
   (October, 1944), 417-18.

1592 Bostetter, E. E. The Romantic Ventriloquists: Wordsworth,
Coleridge, Keats, Shelley, Byron. Seattle: University of Washington
Press, 1973.

1593 Boulger, James D. Coleridge as Religious Thinker. New Haven:
Yale University Press, 1961.

   Reviews: Lucyle Werkmeister in CE, 23 (November, 1961),
   166; in TLS (March 16, 1962), 186; N. P. Stallknecht in
   JEGP, 61 (April, 1962), 429-33; M. J. Svaglic in MP, 61
   (November, 1963), 137-39.

1594 Bowra, C. M. The Romantic Imagination. New York: Oxford
University Press, 1961.

1595 Brandl, Alois. Samuel Taylor Coleridge and the English
Romantic School. New York: Haskell House, 1966.

1596 Brett, R. L. "Coleridge's Theory of Imagination." (In
English Association. English Studies. London. n.s., v. 2, 1949),
75-90.

1597 _____. Fancy and Imagination. London: Methuen, 1969.

1598 _____, ed. S. T. Coleridge: Writers and Their Background.
London: Bell, 1971; Athens: Ohio University Press, 1972.

   Reviews: W. J. B. Owen in RES, 23 (May, 1972), 217-19;
   Gilbert Thomas in English, 21 (1972), 27-28; Christ Wallace-
   Crabbe in AUMLA, 38 (November, 1972), 228-29; J. Robert
   Barth in KSJ, 23 (1974), 154-59.

1599   Brett, R. L. and Jones, A. R., eds. "Lyrical Ballads" by
Wordsworth and Coleridge: The Text of the 1798 Edition, with
Additional 1800 Poems and Prefaces. London: Methuen, 1963.

    Reviews: F. H. Langman in AUMLA, 22 (1964), 309-10; in TLS
    (October 11, 1963), 808; Herbert Huscher in ANGL, 84 (1966),
    473-76.

1600   Brinkley, Roberta Florence, ed. Coleridge on the Seventeenth
Century. Durham N. C.: Duke University Press, 1955.

    Reviews: G. Whalley in UTQ, 25 (January, 1956), 250-62;
    L. Werkmeister in Person, 37 (Summer, 1956), 314-15; in
    PQ, 35 (July, 1956), 253-54; G. Blakemore Evans in JEGP,
    15 (April, 1956), 335-38; M. H. Abrams in MLN, 72 (January,
    1957), 56-60; H. M. Margoliouth in RES, 8 (February, 1957),
    101-02; Pierre Legouis in EA, 10 (1957), 58-59.

1601   Broughton, Leslie Nathan, ed. Sara Coleridge and Henry Reed.
Cornell Studies in English, 27, 1937.

1602   _____. Some Letters of the Wordsworth Family, Now First
Published, With a Few Unpublished Letters of Coleridge and Southey
and Others. Cornell Studies in English, 32, Ithaca: Cornell
University Press; London: Milford, 1942.

    Review: James E. Tobin in THOUGHT, 17 (1942), 754-55.

1603   Brown, John Russell, and Harris, Bernard, ed. Contemporary
Theatre. Stratford-upon-Avon Studies, No. 4, Arnold, 1962.

1604   Burke, Kenneth. Language as Symbolic Action. Berkeley:
University of California Press; London: Cambridge University
Press, 1966.

    Review: George Steiner in CamR, 89A (November 4, 1967),
    69-70.

1605   _____. The Philosophy of Literary Form. Berkeley:
University of California Press, 1974.

1606   Byatt, Antonia S. Wordsworth and Coleridge in Their Time.
London: Nelson, 1970; New York: Crane, Russak, 1973.

1607   Calleo, David P. Coleridge and the Idea of the Modern State.
New Haven: Yale University Press, 1966.

    Reviews: Rudman in BA, 40 (1966), 470; in TLS (Dcember 15,
    1966), 1172; R. J. White in NQ, 14 (August, 1967), 315-16;
    John Colmer in CRIT, 9 (Fall, 1967), 387-89; H. C. Mansfield,
    Jr. in JMH, 40 (September, 1968), 431-33.

1608   Carpenter, Maurice. The Indifferent Horseman: The Divine
Comedy of Samuel Taylor Coleridge. London: Elek Books; Toronto:
Saunders, 1954.

>   Reviews: Kathleen Raine in LM 1 (1954), 84-88; in NSN, 47
>   (June 26, 1954), 841; in TLS (July 2, 1954), 427.

1609   Cash, Arthur Hill. Stern's Comedy of Moral Sentiments.
Foreword by Herbert Read. Pittsburgh: Duquesne University Press,
1966.

1610   Chambers, Edmund K. Samuel Taylor Coleridge: A Biographical
Study. Oxford: The Claredon Press; New York: Oxford University
Press, 1938.

>   Reviews: in YWES, 19 (1938), 217-18; in N&Q, 175 (December
>   24, 1938), 466-67; E. Sackville West in Spect, 162 (January
>   20, 1939), 98-99; K. Burke in NewR, 100 (September 13, 1939),
>   163-64; J. Barryman in NATION, 148 (June 17, 1939), 705-06;
>   A. D. S. in ELH, 6 (March, 1939), 9-10; R. W. King in RES,
>   15 (July, 1939), 266-68; W. Gibson in English 2 (1939),
>   244-46; G. M. Harper in SRL, 19 (March 11, 1939), 11; R. C.
>   Bald in YR, 28 (June, 1939), 855-59; in TLS (January 7,
>   1939), 12; F. Winwar in NYTBR (February 26, 1939), 22;
>   A. D. Snyder in MLN, 55 (1940), 227-29; E. C. Batho in
>   MLR, 35 (1940), 397-99; E. L. Griggs in PQ, 19 (April,
>   1940), 217-20.

1611   Chapman, J. A. Papers on Shelley, Wordsworth and Others.
New York: Books for Libraries Press, 1967.

1612   Chevalier, Charles le. Ethique et Idealisme. Paris: J.
Vrin, 1963.

1613   Chinol, Elio. Il Pensiero di S. T. Coleridge. Venzia:
Neri Pozza, 1953.

>   Reviews: Geoffrey Bullough in YWES, 34 (1953), 257; H. M.
>   Margoliouth in RES, 5 (October, 1954), 436-37.

1614   Cobban, Alfred. Edmund Burke and the Revolt Against the
Eighteenth Century: A Study of the Political and Social Thinking of
Burke, Wordsworth, Coleridge, and Southey. New York: Barnes and
Noble, 1960.

1615   Coburn, Kathleen, ed. Coleridge: A Collection of Critical
Essays. Englewood Cliffs: Prentice-Hall, 1967.

>   Review: Rachel Lowrie in Poet & Critic, 4 (1968), 48-49.

1616 _____. Inquiring Spirit: A New Presentation of Coleridge
from His Published and Unpublished Writings. New York: Pantheon;
London: Routledge; Toronto: McClelland, 1951.

    Reviews: C. D. Thorpe in SatR (October 22, 1951), 11-12;
    Babette Deutsch in NewR (February 25, 1952), 20; I. A.
    Richards in NYTBR (January 13, 1952), 6; D. F. Mercer in
    JAAC, 11 (1952), 84-85; R. J. White in CamJ, 5 (1952),
    506-07; in CanF, 33 (1952), 190; in UTQ, 21 (1952), 297;
    in Listen, 45 (March 24, 1951), 848-49; N. Frye in HR,
    5 (1953), 603-08.

1617 _____. The Letters of Sara Hutchinson from 1800 to 1835.
London: Routledge & Kegan Paul, 1954.

    Review: K. Raine in LM, 1 (1954), 84-88.

1618 Colmer, John. Coleridge: Critic of Society. Oxford:
Clarendon Press, 1959.

    Reviews: Richard Hoggart in NSN, 59 (January 2, 1960),
    16-17; in TLS (February 12, 1960), 98; J. P. Mann in MLR,
    56 (January, 1961), 109-10; Emerson R. Marks in MLN, 76
    (March, 1961), 263-68; W. J. B. Owen in RES, 12 (February,
    1961), 93-95; F. T. Wood in ES, 42 (December, 1961), 400-01;
    Horst Oppel in ANGL, 80 (1962), 213-15.

1619 Colmer, John, ed. On the Constitution of Church and State,
The Collected Works of Samuel Taylor Coleridge, X. London: Routledge
and Kegan Paul; Princeton: Princeton University Press, 1976.

    Review: Anthony J. Harding, WC, 8 (Summer, 1977), 196-200.

1620 Cornwell, Ethel F. "The Still Point": Theme and Variations in
the Writings of T. S. Eliot, Coleridge, Henry James, Virginia Woolf,
and D. H. Lawrence. New Brunswick: Rutgers University Press, 1962.

1621 Cornwell, John. Coleridge: Poet and Revoluntary, 1772-1804.
New York: Allen Lane, 1973.

    Reviews: Amis Martin in NSta (March 23, 1973), 426-28;
    Reeve Parker in WC, 5 (Summer, 1974), 157-60.

1622 Corrigan, Beatrice, ed. Italian Poets and English Critics.
1755-1859. A Collection of Critical Essays. Chicago: University
of Chicago Press, 1969.

1623 _____. Reminiscences of Samuel Taylor Coleridge and Robert
Southey. London: Lime Tree Bower Press, 1970.

1624 Coveney, Peter. Poor Monkey: The Child in Literature. London:
Rockliff, 1957.

    Chapters on Blake, Wordsworth, and Coleridge. Reviewed
    briefly in TLS (January 10, 1958), 24.

1625   Cox, G. Stevens and Cox, J. Stevens. Samuel Taylor Coleridge
and Mary Lamb: Two Recent Discoveries. St. Peter Port, Guernsey:
Toucan Press, 1971.

    Review: Robert Osborn in N&Q, 19 (March, 1972), 82.

1626   Crawford, Walter B. and Odens, Richard S., ed. A Portfolio
of Twenty Drawings Commemorating the Bicentenary of the Birth of
Coleridge. Long Beach: Foundation of the California S. U. 1972.

    Review: Karl Kroeber, WC (Summer, 1973), 173.

1627   Daiches, David. Critical Approaches to Literature. Englewood
Cliffs: Prentice Hall, 1955.

1628   Davies, Hugh Sykes and Watson, George, ed. The English Mind:
Studies in the English Moralists Presented to Basil Willey. Ithaca,
N.Y.: Cornell University Press, 1964.

1630   Deford, Miriam Allen. Thomas Moore. New York: Twayne Publishers,
1967.

1631   Deschamps, Paul. La Formation de la Pensie de Coleridge.
Paris: Didier, 1964.

    Reviews: G. A. Cevesco in BA, 39 (1965), 305; George Cerdt
    in ANGL, 83 (1965), 246-48; in TLS (January 14, 1965), 28;
    James D. Boulger in MP, 63 (May, 1966), 364-67; R. Kerf in
    RLV, 32 (1966), 107-08; M. D. E. de Leve in NEOPHIL, 50 (1966),
    206; S. Vauthier in Bulletin de la Faculte des Lettres de
    Strasbourg, 45 (December, 1966), 332-35; John Colmer in MLR,
    62 (July, 1967), 514-15; G. N. G. Orsini in CRIT, 9 (Fall,
    1967), 383-87.

1632   Deutsch, Babette. Poems of Samuel Taylor Coleridge. New
York: Crowell, 1967.

1633   Dunklin, Gilbert T., ed. Wordsworth Centenary Studies Presented
at Cornell and Princeton Universities. Hamden, Conn.: Shoe String
Press, 1963.

1634   Duffy, John J., ed. Coleridge's American Disciples: The Selected
Correspondence of James Marsh. Amherst: University of Massachusetts
Press, 1973.

    Reviews: Lewis Leary in NEQ, 47 (1974), 620-23; David R.
    Sanderson in WC, 7 (Summer, 1976), 237-38.

1635   Eliot, T. S. On Poetry and Poets. New York: Farrar, Straus,
& Cudahy, 1957.

1636   Ellis, Amanda M. Rebels and Conservatives. Bloomington:
Indiana University Press, 1967.

1637 Elwin, Malcolm. The First Romantics. New York: Longmans,
Green, 1948; New York: Russell & Russell, 1967 (Reprint).

1638 Emden, Cecil S. "Samuel Taylor Coleridge: Unstable Genius."
(In Cecil S. Emdens. Poets in Their Letters. London: Oxford
University Press, 1959), 98-120.

1639 Enscoe, Gerald E. Eros and the Romantics: Sexual Love As a
Theme in Coleridge, Shelley, and Keats: Studies in English Literature.
The Hague: Mouton, 1967.

      Review: John Colmer in YES (1965), 300-01.

1640 Fields, Beverly. Reality's Dark Dream: Dejection in Coleridge.
Kent, Ohio: Kent State University Press, 1967.

      Reviews: in TLS (August 29, 1968), 914; J. B. Beer in RES,
      20 (August, 1969), 358-61; Robin Wells in N&Q, 17 (May,
      1970), 191-93; H. B. DeGroot in ES, 53 (October, 1972),
      466-69; Lawrence Lerner in EIC, 20 (January, 1970), 89-98.

1641 Foakes, R. A., ed. Coleridge on Shakespeare: The Text of the
Lectures of 1812. Folger Monographs on Tudor and Stuart Civ. 3.
Charlottesville: University Press of Virginia, 1971.

      Review: J. K. Walton in N&Q, 20 m.s. (1973), 156-57.

1642 Fogle, Richard H. The Idea of Coleridge's Criticism.
Perspectives in Criticism, 9. Berkeley and Los Angeles: University
of California Press; London: Cambridge University Press, 1962.

      Reviews: in TLS (December 21, 1962), 990; John Colmer
      in MLR, 58 (July, 1963), 464-65; George Watson in EIC,
      12 (October, 1962), 424-26; Charles R. Sanders in SAQ,
      (Spring, 1963), 313-14; W. J. B. Owen in RES, 15 (February,
      1964), 99-100; K. C. Brown in BJA, 4 (1974), 82.

1643 _____ . The Permanent Pleasure: Essays on Classics of
Romanticisim. Athens: University of Georgia Press, 1974.

      Four chapters devoted to Samuel Taylor Coleridge.

      Reviews: W. Paul Elledge in WC, 6 (Summer, 1975), 173-76;
      John Colmer in YES, 7 (1977), 271-72.

1644 Fruman, Norman. Coleridge: The Damaged Archangel. New York:
G. Braziller, 1971; London: Allen and Unwin, 1972.

> Reviews: Paul West in BW, 5 (December 26, 1971), 4;
> in TLS (December 1, 1972), 1463; Owen Barfield in NATION,
> 214 (June 12, 1972), 764-65; G. A. Cevasco in DR, 52 (Spring
> 1972), 143-46; G. A. Cevasco in SIR, 11 (Spring 1972), 158-
> 61; R. H. Fogle in VQR, 48 (Summer 1972), 477-80; L. C.
> Knights in NYRB, 18 (May 4, 1972), 25-26; Hugh Ormsby-Lennon
> in ASch, 41 (Summer 1972), 468-72; Anthony West in NSta,
> (October 20, 1972), 566-67; Christopher Ricks in SaTR, 55
> (January 15, 1972), 31-33, 49; Geoffrey Hartman in NYTBR
> (March 12, 1972), 1, 36; Gabriel Fielding in THE CRITIC,
> 30 (1972), 83-85; Philip C. Rule in AMERICA, 126 (March 25,
> 1972), 323; J. B. Beer in RES, 24 (1973), 346-53; Angus
> Fletcher in CRIT, 15 (1973), 265-75; Basil Cottle in EIC,
> 23 (October, 1973), 413-19; Paul Magnuson in WC, 4 (Summer
> 1973), 175-77; Thomas McFarland in YR, 63 (December, 1973),
> 252-86; Max F. Schulz in MP, 71 (1974), 453-55; Joan T. Knapp
> in ELN, 12 (September, 1974), 46-49; Foakes, R. A. in EIC,
> 24 (October, 1974), 423-27; George Whalley in QQ, 81 (1974),
> 265-77; John Colmer in YES, 4 (1974), 312-14.

1645 Gerard, Albert S. English Romantic Poetry: Ethos, Structure,
and Symbol in Coleridge, Wordsworth, Shelley, and Keats. Berkeley:
University of California Press, 1968.

> Reviews: Eileen Z. Cohen in RBPH 47 (1972), 999-1000;
> Kare Kroeber, in CLS 7 (1972), 117-19.

1646 Gilpin, George H. The Strategy of Joy: An Essay on the Poetry
of Samuel Taylor Coleridge. (ReRt. 3.) Salzburg: Dr. James Hogg.
Inst. für Englische Sprache und Literatur. University of Salzburg
(1972), A-5020.

> Reviews: Anya Taylor, WC, 5 (Summer 1974), 191-94; John
> Colmer in YES, 5 (1975), 301-02.

1647 Gittings, Robert, ed. Omniana; or Horae Otiosiores; By
Robert Southey and S. T. Coleridge. Slough Buckinghamshire: Centaur,
1969; Carbondale: Southern Illinois University Press, 1970.

> Contains the Southey portion, plus Coleridge's contributions,
> including the additions of 1836 and 1884 to the 1812 volume,
> plus several censored portions.

> Reviews: in TLS (May 8, 1969), 496; Jean Raimond in
> EA, 23 (Avril-Juin, 1970), 227-29.

1648 Godwin, William. Uncollected Writings (1785-1822); Articles
in Periodicals and Six Pamphlets, One with Coleridge's Marginalia.
Facsimile Reproductions with Introductions by Jack W. Marken and
Burton R. Pollin. Gainesville, Florida: Scholars' Facsimiles and
Reprints (1968).

> Review: in TLS (March 20, 1969), 290.

1649 Gokak, Vinayak Krishna. <u>Coleridge's Aesthetics</u>. Atlantic
Highlands, New Jersey: Humanities Press, 1975.

1650 Gottfried, Leon A. <u>Arnold and the Romantics</u>. London:
Routledge & Kegan Paul, 1963.

1651 Grant, Allan. <u>A Preface to Coleridge</u>. London: Longman;
New York: Scribner's, 1972.

1652 Griggs, Earl Leslie, ed. <u>Coleridge Fille</u>: <u>A Biography of Sara</u>
<u>Coleridge</u>. Oxford: Clarendon Press, 1940.

    Although about Coleridge's daughter, the book gives a vivid
    picture of the poet's troubled domestic life.

1653 _____. <u>Wordsworth and Coleridge</u>: <u>Studies in Honor of</u>
<u>George McLean Harper</u>. Princeton: Princeton University Press,
1939; New York: Russell, 1962.

    Reviews: R. W. King in RES, 16 (April, 1940), 239-42; R. C.
    Blad in MLN, 55 (June, 1940), 466-69; E. C. Bathos in MLR
    35 (June, 1940), 397-99; A. Cowie in SRL, 20 (July 8, 1939),
    16-17.

1654 Haney, John Louis. <u>The German Influence on Samuel Taylor</u>
<u>Coleridge</u>. New York: Haskell House Publishers, Ltd., 1975.

1655 Hanson, Lawrence. <u>The Life of S. T. Coleridge</u>: <u>The Early Years</u>.
New York: Oxford University Press. London: Allen and Unwin, 1938;
New York: Russell & Russell, 1962.

    Reviews: L. Wolff, in EA, 3 (1939), 270-71; P. Hutchinson
    in NYBTR (June 25, 1939), 2, 16; A. Cowie in SRL,20 (July
    8, 1939), 16-17; E. Sackville West in Spect. 162 (January
    20, 1939), 98-99; J. J. R. in CW, 15 (October, 1939), 116-17;
    K. Burke in NewR, 100 (September 13, 1939), 163-64; in
    NATION, 149 (October 21, 1939), 448; R. C. Bald in MLN, 55
    (1940), 466-69; E. L. Griggs in PQ, 19 (1940), 217-20; C. D.
    Thorpe in CE, 1 (1940), 714-16; E. L. Griggs in YR 29 (1940),
    835-37.

1656 Harding, Anthony John. <u>Coleridge and the Idea of Love</u>: <u>Aspects</u>
<u>of Relationship in Coleridge's Thought and Writing</u>. London: Cambridge
University Press, 1974.

    Reviews: Robert Sternback in SIR, 15 (1976), 150-57;
    Frederick L. Beaty in WC, 7 (Summer 1976), 233-36.

1657 Hart, H. St. J. <u>Confessions of an Inquiring Spirit</u>. With
an introductory note. London: A&C Black, 1956; Palo Alto, California:
Stanford University Press, 1957.

    Ed. from 3rd. ed. of 1853.

    Review: M. Fisch in JEGP, 57 (April, 1958), 347-48.

1658 Hartley, David. Observations on Man (1794). Facsimile reproduction with an introduction by Theodore L. Huguelet. Gainesville, Florida: Scholars' Facsimiles & Reprints, 1966.

1659 Hartman, Geoffrey H. ed. New Perspectives on Coleridge and Wordsworth: Selected Papers from the English Institute. New York: Columbia University Press, 1972.

1660 Haven, Richard. Patterns of Consciousness: An Essay on Coleridge. Amherst: University of Massachusetts Press, 1969.

> Reviews: Thomas McFarland in YR, 59 (Spring, 1970), 444-46; David Ferry in Mass. Rev. 11 (Autumn, 1970), 837-40; J. A. Appleyard in MLQ, 32 (June, 1971), 206-13; Max F. Schulz in MP, 69 (November, 1971), 142-51.

1661 Haven, Richard and Josephine and Maurianne Adams. Samuel Taylor Coleridge: An Annotated Bibliography of Criticism and Scholarship. Vol. I. 1793-1899. Boston: G. K. Hall, 1976.

> Review: Philip C. Rule, S. J. in WC, 8 (Summer, 1977), 205-06.

1662 Hawkes, Terence, ed. Coleridge's Writings on Shakespeare: A Selection of the Essays, Notes, and Lectures of Samuel Taylor Coleridge on the Poems and Plays of Shakespeare. New York: Capricorn Books, 1959.

> Reviews: M. R. A. de Silva Pinto in SQ, 13 (Autumn, 1962), 577-78; T. J. B. Spencer in MLR, 55 (October, 1960), 626; R. C. Bald in NYHTBR, 35 (July 26, 1959), 10.

1663 Hayter, Alethea. Opium and the Romantic Imagination. London: Faber & Faber, 1968.

> Review: in TLS (November 28, 1968), 1343.

1664 _____. A Voyage in Vain: Coleridge's Journey to Malta in 1804. London: Faber & Faber, 1973.

> Review: William Heath, WC, 5 (Summer, 1974), 161-64.

1665 Heath, William. Wordsworth and Coleridge: A Study of Their Literary Relations in 1801-1802. Oxford: Claredon, 1970.

> Reviews: Craig Raine in N&Q, 20 (February, 1973), 69-70; in TLS (April 16, 1971), 453.

1666 Hemphill, George, ed. Discussions of Poetry: Rhythm and Sound. Boston: D. C. Heath, 1961.

1667 Henley, Elton F. and David H. Stamm, ed. Wordsworthian Criticism, 1945-1964: An Annotated Bibliography. New York: New York Public Library, 1965.

> Contains notices of relevant works of Coleridge.

1668 Hodgart, Patricia and Redpath, Theodore, ed. Romantic
Perspectives: The Work of Crabbe, Blake, Wordsworth, and Coleridge
as Seen by Their Contemporaries and by Themselves. New York: Barnes
& Noble: London: Harrap, 1964.

1669 Hough, Graham. "Wordsworth and Coleridge." (In Graham Hough.
The Romantic Poets. Basil Willey, editor. 2d ed. New York: W. W.
Norton), 25-95.

        Review: in Listener, 49, 731.

1670 House, Humphry. Coleridge. London: Rupert-Hart-Davis,
1953. (The Clark Lectures 1951-52).

        Reviews: R. Murphy in Spect. (July 31, 1953), 133-34; in
        TLS (April 10, 1953), 238; Herbert Read in Listen, 49 (March
        26, 1953), 537; D. F. Mercer in JAAC, 13 (1954), 118; Geoffrey
        Bullough in YWES, 34 (1953), 526; in QQ, 60 (1953), 282-83;
        A. Koszul in EA, 7 (1954), 426-27; E. D. H. Johnson in YR,
        43 (December, 1953), 298-301.

1671 Houtchens, Carolyn Washburn, and Houtchens, Laurence Huston.
The English Romantic Poets and Essayists. Revised ed. New York:
New York University Press, 1966.

1672 Jackson, James R. DE J. ed. Coleridge: The Critical Heritage.
London: Routledge and K. Paul; New York: Barnes & Noble, 1970.

        Reviews: Craig Raine in N&Q, 19 (March, 1972), 118-10;
        John Colmer in YES, 2 (1972), 296-98.

1673 _____. Method and Imagination in Coleridge's Criticism.
Cambridge: Harvard University Press; London: Routledge and K. Paul,
1969.

        Reviews: in TLS (March 13, 1969), 259; I. A. Richards in
        UTQ, 40 (Fall, 1970), 102-03; Thomas McFarland ELN, 8 (March,
        1971), 231-34; Max F. Schulze in MP, 60 (November, 1971),
        142-51; Laurence Lerner in EIC, 20 (January, 1970), 89-98.

1674 Jackson, Wallace. Immediacy: The Development of a Critical
Concept from Addison to Coleridge. Amsterdam: Duropi N. V., 1973.

        Review: Roger Lonsdale in N&Q, 22 (January, 1975), 36.

1675 Jordan, Frank, Jr. The English Romantic Poets: A Review of
Research and Criticism. 3d Revised ed. New York: Modern Language
Association of America, 1972.

        Review: R. H. Fogle, WC, 4 (Summer, 1973), 183-84.

1676 Kato, Ryntaro. Coleridge's Literary Criticism. Tokyo:
Kenkyusha, 1971.

1677 Kennedy, Wilma L. The English Heritage of Coleridge of Bristol, 1798: The Basis in Eighteenth Century Imagination and Fancy. New Haven: Yale University Press, 1947; Hamden: Archon, 1969.

     Reviews: in TLS (August 30, 1947), 443; in TLS (September 13, 1947), 460; W. J. Bate in MLN, 62 (December, 1947), 564-66; Barbara Hardy in MLR, 43 (April, 1948), 264-65; R. L. Brett in RES, 24 (October, 1948), 335-36; E. R. Wasserman in JEGP, 47 (1948), 204-07.

1678 Kennedy, William F. Humanist Versus Economist: The Economic Thought of Samuel Taylor Coleridge. Berkeley: University of California Press; London: Cambridge University Press, 1958.

     Review: John Colmer in MLR, 54 (April, 1959), 299.

1679 Kermode, Frank. Romantic Image. New York: MacMillan, 1957.

1680 Knight, G. Wilson. The Starlit Dome: Studies in the Poetry of Vision. London: Oxford University Press, 1941; New York: Barnes & Noble, 1960.

     Essays on Wordsworth, Coleridge, Shelley, and Keats.

1681 Knights, L. C. Metaphor and Symbol: Proceedings of the Twelfth Symposium of the Coston Research Study. Woburn, Mass.: Butterworth, 1960.

1682 _____. Further Explorations. London: Chatto & Sindus; Stanford University Press, 1965.

1683 Kroeber, Karl. Romantic Narrative Art. Madison: University of Wisconsin Press, 1960.

     Christabel, Kubla Khan, and The Rime of the Ancient Mariner.

1684 Lawrence, Berta. Coleridge and Wordsworth in Somerset. Newton Abbot, Devonshire: David and Charles, 1970.

1685 Leavis, Frank Raymond. Scrutiny: A Selection from Scrutiny. 2 vols, London: Cambridge University Press, 1968.

1686 Leech, Clifford, ed. Shakespeare--The Tragedies: A Collection of Critical Essays. Chicago: Chicago University Press, 1965.

1687 Lefebure, Molly. Samuel Taylor Coleridge: A Bondage of Opium. London: Stein and Day, 1974.

     Reviews: H. O. Dendurent in WC, 6 (Summer 1975), 155-58; Norman Fruman in QQ, 82 (August, 1975), 440-44.

1688 Lutri, Corrado. Poemetti e Liriche. Florence: G. C. Sanson, 1953.

     Review: Terence Spencer in MLR, 49 (October, 1954), 541-42.

1689 McFarland, Thomas. Coleridge and the Pantheist Tradition.
Oxford: Clarendon Press, 1969.

Reviews: H. W. Piper in AUMLA, 34 (1970), 325–26; René
Wellek in CL, 22 (Summer 1970), 282–86; J. Robert Barth in
CRIT, 12 (Fall 1970), 353–55; J. A. Appleyard in MLQ, 32
(June 1971), 206–13; John Beer in ELN, 9 (September, 1971),
66–69; John Colmer in YES, 1 (1971), 287–88; Max F. Schulz
in MP, 69 (November, 1971), 142–51; Stephen Prickett in
N&Q, 19 (March, 1972), 116–18.

1690 McKenzie, Gordon. Organic Unity in Coleridge. Berkeley:
University of California Press, 1939.

Review: A. D. Snyder in MLN, 55 (March, 1940), 227–29.

1691 McLuhan, Herbert E. The Major English Romantic Poets,
ed. by Clarence D. Thorpe, et al. Carbondale: Southern Illinois
University Press, 1957.

1692 MacNeice, Louis. Varieties of Parable. London: Cambridge
University Press, 1965.

1693 Magnuson, Paul. Coleridge's Nightmare Poetry. Charlottesville:
University Press of Virginia, 1974.

Reviews: Richard Haven, WC, 6 (Summer, 1975), 159–61; Robert
Sternbach in SIR, 15 (1976), 150–57; John Beer in MLR,
71 (1976), 895–97.

1694 Marcel, Gabriel. Coleridge et Schelling. Paris: Editions
Aubier-Montaigne, 1971.

1695 Margoliouth, Herschel Maurice. Wordsworth and Coleridge, 1795–1834.
London: Oxford University Press, 1953.

Reviews: in TLS (April 10, 1953), 238; Geoffrey Bullough in
YWES, 34 (1953), 255; Helen Darbshire in RES, 5 (1954),
310–11; in N&Q, 198 (1954), 411; in CanF, 33 (1954), 140–41.

1696 Marples, Morris. Romantics at School. London: Faber; New
York: Barnes & Noble, 1967, 48–75.

1697 Mill, John Stuart. Mill on Bentham and Coleridge. London
Chatto, & Windus, 1950; New York: Harper & Row, 1950.

1698 Moorman, Mary. William Wordsworth: A Biography: The Later
Years, 1803–1850. London: Oxford University Press, 1965, passim.

1699 Murray, Roger N. Wordsworth Style. Lincoln: University of
Nebraska Press, 1967.

1700 Noyes, Russell. William Wordsworth. New York: Twayne, 1971.

1701   Ober, Warren U. et al, ed. Young Coleridge: Selected Source
Materials for College Research Papers. Boston: Heath, 1963.

1702   Okamoto, Masao. Coleridge: An Assessment and Study. Kyoto:
Apollon-sha, 1965.

1703   Oppel, Hurst. The Sacred River. Frankfurt: Moritz
Diesterweg, 1959.

1704   Orsini, G. N. G. Coleridge and German Idealism: A Study
in the History of Philosophy with Unpublished Materials from
Coleridge's Manuscripts. Carbondale: Southern Illinois University
Press, 1969.

        Reviews: James D. Boulger in JEGP, 69 (1970), 533-38; Rene
        Wellek in Cl, 22 (Summer 1970), 279-82; Richard Haven in
        CLS, 8 (1971), 93-94.

1705   Owen, W. J. B. Wordsworth as Critic. Toronto: University
of Toronto Press, 1969.

1706   Parker, Reeve. Coleridge's Meditative Art. Ithaca:
Cornell University Press, 1975.

        Reviews: J. D. Gutteridge in N&Q, 24 (1977), 377-78;
        Paul D. Skeats in WC, 7 (Summer 1976), 231-32; Robert
        Sternbach, in SIR, 15 (1976), 150-57.

1707   Payne, William Morton. "Samuel Taylor Coleridge." (In
William Morton Payne. The Greater English Poets of the Nineteenth
Century. New York: Books for Libraries, 1967) 96-127.

1708   Potter, Stephen. Coleridge and S. T. C. New York: Peter
Smith; London, J. Cape, 1935; New York: Russell & Russell, 1965.

        Reviews: in YWES, 16 (1935), 319-21; in TLS (June 6, 1935),
        361; E. Blunden in Spect. 154 (March 3, 1935), 742; R. G.
        Cox in Scrut. 4 (September, 1935), 205-07; M. Roberts in
        Merc. 32 (July, 1935), 292-93; G. West in YR, 25 (June,
        1936), 850-52.

1709   Praz, Mario, ed. La ballata del vacchio marinaro. ('Il
Melagrano' scritti rari e rappresentative di poesie e di pensiero
in versioni d'arte con testo a fronte, N. 13.), Firenze: Fussi
Editore, 1947.

1710   Preyer, Robert. Bentham, Coleridge, and the Science of
History. (BEP41, Heft.), Bochum-Langendreer: Verlag H. Poppinhaus,
1958.

        Review: N. Brooke in N&Q, 7 (March, 1960), 117-19.

1711 Prickett, Stephen. <u>Coleridge and Wordsworth: The Poetry</u>
<u>of Growth</u>. London: Cambridge University Press, 1970.

    Reviews: Craig Raine in DUJ, 63 (1970), 75-77; in TLS
(October 2, 1970), 1129; W. J. B. Owen in MOSAIC, 4 (1971),
111-17; Jack Stillinger in JEGP, 70 (1971), 169-70; Carl
Woodring in MP, 69 (May, 1962), 356-58; H. W. Piper in
SouthR, 5 (June, 1972), 169-71; R. Headlam Wells in N&Q,
20 (February, 1963), 71-72.

1712 _____. <u>Romanticism and Religion: The Tradition of</u>
<u>Coleridge and Wordsworth in the Victorian Church</u>. London:
Cambridge University Press, 1976.

    Review: J. Robert Barth in WC, 8 (Summer 1977), 201-04.

1713 Pritchard, John Paul. <u>Literary Wise Men of Gotham: Criticism</u>
<u>in New York: 1815-1860</u>. Louisiana State University Press, 1963,
<u>passim</u>.

1714 Radley, Virginia L. <u>Samuel Taylor Coleridge</u> Twayne's
English Author Series 36. New York: Twayne Publishers, 1966.

1715 Raine, Kathleen. <u>Coleridge</u>. London: Longman's, 1953.

1716 Read, Herbert. <u>The True Voice of Feelings: Studies in</u>
<u>English Romantic Poetry</u>. London: Faber, 1953.

    Review: E. D. H. Johnson, in YR, (December, 1953), 298-301.

1717 Reardon, B. M. G. <u>From Coleridge to Gore: A Century of</u>
<u>Religious Thought in Britain</u>. London: Longman, 1971.

    Review: Richard A. Soloway in VS, 16 (1972), 104-06.

1718 _____. <u>Religious Thought in the Nineteenth Century</u>
<u>Illustrated from Writers of the Period</u>. London: Cambridge University
Press, 1966.

1719 Reeves, James, ed. <u>Selected Poems of S. T. C., with an</u>
<u>Introduction and Notes</u>. The Poetry Bookshelf. London: Heineman;
New York: Macmillan, 1959.

    Review: in TLS (March 20, 1959), 162.

1720 Reiman, Donald H., ed. <u>The Romantic Poets Reviewed</u>:
<u>Contemporary Reviews of British Romantic Writers</u>. New York
and London: Garland Publishing, 1972.

    Reviews: in TLS (March 30, 1973), 358; Peter F. Morgan in
JEGP, 73 (January, 1974), 129-30.

1721 Richards, Ivor Armstrong. <u>Coleridge on Imagination</u>. Comments
by Kathleen Coburn. New York: W. W. Norton, 1950.

1722 _____. Coleridge on Imagination. New York: Harcourt;
London: Routledge, 1935; Bloomington: Indiana University Press,
1960. Third Edition, with new foreword. London: Routledge and
K. Paul, 1955.

> Reviews: K. John in NSta, 8 (December 29, 1935), 973;
> A. D. Snyder in SRL, 11 (April 20, 1935), 636; R. P. Blackmur
> in NATION, 140 (April 10, 1935), 423-24; C. Brooks, Jr. in
> NR, 85 (November 13, 1935), 26-27; E. L. Walton in NYTBR
> (March 3, 1935), 2; K. Burk in POETRY, 47 (October, 1935),
> 52-54; M. Roberts in Spect. 154 (January 4, 1935), 23-24;
> F. R. Leavis in Scrut, 3 (March, 1935), 382-402; W. Empson
> in Scrut, 4 (June, 1935), 65-67; R. A. Scott-James in Merc,
> 31 (February, 1935), 385-86; R. W. King in MLR, 31 (1936),
> 88-89; C. C. Barnard in E Studien, 71 (1937), 271-73; E. Hunt
> in SR, 44 (January-March, 1936), 103-07; G. West in YR,
> 25 (June, 1936), 850-52; D. J. Hughes in VOICES, 174
> (1961), 54-56.

1723 Roston, Murray. Prophet and Poet: The Bible and the Growth
of Romanticism. London: Faber, 1965.

1724 Rhys, Ernest, ed. The Golden Book of Coleridge. London:
Dent; New York: Dutton, 1945.

1725 Royds, Kathleen E. Coleridge and His Poetry. London:
Harrap, 1971.

1726 Sanders, Charles R. Coleridge and the Broad Church Movement.
Studies in S. T. Coleridge, Dr. Arnold of Rugby, J. C. Hare, Thomas
Carlyle, and F. D. Maurice. Durham: Duke University Press,
1942; London: Cambridge University Press, 1943.

> Reviews: in TLS (January 23, 1943), 42; Richard Brooks in
> MLN, 58 (December, 1943), 646-47; Joseph E. Baker in PQ,
> 22 (1943), 285-86; Charles F. Harrold in JEGP, 43 (1944),
> 137-39.

1727 Schulz, Max F. The Poetic Voices of Coleridge: A Study
of His Desire for Spontaneity and Passion for Order. Detroit:
Wayne State University Press, 1963.

> Reviews: in MLR, 59 (April, 1964), 279-80; Karl Kroeber
> in WHR, 18 (Summer 1964), 278-79; P. M. Zall in ELN, 1
> (March, 1964), 230-33; H. B. de Groot in ES, 45 (1964),
> 482-85; George Whalley in QQ, 71 (1964), 444; in TLS
> (January 30, 1964), 88; W. J. B. Owen in RES, 16 (February,
> 1965), 86-88; George Whalley in SAQ, 64 (Winter 1965),
> 147-49; Wilfred S. Dowden in MP, 62 (1965), 270-72; R. S.
> Woof in N&Q, 12 (1965), 474-76.

1728   Sherwood, Margaret. Coleridge's Imaginative Conception of the Imagination. Wellesley, Mass.: Wellesley Press, 1937.

   Review: in YWES, 19 (1938), 218.

   I. Certain aspects of Coleridge's philosophy of the imagination; II. Coleridge's application of this philosophy in his pleas for a philosophic criticism; III. Notes and bibliography.

1729   Spacks, Patricia M. The Insistence of Horror: Aspects of the Supernatural in Eighteenth-Century Poetry. Cambridge: Harvard University Press, 1962.

1730   Strange, G. Robert, ed. Coleridge. New York: Dell, 1959.

1731   Stevenson, Warren. Divine Analogy: Study of the Creation Motif in Blake and Coleridge. (ReRT 25), Salzburg: Dr. James Hogg, Inst. fur Englische Sprache und Literatur, University of Salzburg, 1972, A-5020.

   Reviews: Anya Taylor in WC, 5 (Summer, 1974), 191-94; Penelope Wilson in YES, 5 (1975), 293-99.

1732   Sultana, David. Samuel Taylor Coleridge in Malta and Italy. New York: Barnes and Noble; Oxford: Blackwell, 1969.

   Reviews: in TLS (June 26, 1969), 713; Thomas McFarland in YR, 59 (Spring, 1970), 441-43; John Duffy in MLJ, 55 (February, 1971), 108-09; George Whalley in MLQ, 32 (March, 1971), 115-19; R. S. Woof in N&Q, 18 (May, 1971), 196-98.

1733   Thorpe, Clarence D., Baker, Carlos, and Weaver, Bennett, eds. "Coleridge." (In Clarence D. Thorpe, et al, eds. The Major English Romantic Poets: A Symposium in Reappraisal. Carbondale: Southern Illinois University Press, 1957), 83-125.

1734   Wain, John, ed. "Coleridge." (In John Wain, ed. Contemporary Reviews of Romantic Poetry. London: Harrap; New York: Barnes & Noble, 1953), 86-113.

1735   Walsh, William. Coleridge: The Work and the Relevance. New York: Barnes and Noble; London: Chatto and Windus, 1967.

   Reviews: Basil Willey in CritQ, 9 (1967), 287-88; Michael Moran in RES, 19 (November, 1968), 444-46; Lore Metzger in MLQ, 30 (March, 1969), 121-31.

1736   _____. The Use of Imagination: Educational Thought and the Literary Mind. London: Chatto and Windus, 1964, 11-29, 52-67, 68-85.

1737   Warner, Francis, ed. Studies in the Arts: Proceedings of the St. Peter's College Library Society. London: Blackwell, 1968.

   Edmund Blunden gives interesting sketches on a remarkable number of relations of S. T. C. who achieved some measure of success or renown.

1738 Watson, George. Coleridge: The Poet. New York: Barnes
and Noble; London: Routledge and K. Paul, 1966.

> Reviews: C. B. Cox in Spect, 217 (October 14, 1966), 487;
> R. L. Brett in CritQ, 9 (1967), 188-89; C. G. Martin in
> RES, 20 (February, 1969), 104-06.

1739 _____ . The Literary Critics: A Study of English Descriptive
Criticism. Totowa: Rowman & Littlefield, 1973, 102-21.

1740 Watters, Reginald. Coleridge. London: Evans, 1971.

> Review: Stephen Gill in N&Q, 219 (June, 1974), 232.

1741 Whalley, George. Coleridge and Sara Hutchinson and the
Asra Poems. Toronto: University of Toronto Press, 1955.

> Reviews: in TLS (May 6, 1955), 238; Kathleen Raine in NSN,
> 49 (May 21, 1955), 726-27; in Listen, 83 (May 26, 1955),
> 947-49; E. Schneider in MP, 54 (August, 1956), 69-70;
> H. M. Margoliouth in RES, 7 (July, 1956), 321-23; Sister
> Maura in DR, 24 (Winter 1956), 393-95; E. E. Bostetter in
> MLQ, 17 (June, 1956), 171-72; F. Priestly in UTQ, 25 (April,
> 1956), 339-40; M. H. Abrams in MLN, 72 (January, 1957),
> 56-60.

1742 _____ . Coleridge Marginalia Lost. London: The Book
Collector, 1968.

1743 _____ . Poetic Process. London: Routledge and K. Paul,
1953.

1744 Willey, Basil. Coleridge on Imagination and Fancy. British
Academy. Warton Lecture on English Poetry. New York: Oxford University
Press, 1946.
> Reviews: in TLS, (November 9, 1946), 555; in N&Q, 192
> (1947), 21-22; in YWES, 27 (1946), 219-20.

1745 _____ . The English Moralists. London, Methuen, 1965.

1746 _____ . Samuel Taylor Coleridge. London: Chatto & Windus;
New York: Norton, 1972.

> Reviews: Graham Martin in Spect. (March 4, 1972), 258-59;
> Geoffrey Grigson in NSta (March 17, 1972), 359-60; in TLS
> (March 31, 1972), 354; Stephen Pricket in WC, 4 (Summer 1973),
> 174; W. J. B. Owen in RES, 2 (May, 1973), 222-25.

1747 Wilson, Raymonrd, ed. A Coleridge Selection. London:
Macmillan; New York: St. Martins Press, 1963.

1748 Wimsatt, William K. Jr., and Brooks, Cleanth. Literary
Criticism: A Short History. London: Routledge and K. Paul, 1957.

1749 Winwar, Frances. Farewell the Banner... Three Persons and
One Soul.: Coleridge, Wordsworth, and Dorothy. New York: Doubleday,
1938.

     Reviews: P. Hutchinson in NYTBR (September 25, 1938), 5, 18;
     G. M. Harper in SRL, 18 (October 1, 1938), 10; G. M. Harper
     in SRL, 18 (October 15, 1938), 13, 38; C. Donahue in Com,
     29 (November 18, 1938), 108; L. B. Salomon in NATION, 148
     (December 31, 1938), 18; in TLS (February 18, 1939), 108;
     S. Harrison in SR, 47 (January-March, 1939), 133-36; G. H. C.
     in QQ, 47 (1940), 94-95.

1750 Wise, Thomas James. Two Lake Poets: A Catalogue of Printed
Books, etc. by William Wordsworth and Samuel Taylor Coleridge.
London: Dawsons, 1965. (Facsim. ed.)

1751 Woodring, Carl R. Politics in the Poetry of Coleridge.
Madison: University of Wisconsin Press, 1961.

     Reviews: in TLS (December 29, 1961), 930; R. A. Gettman in
     JEGP, 61 (April, 1962), 428-29; G. Wills in NR, (July 31,
     1962), 74; Lewis Patton in SAQ, 61 (Summer 1962), 428-29;
     John Colmer in MLR, 57 (Ocotber, 1962), 631; L. Werkmeister
     in Person, 43 (Autumn 1961), 567; W. J. B. Owen in RES,
     13 (November, 1962), 419-21; Derek Roper in N&Q, 10 (May,
     1963) 198-99; R. E. Morsberger in BA, 37 (1963), 79; Max
     F. Schulz in CRIT, 5 (Winter 1963), 88-91; Karl H. Göller
     in ARCHIV, 202 (1965), 66-67.

1752 Wormhoudt, Arthur. The Demon Lover: A Psychoanalytical
Approach to Literature. New York: Exposition Press, 1949, 17-50.

1753 Yarlott, Geoffrey. Coleridge and the Abyssinian Maid. London:
Methuen; New York: Barnes and Noble, 1967.

     Reviews: Basil Willey in CritQ, 9 (1967), 287-88; C. B.
     Cox in Spect, 218 (June 30, 1967), 770-71; W. J. B. Owen
     in RES, 19 (May, 1968), 218-20; Lore Metzger in MLQ, 30
     (March, 1969), 121-31.

Biography

1754 Armour, R. W. and Howes, R. F. "Addenda to Coleridge the Talker." QJS, 32 (October, 1946), 298-303.

1755 Ashbrook, J. "Coleridge's Star Within the Moon." ST, 28 (December, 1964), 335.

1756 Bandy, W. T. "Coleridge's Friend Joseph Hardman: A Bibliographical Note." JEGP, 47 (October, 1948), 395-97.

1757 Barfield, Owen. What Coleridge Thought. Middletown, CT: Wesleyan University Press, 1971.

1758 Bate, Walter Jackson. Coleridge. Masters of World Literature. Macmillan (1968).

1759 Beaty, F.L. "Dorothy Wordsworth and the Coleridges: a New Letter." MLR, 51 (July, 1956), 411-13.

1760 Beer, John Bernard. Coleridge the Visionary. New York: Macmillan, 1959.

1761 _____. Coleridge's Poetic Intelligence. New York: Macmillan, 1977, 318.

1762 Benet, Laura. Coleridge, Poet of Wild Enchantment. New York: Dodd Mead, 1952.

1763 Bottrall, Margaret Florence Saumarez (Smith), ed. Personal Records. London: Hart-Davis, (1961), 24-25, 220.

1764 Beyer, W. W. Coleridge's Early Knowledge of German. MP, 52 (February, 1955), 192-200.

1765 Blunden, Edmund, and Griggs, Earl Leslie, eds. Coleridge:
Studies by Several Hands on the Hundredth Anniversary of His Death.
New York: Russell & Russell, 1970.

1766 Brett, Raymond Laurence, ed. S. T. Coleridge. Writers and
their background. London: Bell, 1971.

1767 Brinkley, R. F. "Coleridge Transcribed." RES, 24 (July,
1948), 219-26.

1768 Burke, C. "Riddle of the Rider." Coronet, 33 (March, 1953),
150, et passim.

1769 Byatt, Antonia Susan. Wordsworth and Coleridge in Their Time.
New York: Cran, Russak, 1973.

1770 Caine, Sir Hall. Life of Samuel Taylor Coleridge. Port
Washington, N.Y.: 1972.

1771 Campbell, James Dykes. Samuel Taylor Coleridge: A Narrative
of the Events of His Life. London: Lime Tree Bower Press, 1970.

1772 _____. Samuel Taylor Coleridge: Narrative of the Events of
His Life, with a memoir of the author by Leslie Stephen. 2d ed.
Folcroft, PA: Folcroft Lib. Editions, 1970.

1773 Carlyle, Thomas. "Samuel Taylor Coleridge." (In Macdonald,
Hugh, ed. Portraits in Prose. New Haven: Yale University Press,
1947), 240-41.

1774 Carpenter, Maurice. Indifferent Horseman: The Divine Comedy
of Samuel Taylor Coleridge. London: Elek Books, 1954.

1775 Chambers, Sir Edmund Kerchener. Samuel Taylor Coleridge, A
Biographical Study. Oxford: Clarendon Press, 1950.

1776 Charpentier, John. Coleridge, the Sublime Somnambulist;
translated by M. V. Nugent. Brooklyn, N.Y.: Haskell House, 1970.

1777 Coleridge, Samuel Taylor. Collected Letters. Edited by
Earl Leslie Griggs. 6 vols. Oxford: Clarendon Press, 1956-1971.

1778 _____. "In a Profound Sleep." (In Dunaway, Philip, and
DeKay, George, eds. Turning Point. New York: Random House, 1958),
285-87.

1779 _____. Inquiring Spirit: A New Presentation of Coleridge
from His Published and Unpublished Prose Writings. Edited by
Kathleen Coburn. New York: Pantheon Books, 1951.

1780 _____. Letters. Selected with an introduction by Kathleen
Raine. London: Grey Walls Press, 1950.

1781 _____. Notebooks. Edited by Kathleen Coburn: 3 vols.
Bollinger ser. L. Princeton, N. J.: Princeton University Press,
1973.

1782 _____. Portable Coleridge; edited and with an introduction
by I. A. Richards. New York: Viking Press, 1950, 1-58.

1783 Cornwell, John. Coleridge, Poet and Revolutionary 1772-1804:
a Critical Biography. New York: Allen Lane, 1973.

1784 Cournos, Helen Sybil Norton (Kestner) and Cournos, John.
Famous British Poets. New York: Dodd, Mead, 1952, 81-88.

1785 Cottle, Joseph. Reminiscences of Samuel Taylor Coleridge
and Robert Southey. London: Lime Tree Bower Press, 1970.

1786 Cox, James Stevens, and Cox, G. Stevens. Samuel Taylor
Coleridge and Mary Lamb; Two Recent Discoveries. Gournsey:
Toucan Press, 1971, 16.

1787 De Selincourt, Aubrey. Six Great Thinkers: Socrates, St.
Augustine, Lord Byron, Rousseau, Coleridge. London: Hamilton,
1958.

1788 De Selincourt, Ernest. Wordsworthian and Other Studies.
New York: Oxford, 1947.

1789 Elwin, Malcolm. The First Romantics. New York: Longmans, Green,
1948.

1790 English Institute. New Perspectives on Coleridge and Wordsworth;
Selected papers from the English Institute, edited with a foreword
by Geoffrey H. Hartman. New York: Columbia University Press, 1972.

1791 Erdman, David V. "Coleridge, Wordsworth, and the Wedgwood
Fund." NYPLB, 60 (September-October, 1956), 486-507.

1792 _____. "Coleridge on George Washington; Newly Discovered
Essays of 1800." NYPLB, 61 (February, 1957), 81-97.

1793 _____. "Immoral Acts of a Library Cormorant; the Extent
of Coleridge's Contributions to the Critical Review." NYPLB, 63
(September-November, 1959), 433-54, 514-30, 575-87.

1794 Fairchild, H. N. "Hartley, Pistorius, and Coleridge."
PMLA, 62 (December, 1947), 1010-21.

1795 Fausset, Hugh I'Anson. Poets and Pundits; a Collection of
Essays. William McKean Brown Memorial Fund, v. 14. New Haven:
Yale University Press, 1947, 150-54.

1796 _____. Samuel Taylor Coleridge. New York: Russell &
Russell, 1967.

1797 Fitzhugh, Harriet Lloyd LePorte and Fitzhugh, P. K. Concise
Biographical Dictionary of Famous Men and Women. Rev & enl ed.
New York: Grosset & Dunlap, 1949, 134-35.

1798   Fox, A. B. "Political and Biographical Background of Coleridge's Osorio." JEGP, 61 (April, 1962), 258-67.

1799   Fruman, Norman. Coleridge, the Damaged Archangel. New York: G. Braziller, 1971.

1800   Garnett, Richard. Coleridge. Folcroft, PA: Folcroft Library Editions, 1972.

1801   Gegenheimer, A. F. "They Might Have Been Americans." SAQ, 46 (October, 1947), 520-21.

1802   Gillman, James. Life of Samuel Taylor Coleridge. Limited ed. Folcroft, PA: Folcroft lib. editions, 1972.

1803   Grant, Allan. Preface to Coleridge. New York: Longmans, 1972, 210

1804   Griggs, E. L. "Ludwig Tieck and Samuel Taylor Coleridge." JEGP, 54 (April, 1955), 262-68.

1805   Grigson, Geoffrey and Gibbs-Smith, C. H. eds. People. New York: Hawthorn, 1956, 94-95.

1806   Haeger, J. H. "Coleridge's Bye Blow: The Composition and Date of Theory of Life." MP, 74 (August, 1976), 20-41.

1807   Hanson, Lawrence. Life of S. T. Coleridge: The Early Years. New York: Russell & Russell, 1962.

1808   Hayter, Alethea. Voyage in Vain: Coleridge's Journey to Malta in 1804. Salem, N.H.: Faber, 1973, 188.

1809   Hazlitt, W. "Hazlitt Meets Coleridge." (In Macdonald, Hugh, ed. Portraits in Prose. New Haven: Yale University Press, 1947), 238-40.

1810   Heath, William. Wordsworth and Coleridge: A Study of Their Literary Relations in 1801-1802. New York: Oxford University Press, 1970, 182.

1811   House, Arthur Humphry. Coleridge. Cambridge University. Trinity College. Clark Lectures, 1951-52. London: R. Hart-Davis, 1953.

1812   House, Humphry. Coleridge. Clark Lectures. Chester Springs, PA.: Dufour, 1965, 167.

1813   "How Great Men Really Looked." Life, 33 (December 22, 1952), 74.

1814   Innes, Kathleen Elizabeth-Royds. Coleridge & His Poetry. New York: AMS Press, 1972.

1815 Jackson, J. R. de J. ed. Coleridge: the Critical Heritage.
New York: Barnes & Noble, 1970.

1816 Johnson, M. L. "How Rare Is a 'Unique Annotated Copy' of
Coleridge's Sibylline Leaves?" NYPLB, 78 (Summer 1975), 451-81.

1817 Jones, Alun Richard, and Tydeman, William, eds. Coleridge:
The Ancient Mariner and Other Poems; a casebook. New York:
Macmillan, 1973.

1818 Jones, Evan, ed. Father: Letters to Sons and Daughters.
New York: Holt Rinehart and Winston, 1960, 14-17.

    Coleridge's letter to his seven-year-old son Derwent.

1819 Kaufman, P. "Coleridge's Use of Cathedral Libraries."
MLN, 75 (May, 1960), 395-99.

1820 Knight, William Angus. Coleridge and Wordsworth in the West
Country, Their Friendship, Work and Surroundings. Limited edition.
Folcroft, PQ: Folcroft Lib. Editions, 1970, 237.

1821 Lawrence, Berta. Coleridge and Wordsworth in Somerset. North
Pomfret, VT: David & Charles, 1970.

1822 Lefebure, Molly. Samuel Taylor Coleridge: A Bondage of
Opium. New York: Stein & Day, 1974.

1823 Link, Arthur S. "Samuel Taylor Coleridge and the Economic
and Political Crisis in Great Britain, 1816-1820." JHI, 9
(June, 1948).

1824 MacGillevray, J. R. "New and Early Poem by Coleridge."
NYPLB, 63 (March, 1959), 153-54.

1825 Magill, Frank Northen, ed. Cyclopedia of World Authors.
New York: Harper, 1958, 223-25.

1826 Mallaby, G. "Dorothy Wordsworth: The Perfect Sister."
AM, 186 (December, 1950), 81-83.

1827 Margoliouth, Herschel Maurice. Wordsworth and Coleridge,
1795-1834. Home University Library of Modern Knowledge, 223.
New York: Oxford University Press, 1953.

1828 Mill, John Stuart. On Bentham and Coleridge; with an
introduction by F. R. Leavis. New York: Stewart, 1951.

1829 "Mr. Coleridge by Washington Allston." Antiques, 55
(January, 1949), 63-64.

1830 Mounts, C. E. Coleridge's Self-Identification with Spenserian
Characters. SP, 47 (July, 1950), 522-33.

1831 Murry, John Middleton. Katherine Mansfield and Other Library
Portraits. London: Nevill (1949), 32-44, 50-90.

1832 Paul-Emile, B. T. "Samuel Taylor Coleridge as Abolitionist."
ARIEL, 5 (April, 1974), 59-75.

1833 Petty, Sallie DeMaree. Famous Authors: Their Lives and Works.
2d ed. Friend, Neb.: Studio News (1948), 30-34.

1834 Potter, S. S. T. Coleridge. (In Strong, Leonard Alfred
George, ed. Sixteen Portraits of People Whose Houses Have Been
Preserved by the National Trust. Contributed by Walter Allen
and Others; Illustrated by Joan Hassall. London: Naldrett Press,
1951.)

1835 Radley, Virginia L. Samuel Taylor Coleridge.   Twayne's
English Authors. Boston: Twayne (1966).

1836 Raine, Kathleen Jessie. Coleridge. Bibliographical Series
of Supplements to British Book News on Writers and Their Work,
no. 43. New York: Longmans, 1967.

1837 Raine, Kathleen J. Coleridge. New York: Longmans, Green, 1955.

1838 Reed, H. "Coleridge as Critic." SR, 56 (October, 1948),
597-624.

1839 Reed, Gwendolyn, comp. Beginnings. New York: Atheneum, 1971.

1840 Richards, Ivor Armstrong. Coleridge on Imagination. 2d ed.
New York: Norton, 1950.

1841 Sanders, Charles Richard. "Background of Carlyle's Portrait
of Coleridge in The Life of John Sterling." John Rylands Library
Bulletin, 55 (Spring 1973), 434-58.

1842 _____. Coleridge and the Broad Church Movement; Studies
in S. T. Coleridge, Dr. Arnold of Rugby, J. C. Hare, Thomas Carlyle,
and F. D. Maurice. New York: Russell & Russell, 1972.

1843 Sastri, P. S. Vision of Coleridge.   Masters in English Literature
Allahabad, India: Kitab Mahal, 1966, 402p.

1844 Saunders, Beatrice. Portraits of Genius. London: J. Murray,
1959, 104-14.

1845 Schilling, Bernard Nicholas. Human Dignity and the Great
Victorians; published for Grinnell College. New York: Columbia
University Press, 1946, 47-60.

1846 Schneider, E. "Unknown Reviewer of Christabel: Jeffrey,
Hazlitt, Tom Moore." PMLA, 70 (June, 1955), 417-32.

1847 Seymour-Smith, Martin. Poets Through Their Letters.
New York: Holt, Rinehart & Winston, 1969.

1848 Shain, C. E. Young Radicals in an Earlier Age of Crisis.
Liberal Education, 58 (December, 1972), 464-77.

1849 Smith, B. "Coleridge's Ancient Mariner and Cook's Second
Voyage." Warburg & Courtauld Inst J, 19 (January, 1956), 117-54.

1850 Stebbins, L. P. "Coleridge and Mrs. Gillman." ConR, 185
(March, 1954), 153-58.

1851 Sultana, Donald. Samuel Taylor Coleridge in Malta and Italy.
New York: Barnes & Noble, 1969.

1852 Super, R. H. "Landor's Letters to Wordsworth and Coleridge."
MP, 55 (November, 1957), 73-83.

1853 Suther, Marshall Edward. Dark Night of Samuel Taylor Coleridge.
New York: Columbia University Press, 1960.

1854 Thompson, Laurence Victor, ed. Blue Plaque Guide to Historic
London Houses and the Lives of Their Famous Residents. London:
Newman Neame, 1953.

1855 Traill, H. D. Coleridge. Library of Lives and Letters: British
Writers. Detroit: Gale Research, 1968.

1856 Untermeyer, Louis. "Lost Utopias: Wordsworth, Coleridge,
Southey." (In Louis Untermeyer. Lives of the Poets. New York:
Simon & Schuster, 1959), 338-70.

1857 _____. "Coleridge." (In Louis Untermeyer. Paths of Poetry.
New York: Delacorte Press, 1966), 118-25.

1858 Watson, George. Coleridge the Poet. New York: Barnes &
Noble, 1966.

1859 Watters, Reginald. Coleridge: Literature in Perspective. London:
Evans, 1971.

1860 Werkmeister, L. "High Jinks at Highgate." PQ, 40 (January, 1961),
104-11.

1861 Whalley, George. Coleridge and Sara Hutchinson, and the Asra
Poems. Boston: Routledge & Kegan Paul, 1955.

1862 Whalley, G. "Coleridge and Southey in Bristol, 1795." RES
m.s. 1 (October, 1950), 324-40.

1863 Whitehill, J. "Samuel Taylor Coleridge: Prisoner and Prophet
of System." A Sch, 37 (Winter, 1967), 145-58.

1864 Willey, Basil. Samuel Taylor Coleridge. New York: W.W.
Norton, 1972.

Dissertations and Abstracts
of Dissertations

1865 Adams, Maurianne Schiffreen. "Coleridge and the Victorians:
Studies in the Interpretation of Poetry, Scripture, and Myth."
Indiana University, DA,28 (March, 1968), 3662A-63A.

1866 Adams, Michael W. "David Masson: A Study of His Literature
Criticism." University of Texas at Austin, DAI,34 (November, 1973),
2544A.

1867 Anderson, Augustus Edwin. "Theory of Fancy and Imagination in
English Thought from Hobbs to Coleridge." Vanderbilt University,
DA,13 (February, 1953), 226.

1868 Anderson, Erland Gregory. "Harmonious Madness: A Study of
Musical Metaphors in the Poetry of Coleridge, Shelley, and Keats."
University of Washington, DAI,34 (January, 1974), 4185A.

1869 Appleyard, Joseph Albert. "The Development of Coleridge's
Philosophy of Literature, 1791-1818." Harvard University, Unpublished
Doctoral Dissertation. (1964).

1870 Archer, Lewis Franklin. "Coleridge's Definition of the Poet
and the Works of Herman Melville and William Faulkner." Drew University,
DA,28 (November, 1967), 1810A-11A.

1871 Bailey, June Dudley. "Coleridge's Revisions of The Friend:
A Study of His Thought and Method." University of Urbana, DA,15
(January, 1955), 120-21.

1872 Baker, James Volant. "The Subterranean Fountain: The Role of
the Unconscious in Coleridge's Theory of Imagination." University
of Michigan, DA,14 (April, 1954), 670-71.

1873 Banks, Thomas Wilson. "The Dramatic Career of Samuel Taylor
Coleridge." Emory University, DA,27 (February, 1967), 2494A-95A.

1874 Barcus, James Edgar. "The Homogeneity of Structure and Idea
in Coleridge's Biographia Literaria, Philosophical Lectures, and Aids
to Reflection." University of Pennsylvania, DA, 29 (January, 1969),
2205A-06A.

1875 Barnett, Gail Z. "The Endless Journey: An Ontogenetic Study
of Three Poets." University of Maryland, DAI, 33 (November, 1972),
2314A.

      Tennyson, T. S. Eliot, S. T. Coleridge.

1876 Barsky, Arthur. "The Thoughts of Coleridge on the Events of
His Times with Some Possible Influences on His Thoughts." University
of California, L. A., DA, 26 (March, 1966), 539A.

1877 Baum, Joan Mandell. "The Theatrical Compositions of the Major
English Romantic Poets." Columbia University, DA, 30 (November,
1969), 1976A.

1878 Benziger, James G. "The Background of Coleridge's Doctrine of
Organic Form." Princeton University, DA, 12 (1952), 59.

1879 Berkoben, Lawrence David. "Symbolic Action in the Poetry of
Samuel Taylor Coleridge." University of Washington, DA, 24 (May,
1964), 4674A.

1880 Boulger, James Denis. "Coleridge as Religious Thinker." Yale
University, Unpublished Doctoral Dissertation, (1957).

1881 Bouslog, Charles S. "Coleridge's Defection." Harvard University,
Unpublished Doctoral Dissertation, (1951).

1882 Brennan, Maynard James. "Organic Unity: The Principle and Its
Application in the Criticism of Coleridge." University of Michigan,
DA, 13 (May, 1953), 792-93.

1883 Brown, Ella L. "The Uses of Landscape: A Study in Eighteenth
Century Poetry." University of Washington, DAI, 33 (September,
1972), 1160A.

1884 Bundy, Nancy Annis. "Samuel Taylor Coleridge, A Chronology:
August 20, 1795-January 14, 1805." University of Southern California,
DAI, 34 (August, 1974), 1089A.

1885 Caliri, Sister Flavia Mary. "Leopardi and Coleridge: A Study
in Poetic Theory." Boston College, DAI, 36 (September, 1975), 1487A.

1886 Camp, George C. "Some Philosophical Aspects of the Early
Coleridge with Special Attention to the Philosophy of George Berkeley
and the Works of Thomas Taylor." University of Illinois at Urbana,
Unpublished Doctoral Dissertation, (1952).

1887 Chayes, Irene Hendry. "The Circle and the Stair: Pattern of
Blake, Wordsworth, Coleridge, Shelley, and Keats." The John Hopkins
University, Unpublished Doctoral Dissertation, (1960).

1888 Chiang, Oscar A. "Idealism in Plays Written by Early Nineteenth-
Century Poets." St. Johns University, DAI, 32 (August, 1972), 720-21A.

     Includes discussion of Southey, Coleridge, Byron, Shelley, and
     Keats.

1889 Cierpial, Leo Joseph. "Degeneration and the Religion of
Beauty: A Traditional Pattern in Coleridge's The Rime of the Ancient
Mariner, Pater's The Renaissance, Maugham's Of Human Bondage, and
Joyce's Ulysses. Wayne State University, DA, 23 (October, 1962),
1361A-62A.

1890 Clatanoff, Doris A. R. "Poetry and Music: Coleridge, Shelley,
and Keats and the Musical Milieu of Their Day." University of
Nebraska, DAI, 34 (November, 1973), 2551A-52A.

1891 Creed, Howard H. "Coleridge as Critic." Vanderbilt University,
Unpublished Doctoral Dissertation, (1943).

1892 Daly, Michael Joseph. "The Marriage Metaphor and the Romantic
Prophecy: A Study of the Uses of the Epithalamium in the Poetry of
Blake, Wordsworth, and Coleridge." University of Southern California,
DA, 29 (January, 1969), 2254A.

1893 Deen, Leonard W. "The Development of Coleridge's Political
Thought." University of Chicago, Unpublished Doctoral Dissertation,
(1958).

1894 Demarest, Anthony Kevin. "Coleridge and the Elder Edda: 1795-
1798." Fordham University, DAI, 36 (September, 1975), 1521A.

1895 Dendurent, Harold O. "The Texts and Textual Relationships of
Coleridge's Osoris and Remorse." Northwestern University, DAI, 33
(April, 1973), 5718A.

1896 D'Itri, Patricia A. Ward. "A Study of Samuel Taylor Coleridge's
Critical Reception in Five Major Nineteenth Century Periodicals."
Michigan State University, DA, 39 (December, 1969), 2479A-80.

1897 Dramin, Edward I. "Amid the Jagged Shadows': Parody, Moral,
Realism, and Metaphysical Statements in Coleridge's Christabel."
Columbia University, DAI, 34 (July, 1973), 310A.

1898 Elliott, John W., Jr. "A Critical Index to the Letters of
Samuel Taylor Coleridge from 1785 to 1801 on the Subjects of Philosophy
and Religion, and Literature and Literary Theory: A Presentation of
His Thought." Columbia University, DAI, 34 (April, 1974), 6587A-88A.

1899 Elliot, Maurice Slater. "The Prose Writings of Samuel Taylor
Coleridge, 1795-1830: An Inquiry into Coleridge's Search for an
Appropriate Public and an Appropriate Form for His Prose Works."
University of Toronto, DAI, 35 (March, 1975), 6095A.

1900 Enscoe, Gerald Eugene. "Eros and the Romantics: Sexual Love
as a Theme in Coleridge, Shelley and Keats." University of Washington,
DA, 24 (July, 1963), 296A-97A.

1901 Fernelius, Alfred C. "Three Essays on Johnson and Coleridge."
Wayne State University, DAI, 33 (May, 1973), 6306A-07A.

   Comparison of Johsnon's and Coleridge's criticism.

1902 Ferrell, Mary Key Wynne. Tennyson's Ulysses: An Analysis
According to Coleridge's Critical Principles. University of Georgia,
DAI, 35 (April, 1975), 6664A.

1903 Fields, Beverly Franke. "Reality's Dark Dream: A Study of
Dejection in Coleridge." Northwestern University, DA, 26 (December,
1965), 3333A-34A.

1904 Finch, John Alban. "Wordsworth, Coleridge, and The Recluse,
1798-1814." Cornell University, DA, 25 (September, 1964), 1911A.

1905 Fitzpatrick, James Joseph. "Obstinate in Resurrection: An
Interpretation of Coleridge's Envisioning of Reality." University
of Southern California, DAI, 32 (April, 1972), 5735A-36A.

1906 Flothow, Rudolph Carl. "The Ecclesiastical Policy of Richard
Hooker and Samuel Taylor Coleridge: A Study of the Continuity of
Historical Issues." University of Southern California, Unpublished
Doctoral Dissertation, (1959).

1907 Frese, John H. "Four Voices: Studies in Consciousness and the
Romantic Ode." University of Iowa, DAI, 33 (October, 1972), 1681A.

1908 Frothingham, Richard. "The Unitarianism of Samuel Taylor
Coleridge." Columbia University, DA, 27 (June, 1967), 4250A.

1909 Fruman, Norman. "Coleridge: A Reexamination of His Character
and Creative Status." New York University, DA, 27 (December, 1966),
1784A-85A.

1910 Fussell, Iva M. "The Political Thought of S. T. Coleridge."
The University of Texas at Austin, Unpublished Doctoral Dissertation,
(1955).

1911 Gaskins, Avery Freeman. "His Gifted Ken: Coleridge's Poetry
and Criticism as Used by Certain Critics and Poets, 1817-1850."
Indiana University, DAI, 33 (July, 1972), 273A.

1912 Gerrietts, John S. "A Study of the Imaginal Qualities of
Poetry Based on Descriptive Passages of Milton and Coleridge."
Loyola University of Chicago, Unpublished Doctoral Dissertation, (1954).

1913 Gibbons, Edward Earl. "The Conversation Poems of Samuel Taylor
Coleridge: Coleridgean Art and Coleridgean Theory." University of
Pennsylvania, DAI, 30 (February, 1970), 3429A.

1914 Gilpin, George Heyburn. "Visions of Joy: A Study of the Poetry
of Samuel Taylor Coleridge." Rice University, DA, 28 (November, 1967),
1784A-85A.

1915   Glimm, James York. "Five Essays on Mystical Experience in the
Works of Wordsworth, Coleridge and Shelley." University of Texas
at Austin, DAI, 30 (October, 1969), 1525A.

1916   Good, James Milton. "The Coleridge-Figure in Wordsworth's
Prelude." Columbia University, Columbia University, DAI, 33 (July,
1972), 273A.

1917   Goodin, George Vincent. "The Comic Theories of Hazlitt, Lamb,
and Coleridge." University of Illinois at Urbana-Champaign, DA, 23
(August, 1962), 632A.

1918   Goodman, Hardin McDonald. "The German Influence on Samuel
Taylor Coleridge." University of Florida, DA, 22 (February, 1962),
2785A.

1919   Goodson, Alfred C., Jr. "Coleridge and Hölderlin: Studies
in the Poetics of Space." State University of New York, Buffalo,
DAI, 34 (August, 1973), 770A-71A.

1920   Grantz, Carl Leon. "Letters of Sara Coleridge: A Calendar
and Index to Her Manuscript Correspondence in the University of
Texas Library." University of Texas at Austin, DA, 29 (November,
1968), 1539A.

1921   Grow, Lynn Merle. "The Prose Style of Samuel Taylor Coleridge."
University of Southern California, DAI, 32 (December, 1971), 3251A.

1922   Haeger, Jack Howard. "The Scientific Speculations of Samuel
Taylor Coleridge Manuscript Transcriptions and a Commentary."
University of Washington, DAI, 32 (November, 1971), 2642A.

1923   Hager, Philip E. "Wordsworth, Coleridge, and Southey."
University of Washington, Unpublished Doctoral Dissertation, (1951).

1924   Hall, William Thomas. "Coleridge's Religious Doctrines and
Significant Parallels in Calvinism." University of Texas at Austin,
DA, 23 (July, 1962), 224-225.

1925   Haven, Richard. "Vision and Intellect: The Role of Mystical
Experience in the Work of Samuel Taylor Coleridge." Princeton
University, DA, 20 (July, 1959), 289-90.

1926   Henry, William Harley. "Coleridge's Meditative Poems and His
Early Religious Thought: The Theology of The Eolian Harp, This Lime
Tree Bower My Prison, and Frost at Midnight." John Hopkins University,
DAI, 31 (November, 1970), 2345A.

1927   Howard, John Douglas, Jr. "The Child-Hero in the Poetry of
Blake, Shelley, Byron, Coleridge, and Wordsworth." University of
Maryland, DA, 28 (January, 1968), 2647A.

1928   Hoyle, James F. "The Coleridgean Landscape: An Essay in
Historical Criticism of His Poetry." Princeton University, DA, 22
(December, 1961), 1999A.

1929 Hughes, Daniel John. "Coleridge and Valery: An Essay in Modern
Poetics." Brown University, DA, 19 (January, 1959), 1758.

1930 Jackson, J. R. de J. "The Influence of the Theater on Coleridge's
Shakespearean Criticism." Princeton University, DA, 22 (December, 1961),
2000.

1931 Jackson, Wallace. "Immediacy: The Development of a Critical
Concept from Addison to Coleridge." University of Pennsylvania,
DA, 25 (December, 1964), 3574-75.

1932 Jenkins, Patricia Movis (Dardano). "Coleridge's Literary
Theory: The Chronology of Its Development, 1790-1817." University
of Maryland, DAI, 35 (March, 1975), 6141A.

1933 Kennedy, Wilma Lucile. "Theory of the Imagination." Yale
University, Unpublished Doctoral Dissertation, (1940).

1934 Kirkwood, James Johnston. "Coleridge on Nature." Duke University,
DA, 29 (April, 1969), 3614A.

1935 Kline, Alfred Allan. "The English Romantics and the American
Republic: An Analysis of the Concept of America in the work of Blake,
Burns, Wordsworth, Coleridge, Byron, and Shelley." Columbia University,
DAI, 4 (January, 1954), 112.

1936 Kovitz, Miriam G. "The Lake Poets: Their Humor." Ohio State
University, DAI, 32 (May, 1972), 6430A.

1937 Lacey, Paul Alvin. "Samuel Taylor Coleridge's Political and
Religious Development, 1795-1810." Harvard University, Unpublished
Doctoral Dissertation. (1966).

1938 Larkin, John E., Jr. "The Theory and Methods of Criticism
in Coleridge and Carlyle." Duke University, DAI, 34 (August, 1973),
729-30A.

1939 Lattin, Vernon Eugene. "Samuel Taylor Coleridge's The Friend:
A Study in Argument and Methods of Expression." University of
Colorado, DAI, 31 (March, 1971), 4777A.

1940 Litchfield, Lawrence. "The Conservative Response to the Problem
of Authority in Nineteenth Century Britain: Coleridge, Carlyle,
Bagehot." State University of New York at Buffalo, DAI, 34 (August,
1973), 837A.

1941 Lockridge, Laurence Shockley. "The Moral Philosophy of Samuel
Taylor Coleridge." Harvard University, Unpublished Doctoral
Dissertation. (1969).

1942 Lott, Nelda Jackson. "The Tragedies of Scott, Lamb, and
Coleridge: Their Elizabethan Heritage." University of Southern
Mississippi, DAI, 32 (March, 1972), 5189A.

1943 Lupton, Mary Jane. "A Psychoanalytic Study of the Poetry
of Samuel Taylor Coleridge." Temple University, DAI, 30 (October,
1969), 1531A-32A.

1944 McCreadie, Marsha Anne. "T. S. Eliot and the Romantic Poets:
A Study of the Similar Poetic Themes and Methods Used by Eliot and
Wordsworth, Coleridge, Keats, Byron, and Shelley." University of
Illinois at Urbana-Champion, DAI, 34 (June, 1974), 7713A-14A.

1945 McFarland, Thomas A. "Nine Fathom Deep: The Background,
Imagery, and Symbolic Unity of Coleridge's Ancient Mariner." Yale
University, Unpublished Doctoral Dissertation. (1953).

1946 MacLean, Norman F. "The Theory of Lyric Poetry in England
from the Renaissance to Coleridge." University of Chicago, Unpublished
Doctoral Dissertation. (1941).

1947 Magnuson, Paul Andrew. "The Problems of Personal Identity
and Guilt in Coleridge's Poetry." University of Minnesota, DAI, 30
(February, 1970), 2466A-67A.

1948 Malik, Naseem. "The Poetical Development of Samuel Taylor
Coleridge Between 1787 and 1800." University of Washington, DA, 22
(March, 1962), 3202A-03A.

1949 Marnell, William H. "The Relations of Coleridge and Southey
in the Pantisocracy." Harvard University, Unpublished Doctoral
Dissertation. (1938).

1950 Martin, Richard Thomas. "A Reappraisal of Samuel Taylor
Coleridge's Conversation Poems." University of Illinois at
Urbana, DA, 25 (May, 1965), 6598A.

1951 Matthews, Jerry B. "Coleridge's Principle of the Reconciliation
of Oppositions as Manifested in His Poetry." University of Texas
at Austin, DAI, 35 (February, 1975), 5354A.

1952 Michaels, Judith Rowe. "The Bounds of the Self: Coleridge's
Philosophy of Love and Its Effect on His Poetic Vision." Bryn
Mawr College, DAI, 35 (April, 1975), 6674A.

1953 Millar, Kenneth. "The Inward Eye: A Revaluation of Coleridge's
Psychological Criticism." University of Michigan, DA, 12 (1952), 190.

1954 Miller, Craig William. "An Examination of the Key Terms in
Coleridge's Prose Writings." University of Washington, DA, 17 (May,
1957), 1075-76.

1955 Modiano, Raimonda. "Spatial and Sensory Modes of Experience in
Coleridge." University of California at San Diego, DAI, 34 (February,
1974), 5112A.

1956 Monroe, Dougald McDaugald. "Coleridge's Theories of Dreams,
Hallucination, and Related Phenomena in Relation to His Critical
Theories." Northwestern University, DA, 13 (1953), 1186-87.

1957   Mounts, Charles Eugene.   "The Influence of Spenser on Wordsworth
and Coleridge.   Duke University, Unpublished Doctoral Dissertation.
(1941).

1958   Mulvey, Thomas Vincent.   "The Fractured Dome: A Study of the
Unity of Coleridge's Kubla Khan."   Fordham University, DAI, 35
(November, 1974), 3000A-01A.

1959   Nichelson, Floyd Patrick.   "A Romantic Motif in Theological
Ethics: An Expository Study of the Doctrines of God and Original
Sin in Samuel Taylor Coleridge's Friend of 1818."   University of
Southern California, DAI, 35 (December, 1974), 3872A-73A.

1960   O'Hear, Michael Francis.   "The Constant Dream: Coleridge's
Vision of Woman and Love."   University of Maryland, DAI, 31 (February,
1971), 4174A-75A.

1961   Orsinski, Sister Mary Lucilla, O.S.F.   "A Study of the Structure
of Coordination in a Representative Sample of the Biographia Literaria."
The Catholic University of America, DA, 24 (March, 1964), 3731A-32A.

1962   Pachori, Satya Sheel.   "The Transcendentalism of Samuel Taylor
Coleridge."   University of Missouri-Columbia, DAI, 30 (April, 1970),
4421A-22A.

1963   Parker, Alan Reeve.   "The Way of Resurgence: A Study of Attitude
and Craft in Coleridge's Conversation Poems."   Harvard University,
Unpublished Doctoral Dissertation.   (1965).

1964   Patterson, Charles Ivey, Jr.   "The Romantic Critics' Conception
of the Novel: Hazlitt, Coleridge and De Quincey."   University of
Illinois at Urbana-Champaign, DA, 10 (1950), 116A-117.

1965   Patton, Lewis.   "The Watchman by S. T. Coleridge."   Yale
University, Unpublished Doctoral Dissertation.   (1937).

1966   Paul-Emile, Barbara Taylor.   "Slavery and the English Romantic
Poets: Coleridge, Wordsworth, and Southey."   University of Colorado,
DAI, 32 (March, 1972), 5196A.

1967   Pedrini, Lura Nancy Gregory.   "Serpent Imagery and Symbolism
in the Major English Romantic Poets: Blake, Wordsworth, Coleridge,
Byron, Shelley, Keats."   University of Texas at Austin, DAI, 20
(December, 1959), 2277A.

1968   Preyer, Robert Otto.   "The Benthamite and Coleridgean Versions
of History."   Columbia University, DA, 14 (October, 1954), 1727.

1969   Priestley, Mary Ellen.   "English Syntax in the Early Prose of
Samuel Taylor Coleridge: A New Reading of The Watchman, 1796."
University of Alabama, DA, 28 (February, 1968), 3195A-96A.

1970   Purves, Alan Carroll.   "A Catalogue and Index of the Letters
to Ernest Hartley Coleridge."   University of Texas at Austin, DA, 21
(July, 1960), 190-91.

1971   Quillen, Kathleen K.   "The Dimensions of the Sacred in Poetry:
Coleridge's The Rime of the Ancient Mariner and Poems of George
Macbeth." Emory University, DAI, 36 (January, 1976), 4464A.

1972   Ray, Charlotte Walters.   "A Catalogue and Index of the Letters
to Ernest Hartley Coleridge." University of Texas at Austin,
DAI, 32 (May, 1972), 6389A.

1973   Rhodes, Jack Lee.   "A Study in the Vocabulary of English
Romanticism: Joy in the Poetry of Blake, Wordsworth, Coleridge,
Shelley, Keats, and Byron." University of Texas at Austin, DA, 27
(April, 1967), 3434A.

1974   Richards, Michael R.   "The Romantic Critics' Opinion of
Elizabethan Non-Dramatic Literature." University of Tennessee,
DAI, 33 (February, 1973), 4361A.

1975   Robinson, Forest Elmo.   "The Peninsular War in the Political
Evolution of Five English Romantic Poets." University of Colorado,
DA, 27 (September, 1966), 782A.

1976   Rosen, Marvin Stanley.   "Authorship in the Days of Coleridge
and Wordsworth." University of California at Berkeley, DA, 26
(April, 1966), 6026A.

1977   St. George, Priscilla P.   "Romantic Poetry as Wisdom: The
Contemplative Metaphor in Wordsworth, Coleridge, and Shelley."
Yale University, DA, 27 (February, 1967), 2544A.

1978   St. Louis, Ralph F.   "The Middle Ages as a Political and
Social Ideal in the Writings of Edmund Burke, Samuel Taylor Coleridge,
Thomas Carlyle, and John Ruskin." University of Nebraska, DAI, 33
(January, 1973), 3600A-01A.

1979   Schulz, Max F.   "The Voices of Coleridge's Poetry: A Study
of the Desire for Spontaneity and the Rage for Order." Wayne State
University, DA, 25 (October, 1964), 2500A.

1980   Shaffer, Elinor Stoneman.   "Studies in Coleridge's Aesthetics."
Columbia University, DA, 28 (October, 1967), 1409A.

1981   Shen, Yao.   "Some Chapters on Shakespearean Criticism: Coleridge,
Hazlitt, and Stoll." University of Michigan, DA, 7 (1944), 91.

1982   Siegel, Robert Harold.   "The Serpent and the Dove: The Problem
of Evil in Coleridge's Poetry." Harvard University, Unpublished
Doctoral Dissertation. (1968).

1983   Smithey, Robert Arthur.   "Coleridgean Elements in Browning's
The Ring and the Book." University of Wisconsin, DAI, 32 (October,
1971), 2070A.

1984   Snipes, Wilson Currin.   "An Analysis of the Critical Principles
in Coleridge's Shakespearean Criticism with Some Attention to Their
Background and Development." Vanderbilt University, DA, 17 (November,
1957), 2601.

1985 Stabenau, Heinrich H. "Theories of Poetic Meaning and the Function of Poetry: 1700-1850." Princeton University, DAI, 32 (May, 1972), 6455A-56A.

1986 Stebelman, Scott David. "The Theme of Betrayal in Coleridge's Poetry." University of Wisconsin, DAI, 34 (July, 1974), 418A.

1987 Stephens, Frances Anne Carlock. "The Hartley Coleridge Letters at the University of Texas: A Calendar and Index." University of Texas at Austin, DAI, 31 (October, 1970), 1773A-74A.

1988 Stevenson, Stanley Warren. "The Creation Motif in Romantic Poetry and Theory with Particular Reference to the Myth of Blake and Coleridge." Northwestern University, DA, 19 (December, 1958), 1368-69.

1989 Stuart, John A. "Emerson's Nature: Its Relation to Coleridge's Transcendental Idealism." Northwestern University, Unpublished Doctoral Dissertation. (1945).

1990 Sullivan, Ruth E. "Some Variations on the Oedipal Theme in Three Pieces of Fiction: A Rose for Emily, Three Hours After Marriage, and Christabel." Tufts University, DAI, 33 (February, 1973), 4366A.

1991 Suppan, Adolph A. "Coleridge: The Shaping Mind." University of Wisconsin, Unpublished Doctoral Dissertation. (1947).

1992 Suther, Marshall Edward, Jr. "The Dark Night of Samuel Taylor Coleridge." Columbia University, DA, 19 (July, 1958), 132-133.

1993 Sypher, Richard B. "Coleridge at Christ's Hospital: The Progress of Genius." Northwestern University, DAI, 33 (April, 1973), 5694A.

1994 Taylor, Anya Boxeman. "Magic and the Spell in Coleridge and His Tradition." The City University of New York, DAI, 31 (December, 1970), 2891A.

1995 Terrett, Dulany. "Coleridge's Politics, 1789-1810." Northwestern University, Unpublished Doctoral Dissertation. (1941).

1996 Thomas, George Stephen. "Wordsworth, Scott, Coleridge, Southey, and De Quincey on Catholic Emancipation, 1800-1829: The Conservative Reaction." New York University, DA, 25 (July, 1964), 487A-488A.

1997 Twitchell, James B. "The Romantic Psychodrama: An Interpretation of The Rime of the Ancient Mariner, Manfred and Prometheus Unbound, Act IV." University of North Carolina at Chapel Hill, DAI, 32 (March, 1972), 5204A-05A.

1998 Valenti, Peter Louis. "Picturesque Aesthetics and Associationist Theory in the Early Poetry of Wordsworth and Coleridge." University of North Carolina at Chapel Hill, DAI, 35 (February, 1975), 5369A.

1999 Van Haitsma, Glenn Allyn. "Coleridge and the Idea of Culture." Syracuse University, DA, 22 (June, 1962), 4346.

2000 Waldoff, Leon. "The Mythic Basis of Three Major Poems of the
Romantic Period." University of Michigan, DA, 28 (January, 1968), 2699A.

2001 Waters, Leonard Adrian. "Coleridge and Eliot: A Comparative
Study of Their Theories of Poetic Composition." University of
Michigan, DA, 8 (1948), 112-113.

2002 Weinberg, Marcel. "Coleridge on Dreams: Their Relationship
to His Own Experiences and to His Psychological Esthetic, and
Theological Speculations." University of Chicago, Unpublished
Doctoral Dissertation. (1970).

2003 Wendling, Ronald Charles. "The Art of Coleridge's Conversation
Poems." Case Western Reserve University, DAI, 32 (July, 1971),
405A-06A.

2004 Werkmeister, Lucyle. "The First Two Editions of Coleridge's
Friend, edited by Lucyle Werkmeister." University of Nebraska,
Lincoln, DA, 17 (July, 1957), 1560A.

2005 Whitmer, Anne Bernadine. "American Reaction to the Literary
Criticism of Samuel Taylor Coleridge, 1830-1860." Ohio State University,
Unpublished Doctoral Dissertation. (1939).

2006 Wieden, Fritz Maximillian. "Samuel Taylor Coleridge as a
Student of German Literature." University of Toronto, Canada,
Unpublished Doctoral Dissertation. (1963).

2007 Wilkinson, Loren E. "Meaning, Man, and Earth: A Romantic
Dilemma in Contemporary Part." Syracuse University, DAI, 34 (April,
1974), 6609A-10A.

2008 Wilson, Douglas Brownlow. "Studies in Coleridge." Harvard
University, Unpublished Doctoral Dissertation. (1967).

2009 Woof, Robert Samuel. "The Literary Relations of Wordsworth and
Coleridge, 1795-1803: Five Studies." University of Toronto, Canada,
Unpublished Doctoral Dissertation. (1960).

2010 Wynn, Lawrence. "The Reputation of Samuel Taylor Coleridge Among
His Contemporaries in England." Princeton University, DA, 15 (May,
1955), 834A-35.

Bibliography of Sources

2011 Abstracts of English Studies: An Offical Publication of the
National Council of Teachers of English. 1(1958) -20 (1977).

2012 Altick, Richard D. and Wright, Andrew. Selective Bibliography
for the Study of English and American Literature. New York:
Macmillan, 1960.

2013 Arms, George, and Kuntz, Joseph M. Poetry Explication: A
Checklist of Interpretation Since 1925 of British and American
Poems, Past and Present. New York: Swallow Press and William
Morrow, 1950.

2014 Baldensperger, Fernand and Friederich, Werner P. Bibliography
of Comparative Literature. Chapel Hill, N. C.: University of North
Carolina Studies in Comparative Literature, 1950. UNCSCL, 1.

2015 Bateson, F. W., ed. The Cambridge Bibliography of English
Literature. 4 vols. New York: Macmillan, 1941.

2016 _____. A Guide to English Literature. Garden City, N.Y.:
Doubleday, 1965.

      A Coleridge reading list, pp. 159-60.

2017 Besterman, Theodore. A World Bibliography of Bibliographies
and of Bibliographical Catalogues, Calendars, Abstracts, Digests,
Indexes, and the Like. 4th ed., rev. and greatly enl., 5 vols.
Lausanne, Societas Bibliographica, 1965-66.

2018 Bibliographic Index: A Cumulative Bibliography of Bibliographies.
1936-1977. New York: H. W. Wilson, 1935-1977.

2019 Biography Index: A Cumulative Index to Biographical Material in
Books and Magazines. 1946-1977. New York: H. W. Wilson, 1949-1977.

2020 Books for College Libraries; a Selected List of Approximately
53,400 Titles Based on the Initial Selection Made for the University
of California's New Campuses Program and Selected with the Assistance
of College Teachers, Librarians, and Other Advisers. Prepared under
the direction of Melvin J. Voigt and Joseph H. Treyz. Chicago:
American Library Association, 1967.

2021 Cambridge Bibliography of English Literature. Edited by F. W.
Bateson. Cambridge: University Press, 1940–57; New York: Macmillan,
1941–57. 5 vols.

2022 Cumulative Book Index: A World List of Books in the English
Language. 1933–1978. Supplementing the United States Catalog, 4th ed.
New York: H. W. Wilson, 1936–1977.

2023 Dissertation Abstracts. Ann Arbor, Michigan: University Microfilms, 1952–1961.

2024 Doctoral Dissertations Accepted by American Universities. New
York: H. W. Wilson, 1935–1955.

2025 E. L. H., A Journal of English Literary History. 3 (1936),
14 (1948).

2026 English Association. The Year's Work in English Studies. 1935–
1974. Oxford: University Press, 1937–1976, Vols. 16–55.

2027 English Literature, 1660–1800. Studies compiled for Philological
Quarterly by Ronald S. Crane et at. 6 vols. Princeton: Princeton
University Press, 1950–72.

2028 Essay and General Literature Index. 1934–1977. New York: H. W.
Wilson, 1941–1977.

2029 Fogle, Richard Harter. Romantic Poets and Prose Writers. New
York: Appleton – Century-Crofts, 1967.

2030 Green, David Bonnell and Wilson, Edwin Graves, eds. Keats,
Shelley, Byron, Hunt, and Their Circles, A Bibliography: July 1,
1950–June 30, 1962. Compiled by David Bonnell Green and others.
Lincoln: University of Nebraska Press, 1964.

2031 Gregory, Winifred, ed. Union List of Serials in Libraries of
the United States and Canada. 2d ed. New York: H. W. Wilson, 1943.
Supplement 1941–1943; Second Supplement 1944–1949.

2032 Hall, Thomas. "A Check List of Coleridge Criticism." BB 25
(January–April, 1968), 124–31.

2033 Haven, Richard; Haven, Josephine; and Adams, Maurianne, eds.
Samuel Taylor Coleridge: An Annotated Bibliogrpahy of Criticism.
Vol. 1: 1793–1899. Boston: G. K. Hall, 1976.

2034 Howard, Patsy C. Theses in English Literature, 1894–1970.
Ann Arbor, Michigan: Perian Press, 1973.

2035 Humanities Index. 1974-1977. New York: H. W. Wilson, 1974-1976.

2036 Index to American Doctoral Dissertations. Ann Arbor, Michigan:
University Microfilms, 1957-1961.

2037 International Index to Periodicals: A Quarterly Guide to
Periodical Literature in the Social Sciences and Humanities. 7 (July,
1934-June, 1937), - 18 (April, 1964-March, 1965).

2038 Kennedy, Virginia Wadlow and Barton, Mary Neill. Samuel Taylor
Coleridge: A Selective Bibliography of the Best Available Editions of
His Writings, of Biographies and Criticisms of Him and of References
Showing His Relations With Contemporaries, for Students and Teachers.
Baltimore: Enoch Pratt Free Library, 1935.

2039 Library of Congress Author Catalog: A Cumulative List of Works
Represented by Library of Congress Printed Cards, 1948-1952. Ann
Arbor, Michigan: J. W. Edwards, 1953. 24 vols.

2040 McNamee, Lawrence F. Dissertations in English and American
Literature; Theses Accepted by American, British and German Universities,
1865-1964. New York: Bowker, 1968.

2041 _____. Supplement 1-2. New York: Bowker, 1969-74.

2042 Microfilm Abstracts. Ann Arbor, Michigan: University Microfilms,
1938-1951.

        Succeeded by DA in 1952.

2043 Modern Humanities Research Association. Annual Bibliography
of English Language and Literature. 1936-1958. Cambridge: Cambridge
University Press. Vols. 17-33.

2044 Modern Language Association of America. MLA International
Bibliography of Books and Articles on the Modern Languages and
Literatures. 1936-1975.

2045 National Union Catalog: A Cumulative Author List Representing
Library of Congress Printed Cards and Titles Reported by Other American
Libraries, 1953-1957. Ann Arbor, Michigan: J. W. Edwards, 1958. 28
vols. 1958. Washington: Library of Congress, 1959. 5 vols. 1959.
Washington: Library of Congress, 1960. 5 vols.

2046 The New Cambridge Bibliogrpahy of English Literature. Cambridge:
University Press, 1969-74. 5 vols.

2047 New Serial Titles: A Union List of Serials Commencing Publication
After December 31, 1949. Washington: Library of Congress, 1956-1960.

2048 Philological Quarterly. 28 (1950), 55 (1976).

2049 Sheehy, Eugene P., comp. Guide to Reference Books. 9th ed.
With the Assistance of Rita G. Keckeissen and Eileen McIlvaine.
Chicago: American Library Association, 1976.

2050   Social Science and Humanities Index.   19 (April, 1965-March,
1966) - 27 (April, 1973-March, 1974).

2051   Studies in Romanticism.   14 (1935) - 55 (1977).

2052   U. S. Library of Congress.   A Catalog of Books Represented by
Library of Congress Printed Cards, Issued to July 31, 1942.   Ann
Arbor, Michigan: Edward Bros., 1942-1946.   167 vols.   Supplement:
Cards issued August 1, 1942-December 31, 1947.   Ann Arbor, Michigan:
J. W. Edward, 1948.   42 vols.

2053   Watson, George, ed.   The Cambridge Bibliography of English
Literature.   Vol. 5, Supplement: A. D. 600-1900.   Cambridge: University
Press, 1957.

2054   Winchell, Constance M.   Guide to Reference Books.   8th ed.
Chicago: American Library Association, 1967.

Author Index

Emerson, Donald, 902

Emerson, Francis Willard, 277

Emery, Clark, 903

Emmett, Dorothy, 904

Empson, William, 475, 476

Endicott, N. J., 905

England, A. B., 278

England, Martha Winburn, 906

Enrico, Harold, 477

Everett, Edwin M., 478

Enscoe, Gerald E., 50, 279, 280,
1639, 1900

Epstein, Arthur D., 907

Erdman, David V., 51, 908, 909,
910, 911, 912, 913, 914, 915,
916, 917, 918, 919, 920, 921,
922, 923, 924, 1791, 1792, 1793

Evans, B. Ifor, 139, 925, 926

Everett, Edwin M., 52, 927

Ewen, Frederic, 928

Fairbanks, A. Harris, 140, 186,
929, 930

Fairchild, Hoxie N., 931, 1794

Farrison, W. Edward, 53

Fausset, Hugh I'Anson, 1795, 1796

Fenner, Theodore L., 933

Fernelius, Alfred C., 1901

Ferrell, Mary Key Wynne, 1902

Ferry, David, 934

Fields, Beverly Frankel, 54, 281,
479, 1640, 1903

Finch, Jeremiah S., 935

Finch, John A., 936, 1904

Fisch, M. H., 937

Fiske, Roger, 938

Fitzhugh, Harriet Lloyd LePorte,
1797

Fitzhugh, P. K., 1797

Fitzpatrick, James Joseph, 1905

Fleissner, Robert F., 282, 283,
284, 285, 286, 287, 288, 480,
939, 940

Flory, Wendy Stallard, 55

Flothow, Rudolph Carl, 1906

Foakes, R. A., 941, 942, 1641

Fogel, Daniel Mark, 9

Fogle, Ephim G., 943

Fogle, Richard Harter, 56, 141,
187,, 213, 289, 290, 291, 481,
482, 944, 945, 946, 947, 948,
949, 950, 951, 952, 953, 1642,
1643, 2029

Fogle, Stephen F., 142

Ford, George H., 954

Ford, Newell F., 483

Forstman, H. Jacksoh, 955

Forstner, Lorne J., 484

Fox, Arnold B., 956, 1798

Frankebert, Lloyd, 292

Freedman, R., 485

French, Richard, 57

French, Richard, 957

ABOUT THE COMPILERS

Jefferson D. Caskey, a librarian and professor of library science for many years, is currently professor of library science and instructional media at Western Kentucky University. He has had articles published in *Language Arts, English in Texas, Media: Library Services Journal,* and *Rainbow Magazine,* and will have a short fictional piece published in *Sandlapper Magazine* in 1978.

Melinda M. Stapper is librarian at San Marcos High School and has taught high school English for several years.